Writing from the Left

THE HAYMARKET SERIES

Editors: Mike Davis and Michael Sprinker

The Haymarket Series offers original studies in politics, history and culture, with a focus on North America. Representing views across the American left on a wide range of subjects, the series will be of interest to socialists both in the USA and throughout the world. A century after the first May Day, the American left remains in the shadow of those martyrs whom the Haymarket Series honors and commemorates. These studies testify to the living legacy of political activism and commitment for which they gave their lives.

Writing from the Left

New Essays on Radical Culture and Politics

ALAN M. WALD

VERSO

London · New York

First published by Verso 1994
© Alan M. Wald 1994
All rights reserved

Verso
UK: 6 Meard Street, London W1V 3HR
USA: 29 West 35th Street, New York, NY 10001-2291

Verso is the imprint of New Left Books

ISBN 1-85984-906-7
ISBN 1-85984-001-9   (pbk)

British Library Cataloguing in Publication Data
A catalogue record for this book is available from the British Library

Library of Congress Cataloging-in-Publication Data
Wald, Alan M., 1946–
Writing from the left : new essays on radical culture and politics
/ Alan Wald.
p.   cm.
Includes bibliographical references and index.
ISBN 1-85984-906-7. – ISBN 1-85984-001-9 (pbk.)
1. Radicalism—United States—History—20th century.
2. Communism—United States—History—20th century. 3. Communism
and culture—United States—History—20th century. 4. Communism and
literature—United States—History—20th century. 5. Communism and
intellectuals—United States—History—20th century. I. Title.
HN90.R3W355   1994
303.48'4—dc20
94-20993
CIP

Typeset by Servis Filmsetting Ltd, Manchester
Printed and bound in Great Britain by
Biddles Ltd, Guildford and King's Lynn

**In Memory of
My Beloved Celia (1946–92)**

always . . . and forever . . .

Contents

CONTENTS

Acknowledgments

I am grateful to the following publications and publishing houses for permission to reprint:

Columbia University Press for "The Legacy of Daniel Aaron," which appeared as the "Introduction" to the reprint of *Writers on the Left* (1992) and for "James T. Farrell in the 1930s: The Athanasius of Union Square," which appeared as the "Introduction" to the reprint of *A Note on Literary Criticism* (1993); *Reviews in American History* for "Alfred Kazin in Retrospect," 20 (1992); *In These Times* for "Premature Socialist-Feminists," March 25–31, 1992; *Cineaste* for "An Earlier 'Time of the Toad,'" 20, no. 2 (Summer 1993); *Journal of American History* for "The 'Radical Impressario' Revisited" (September 1993); *Journal of English and Germanic Philology* for "Edwin Rolfe, *Presente!*" 91, no. 3 (July 1992); Monthly Review Press for "Culture and Commitment: US Communist Writers Reconsidered" from Michael Brown et al., eds, *New Studies in the Culture and Politics of US Communism* (1993); University of Delaware Press for "Communist Writers Fight Back in Cold War Amerika," in Philip Goldstein, ed., *Styles of Cultural Activism: From Theory and Pedagogy to Women, Indians and Communism* (1994); *Journal of Trotsky Studies* for "Leon Trotsky's Contribution to Marxist Cultural Theory and Literary Criticism," 2 (Summer 1994); *Science and Society* for "Literary 'Leftism' Reconsidered," 57, no. 2 (Summer 1993); *Against the Current* for "The Utopian Imagination," forthcoming (1994), and for "The Roots of African-American Communism," 8, no. 4 (September–October 1993); *Monthly Review* for "The Subaltern Speaks," 43, no. 11 (April 1992), and for "The Anti-racist Imagination," 45, no. 3 (July–August 1993).

"The 1930s Left in US Literature Reconsidered" was presented at the April 30–May 2, 1992 Youngstown State University Conference on "The Thirties" and a version will appear in a collection to be published by University of Illinois Press called *Re-Visioning 30s Culture: New Directions in Scholarship*, edited by Bill Mullen and Sherry Linkon. "From Old Left to New in US Literary Radicalism" is based on talks delivered at the "Interdisciplinary Conference on the History of the 1960s" in April 1993 at Madison, Wisconsin, and at the American Studies Association national convention in November 1993 in Boston, Massachusetts; "Cultural Cross-Dressing: Radical Writers Represent African-Americans and Latinos in the McCarthy Era" is a paper from the April 1992 national convention of the Society for Multi-ethnic Literature in the US at UCLA in Los Angeles, California; "Belief and Ideology in Robert Hayden" is a paper from the Robert Hayden Memorial Conference in February 1990 in Ann Arbor, Michigan; "John Sanford and 'America Smith'" is based on a talk given at the 1993 national convention of the Modern Languages Asssociation and a version will also appear as the "Introduction" to the University of Illinois Press reprint of *The People from Heaven*; "Lloyd Brown and the African-American Literary Left" is based on a talk given at the Center for the Study of Black Literature and Culture at the University of Pennsylvania in March 1994, and a version will also appear as the "Introduction" to the Northeastern University Press reprint of *Iron City*. I am grateful to the above universities and conferences of professional organizations for inviting me to present early versions of papers that are included in this volume.

Political Chronology

1965 Malcolm X assassinated. SDS March on Washington against Vietnam War. Watts Rebellion.

1968 Tet Offensive in Vietnam. Prague Spring in Czechoslovakia. Student rebellion in Mexico City. American Indian Movement (AIM) formed. Martin Luther King assassinated.

1969 Rebellion at Stonewall Inn, a gay bar in New York's Greenwich Village.

1973 Supreme Court legalizes right to abortion.

1979 Sandinista Revolution in Nicaragua. FMLN formed in El Salvador.

1989 Collapse of USSR.

1990–91 Gulf War.

1991 Ron Carey reform slate elected to leadership of Teamsters Union.

1992 Mass uprising in Los Angeles.

1992 November 3 – End of Reagan–Bush Era.

1993 War in ex-Yugoslavia.

Introduction

The Marxist Literary Tradition

in the United States

Readers may profit from an explanation for why this unabashedly "presentist" volume on the US Marxist literary tradition allocates so much attention to cultural workers associated with the Communist Party between the early 1930s and late 1950s. Such a focus may seem even more perplexing once the reader learns that the author has defined his politics as resolutely "anti-Stalinist" (albeit within the tradition of revolutionary Marxism[1]) since he began writing from the Left, as well as about the Left, as an undergraduate and graduate student in the 1960s and 1970s.[2] Part of the explanation for the central role of literary Communism in this volume, and, indeed, its continuing relevance, is its foundational role within an interpretation of a Marxist cultural tradition separated into two interrelated yet distinct phases.

In the first phase, the decisive features of the phenomenon were established in the decades following the Russian Revolution of 1917 as Communist theory and activism intersected with the US social crisis of the Great Depression. What was built between the early 1930s and the crisis of international Communism in 1956–58 was a relatively coherent, though not monolithic or always consistent, Marxist cultural movement allied with the political dynamism of the US Communist Party. A distinctive feature of this tradition, to which I pay homage in *Writing from the Left*, was that its great theme was anti-racism, which I believe should continue to remain a primary concern of any US cultural Left at the present and in the future.

The Communist Party itself during these years was the most successful multi-racial class struggle political organization ever built on the US Left, even though its legacy leaves at least as many problems to haunt us as it does admirable achievements to inspire. On the negative side, the Party was forged by activists with a semi-religious belief that the Soviet Union under Stalin (a vile dictator misperceived as a benign leader) was the vanguard of humanity, advancing toward a classless society devoid of racism which provided exceptional opportunities for women. In the 1930s, the Party was also shaped by the heat of

1

anti-fascist struggles around the world, and amidst militant combat against racism at home. These strident campaigns gave the Party at times certain features of an authoritarian military machine; the focus on such dangerous and vicious enemies also helps explain why the Soviet Union's brutally undemocratic regime was not subjected to the same critical scrutiny as those in capitalist and fascist countries. More positively, the Party and the movements it influenced were exceedingly proletarian in composition and orientation (at least through the mid 1940s). This assisted the Party's ability to attract large number of extraordinarily able intellectuals, students, and cultural workers who felt that they had something to give to, and learn from, the struggles in which it was engaged.

In literary and cultural matters, it is useful to note that the bulk of activists in cultural movements during the 1930s–50s phase, which were considerably broader than strict Party membership, were not affiliated with colleges or universities. A few were academics, but almost all of these were eventually fired or forced out of academe if they maintained their pro-Communist stances. Others worked for the Party apparatus or affiliated cultural organizations, were in publishing and journalism, had "regular jobs," or were supported by spouses (mostly instances of women supporting men).

Moreover, in contrast to the Left of the second phase, after the 1960s, creative practice took precedence over literary criticism and theory in the Marxist cultural critique of the 1930s–50s era. That is, prominent left-wing novelists such as Mike Gold, Richard Wright, and Isidor Schneider proclaimed their fiction to be explicitly within Marxist culture, and accordingly built a body of literary criticism that complemented the centerpiece of their fiction. Of the four men who published book-length works of Marxist literary criticism in the United States in the 1930s – V. F. Calverton, James T. Farrell, Granville Hicks, and Bernard Smith – the first three also wrote novels and short stories.[3] Among the many women writers on the Left, Genevieve Taggard, primarily known as a poet, wrote the single critical work in that period about US literature.[4]

Finally, a strong faith in the progressive role and real achievements of the USSR was one factor supporting tremendous political commitment, rarely surpassed in later generations, in the personal lives of Marxists. Writers in the 1930s risked danger and violence to investigate the conditions of workers in the mines or in racist strongholds such as Alabama. They undertook difficult journeys to expose ruthless dictatorships in countries such as Nazi Germany. And they volunteered to fight in Spain in the gallant but ill-equipped International Brigades. During the post-war McCarthyite witch-hunt, many writers defied US government investigating committees, sometimes went to prison, almost always lost their jobs, and not infrequently had to flee to exile in Mexico or Europe.

None of this should be seen as an effort to idealize the personal qualities of this generation of Marxist cultural workers, as if they were superhuman exemplars compared to those who came after. An individual's motivations for what appear to be acts of martyrdom and self-sacrifice can sometimes be less than altruistic. No doubt a few benefited psychologically and perhaps even modestly materially from their inflated reputations in Party cultural circles and from sales of translations of their books in Communist countries. Others possibly combined their self-sacrifice with arrogance and self-righteousness, not always apparent to those younger people who encountered them in later decades through documentary films such as *Seeing Red* (1981), by which time they had mellowed considerably. Yet, on the whole, this generation's devotion to social change at considerable risk to their personal wellbeing may not have been matched by their successors, with the exception of some participants in the early civil rights movement and long-term anti-racist activists, and individuals who went to jail or fled the country following their involvement in militant opposition to racism in Monroe, North Carolina, and Wounded Knee, South Dakota, during the 1960s and after.

Moreover, we should not forget that, from the early 1930s on, there were also Marxist cultural workers allied with rival political currents to the Communist Party – Trotskyists, socialists, Bukharinists, council communists, anarcho-communists, and unaffiliated radicals. In the body of cultural work left by these alternative Marxist traditions, especially that of the Trotskyists, there are many indispensable correctives to the Communist cultural tradition.[5]

In particular, since Trotskyists were anti-Stalinist Marxist-Leninists, they could be especially astute in pointing out possible connections between Communist cultural practice and political subservience to the Soviet Union. This sensitivity perhaps led to more flexibility in distinguishing strictly political from literary judgments, although the two can never be totally separated. Moreover, among the Trotskyists, there was a greater tolerance for modernist experimental and other difficult literature, which was frequently decried as elitist if not reactionary by leading critics in the Communist publications. In addition, since the Trotskyists were quick to accuse the Communists of the utilitarian exploitation of literature and of trying to foist a political line on literary movements, the Trotskyists were, methodologically, more inclined to give greater attention to mediating factors between what are traditionally called the economic "base" and ideological "superstructure."

Trotskyism in politics and literature, arguably the most significant Marxist alternative to the Communists, made a memorable "mark" on radical cultural practice, but never by itself sustained for any length of time anything approximating a mass movement. Indeed, Trotskyism is probably remembered today more because a number of its adherents detached themselves from the Left before and during the Cold War, and made names for themselves in New York cultural circles based upon the universities and intellectual journals. What is recuperable from this tradition is important, and in certain respects even crucial, but hardly constitutes the foundation of an autonomous Marxist cultural tradition that could rival the actual record of the Communist-led movement.

Another feature of the Communist cultural tradition is that, even after the near destruction of the Communist Party as a credible political force in 1956–58, its cultural tradition survived through intersections with the early New Left. This can be seen in relation to the African-American movement, where the older Black Communist cultural Left intersected with the new "Black Arts" movement. During the 1950s, Black Arts ideas were somewhat prefigured through Communist-influenced cultural leaders such as John O. Killens, Lorraine Hansberry, Paul Robeson, and W. E. B. Du Bois. The Black Arts movement also treated with respect prominent writers who had been influenced by Communism, such as Richard Wright and Langston Hughes.

Another intersection between the Old and the New Lefts can be seen in the reappearance of one-time Communist women writers, such as Tillie Olsen and Meridel Le Sueur, in the feminist literary movement. Their resurgence that emerged from the 1960s was followed by reprintings through the Feminist Press publishing house of works by other writers such as Josephine Herbst, Myra Page, Fielding Burke, and Josephine Johnson.

A third intersection can be seen in poetry: Walter Lowenfels, a well-known Communist poet, was central in organizing popular anthologies of anti-Vietnam War poets and anti-racist poets; Thomas McGrath, an important modernist poet who was in and out of the Communist Party, influenced many younger poets; Muriel Rukeyser, intimately connected with the Old Left, was a mentor of Alice Walker and was highly regarded by feminist and lesbian writers; and Kenneth Fearing, perhaps the most widely respected revolutionary poet of the 1930s, is acknowledged by critics as having anticipated some of the styles and themes of Beat and early New Left poetry. In addition to these literary lines of communication, there were Communist influences across the generations in folk music, most notably by Pete Seeger and Woody Guthrie, and in some areas of theater and film. The popularity in the 1960s and after of the 1951 film *Salt of the Earth* is a notable instance.[6] Also, the memory of resistance against the McCarthyite witch-hunt by Hollywood and other cultural workers was inspirational to New Leftists, who frequently paid homage to blacklistees at teach-ins, rallies, and in publications.

The Marxist literary criticism stemming from the 1930s–50s phase of the Marxist cultural movement was, however, usually not taken seriously by the New Left rebels of the 1960s. If they paid any attention at all, they regarded Communist critics such as Granville Hicks and Mike Gold as vulgar and simplistic, and the Trotskyist-influenced *Partisan Review* writers as elitist and sell-outs. Thus, while some cultural phenomena sustained continuity across the generations, others provided the 1960s radicals with the political consciousness that set it apart from its forebears. The first phase of Marxist cultural critique gave way to its successor which simultaneously drew from and broke with its legacy of experiences and cultural expressions. In complex ways, then, the 1960s saw a dying out of and reaction against the traditions of the older generation, and the coming together of the basis for a new kind Marxist culture, even though this new type didn't materialize instantaneously and there were the notable if exceptional link-ups mentioned earlier.

Significantly, the basis of the New Left Marxist cultural critique, which influences the outlook, priorities, and methodology of the essays in this book, was first of all the student movement. As a result, in the second phase the terrain for Marxist cultural criticism shifted from a creative cultural practice closely allied with proletarian and anti-racist movements to the academy. The appearance in 1971 of Fredric Jameson's *Marxism and Form* heralded the new US Marxist criticism. Jameson's audience was the elite university campus, not the community college or the working-class institution.

Where the university now took priority over the workplace and social settings of the US working class, the new cultural critique reflected the middle-class underpinnings of the academy. Single-issue and then separatist politics increasingly characterized the social movements associated with the New Left. The early Civil Rights movement had a major student component at the outset, although it became more plebeian as manifested in the ghetto-based Black Power movement. The Free Speech, sexual freedom, and cultural lifestyle struggles concomitant with growing anti-war and anti-draft campaigns emerged in the mid and late 1960s. The mass student organization, Students for a Democratic Society (SDS), which in its early phase rejected Marxism, self-destructed a few years later because of virulent disagreement among Maoist Marxist-Leninist factions that unexpectedly appeared. The anti-Vietnam War movement was university-based at its inception, although it gradually extended into broader reaches of society. Simultaneously there emerged the Second Wave of Feminism; nationalist struggles of Chicanos, Asian-Americans, Puerto Ricans, and Native Americans; and, especially after the 1969 rebellion at the Stonewall Inn, a gay bar in New York City, more visible gay and lesbian struggles. In the 1980s, while there was an overall decline in radical activities, there appeared small ongoing solidarity movements with revolutionary struggles in South Africa, Nicaragua, and El Salvador; nuclear disarmament movements; and a new environmental movement.[7]

The 1990s, however, have tended to put the Left on the defensive, perhaps more than ever before. Early hopes for a positive outcome to the collapse of the oppressive regime in the USSR were dashed by the rise of nationalist reaction and the weakness of working-class self-mobilization. The "Vietnam Syndrome" was clearly broken by the US-led Gulf War. Developments in Nicaragua, El Salvador, and South Africa have shifted revolutionary strategy onto new and unfamiliar terrain. Although there have been positive developments such as the election of Ron Carey's reform slate to the leadership of the International Brotherhood of Teamsters in 1991, and the inspirational rise of the Workers' Party in Brazil, much of the US Left misplaced its hopes by supporting the

election of Bill Clinton, forgetting key lessons of past decades about the incapac-
ity of the Democratic Party to carry out genuine reform.

What can one expect from a Marxist cultural movement in the coming
decades? Of course, it is far easier to theorize *post facto* than *a priori*. As I argued
in *The New York Intellectuals* (1987), most of the participants in that strand of the
1930s radicalization grandly misestimated at the outset of their journey the trajectory that they would eventually follow. This set the stage for many of them to
succumb to the very kind of deradicalization against which they had originally
inveighed, with blithe rationalizations amounting to little more than the truism
that "things are different now." It would be foolhardy, and against the method
I proposed in that book, to prognosticate, especially in terms of a "master narrative," about the fate of the current generation of Marxist intellectuals in the
United States. Even worse would be to count upon a new economic depression
or other cataclysmic event to jar a new generation to the Left. Not only are such
predictions of dubious scientific value, but they contribute to a fatalistic version
of socialism and imply that Marxists hope for greater suffering as an instrument
to realize their dreams.

The preponderance of my literary work involves reconstructing, from a
frankly contemporary perspective, past models and paradigms for a critical
contemplation that may precipitate self-induced action. Such retrospective
experience cannot, however, predict or mandate behavior in a new political era.
The present category of "Marxist intellectuals" must be significantly retheor-
ized in the mid 1990s. It consists of overlapping generations that include a
rapidly vanishing breed of veterans from the 1930s, such as surviving older
editors of *Monthly Review, Jewish Currents,* and *Science and Society*; a university-
based layer of scholars who were radicalized in the 1960s as young academics
or students; and a younger generation which has grown up with little experience of mass social struggles. Marxist scholarship has largely been subsumed by
post-Marxist and post-modernist debates, with a much greater emphasis on
independent subject positions as women, people of color, and gays and lesbians.

I see part of my role as a scholar as making accessible and relevant to present
and potential socialist activists the experiences of like-minded people from the
past, especially hitherto obscure cultural workers or those who have been rele-
gated as "minor." I certainly encourage other scholars to extend this method
into new areas in order to recover the contributions of not only cultural workers
in fields outside literature (painting, sculpture, cartooning, music, dance) but
also union activists and political militants, especially women and people of color.

If I had to cite one "danger" for radical and socialist intellectuals and cultural
workers that has cropped up repeatedly in my study of the past, and that is
therefore quite likely to be the "Achilles' heel" of any future Left, it is the recur-
rent tendency to misunderstand the indispensability of socialist organization. I
simply cannot believe that intellectuals will be able to ally with people in struggle against oppression and repression without developing a serious alternative

political organization. While we have no dearth of examples of failed and dreary organizations, especially self-proclaimed "revolutionary vanguards," that have degenerated and self-destructed, intellectuals cannot afford to turn their backs on organizational commitment and responsibility; abstention is only guaranteed to make things worse for themselves and everybody else who desperately needs unity in constructive action. Marxist cultural workers must continue to devote their skills and goodwill to the serious and admittedly very difficult task of creating an intelligent, broad, and militant socialist organization that can harmoniously represent the aspirations of working people, oppressed nationalities, women, gays and lesbians, and all others who suffer the consequences of a callous, exploitative, and destructive capitalist system.

Since *Writing from the Left* is a collection taking up reprints of influential critical writings and "lost" novels, new works of scholarship, and conference topics of the early 1990s, its contents and emphases have been partially determined by factors beyond my control. Although feminist aspects of this book may be a modest improvement over my earlier ones, they still remain too weak; the space given here to Latino, Asian-American, Native American, and gay and lesbian issues, and to mass culture, scarcely reflects the actual research and attention I have devoted to these topics in the last few years. Following the policy used in *The Responsibility of Intellectuals* (1992), my collection of essays from the 1980s, I have made only minimal corrections to previously published texts and have restored only passages that were cut from the original writings for reasons of space. Since these essays, reviews, and talks were prepared for various occasions, it is inevitable that there should be some overlap and, in a few cases, repetition of key conceptual points and examples. This accounts for some divergence in style and in the amount and length of notes, which are more academic and detailed in articles that appeared in scholarly journals, and lighter and less dense in those from more popular publications or from conference papers. Also, I continue to follow the policy of capitalizing "Communism" whenever it refers to political movements or ideas associated with the Third International, regardless of grammatical form; I wish other scholars would do the same, so as to preserve the uncapitalized "communism" for broader use as a term embracing the other varieties of revolutionary Marxism as well. In general, I use the styling "anticommunism" rather than "anti-Communism" when referring to right-wing persecution because, in the United States, attacks on the official Communist movement have invariably led to repression of the entire far Left.

At the beginning of this book I have included a brief and highly selective political chronology of the US Left, extending from the origins of the Communist Party to the present. The most distinctive part of the argument of this book, as elaborated in the paper "From Old Left to New in US Literary

7

Radicalism," is its dual challenge to the historiographical conventions of identifying the Communist cultural achievement with "The Thirties," and of treating the "New Left" as far too "new." In fact, the identification of the Marxist literary Left with "The Thirties" has been so great that, even though none of my four past books are about the 1930s, and I have no expertise in the 1930s outside of radical developments, I am frequently described as a "specialist in the 1930s." The reduction of a long-term and central cultural tradition into one decade is a major factor obscuring the extraordinary writing by Marxist cultural workers who grew up in that period but started publishing in the 1940s and 1950s. Moreover, it tends to "type" radical literature as a whole according to 1930s genres and paradigms based on Mike Gold's *Jews Without Money* (1930), Jack Conroy's *The Disinherited* (1933), and John Dos Passos's *USA* (1938). The result has been the "loss" of much extraordinarily good radical writing that somehow looks "different" for various reasons – because it appeared in mass culture forms, emanated from regions of the country not valued in canonical studies of "The Thirties," or was produced by writers not from the Euro-American and African-American milieux usually associated with the 1930s.

There has been a steady stream of competent books and dissertations on the US literary Left since I completed graduate school in late 1974, which I document in my opening essay on "The Legacy of Daniel Aaron." But none has the freshness nor the impact of books published in the past few years, some of which I refer to in passing as manuscripts-in-progress in essays reprinted in this book. The new Marxist theory, largely Eurocentric and applied to elite texts, that became attractive in the 1970s took a long time to "trickle down" to those few scholars, myself included, working on the literary Left. I had been reading Lukács, Gramsci, and Fanon since I was an undergraduate at Antioch College in the 1960s, but I found no encouragement to work on the literary Left from a theoretical perspective at the time I wrote my dissertation on James T. Farrell in 1974.

In 1983, however, I made an argument for the unity of the new Marxism and the reconsideration of the US literary Left in my book *The Revolutionary Imagination*. Despite strong reviews in the academic press, the book, unfortunately, had no impact in Marxist cultural circles at that time. Although I incorporated a dimension of literary theory in *The New York Intellectuals*, especially regarding the treatment of ideology in the section "The New York Intellectuals in Fiction," I was surprised, albeit pleasantly, by the appearance in 1989 of Cary Nelson's remarkable *Repression and Recovery: Modern American Poetry and the Politics of Cultural Memory, 1910–1945*. In generating excitement about forgotten Marxist poets, Nelson accomplished exactly what I had failed to do six years earlier in *The Revolutionary Imagination*.

The most important work following Nelson's was Paula Rabinowitz's 1991 *Labor and Desire: Women's Revolutionary Fiction in Depression America* (which had been preceded by her 1987 anthology of left-wing women writers co-edited with

Charlotte Nekola, *Writing Red*). While Rabinowitz's texts were mainly restricted to the 1930s, and her research less biographically based than mine, she brilliantly managed to demonstrate the contemporary relevance of 1930s literature by women to the practical concerns of the present generation through the revision of the typologies for interpreting narrative form. Appearing a year later was James Bloom's *Left Letters: The Culture Wars of Mike Gold and Joseph Freeman* (1992), an impressive book from the point of view of situating earlier radicals in the tradition of canon debate. In late 1993, Barbara Foley's *Radical Representations: Politics and Form in US Proletarian Fiction, 1929–1941* was published. Foley focuses on the 1930s alone, and her selections are weighted toward canonical versions of what constitutes radical literature. Still, despite her error in declaring anti-Stalinism to be the same as anti-Marxism, she is an exceptionally able scholar and admirably serious about her subject, which she explores with unusual rigor and from many fresh angles. In particular, her chapter on "Race, Class and the 'Negro Question'" is a fine critical survey of the scholarship in that field and contains an excellent application of her ideas to the writings of Richard Wright and William Attaway.

The latest major step forward has been Douglass Wixson's *Worker-Writer in America: Jack Conroy and the Tradition of Midwestern Literary Radicalism, 1889–1990* (1994). This is a monumental study with extraordinary biographical detail and intelligent observations about the works of a large number of neglected figures.

I also wish to emphasize that the scholarly essays in this collection are only one aspect of my political-intellectual life in the last few years. As an activist in the socialist organization Solidarity, and a member of the editorial board of *Against the Current*, I have devoted considerable time and effort to projects inappropriate in their topics for inclusion in this volume, which nonetheless help inform its context. In November 1986 I was fortunate to be part of a delegation from the City of Ann Arbor that traveled to Nicaragua to establish Sister City relations with Juigalpa in Region Five during the Contra War, and I wrote about the Nicaraguan Revolution in "Perspectives on the Sandinista National Liberation Front," *Against the Current* 7 (January–February 1987). About the same time, I was involved in anti-racist struggles at the University of Michigan, and expressed my views on racism in "The 'New Racism' in the US," *International Viewpoint* 138 (April 4, 1988). In early 1989 I traveled to the mountains of northern New Mexico to report on armed seizures of land there by the Mexicano population, which I described in "Land or Death in New Mexico," *Against the Current* 19 (March–April 1989). In 1991 I gave a number of public talks on "The Campaign Against 'Political Correctness,'" which became a pamphlet published by Solidarity. In June 1992 I had the opportunity to travel to Cuba to deliver a paper at the University of Havana and to study the current stage of the Cuban Revolution; and in July 1992 I participated in a human rights fact-finding delegation to Haiti, which I described in "Haiti Under the Iron Heel" in *International Viewpoint* 249 (October 1993). Some of my opinions about political perspectives for the socialist Left in the United States appear in "Remaking Marxism in the 1990s," in *Monthly Review* 43, no. 5 (October 1991), and in "From the Old Left to the New and Beyond: The Legacy and Prospects for Socialism in the United States," in the Winter 1992 issue of *International Marxist Review* (No. 14).

Finally, I wish to express my gratitude to a few friends and comrades who have assisted the preparation of this volume in various ways: Patrick Quinn, Aaron Kramer, Franklin Folsom, Sender Garlin, Lloyd Brown, Paula Rabinowitz, Michael Löwy, Ellen Poteet, Christopher Phelps, Constance Coiner, Marcia Endore Goodman, Alexander Saxton, Larry Goldstein, Xavier Nicholas, and John Sanford.

Notes

1. I have always argued that "anti-Stalinism," if *detached* from a revolutionary socialist framework, can easily evolve in a rightward direction.

2. These early writings, uncollected, appeared in student newspapers and magazines as well as publications of the Young Socialist Alliance and Socialist Workers' Party, such as the *Young Socialist*, *Militant*, *International Socialist Review*, and *Intercontinental Press*, during the 1960s and 1970s.

3. See V. F. Calverton, *The Liberation of American Literature* (1932); James T. Farrell, *A Note on Literary Criticism* (1936); Granville Hicks, *The Great Tradition* (1933; revised 1935); and Bernard Smith, *Forces in American Criticism* (1939).

4. Genevieve Taggard, *The Life and Mind of Emily Dickinson* (1930). However, Barbara Giles, whose major work was the novel *The Gentle Bush* (1947), wrote a body of reviews and essays for the *New Masses* and *Masses & Mainstream* that might eventually be collected, and Josephine Herbst, also mainly a novelist, produced critical reminiscences that were posthumously published as *The Starched Blue Sky of Spain* (1991).

5. Establishing the legitimacy of these correctives was a major purpose of my books *James T. Farrell: The Revolutionary Socialist Years* (1978), *The Revolutionary Imagination* (1983), and *The New York Intellectuals* (1987), and part of *The Responsibility of Intellectuals* (1992).

6. See the Feminist Press edition of *Salt of the Earth* (1978) for a good example of the New Left's identification with this aspect of the Old Left's cultural achievement.

7. See the valuable collection *Reshaping the US Left: Popular Struggles in the 1980s* (1988), edited by Mike Davis and Michael Sprinker.

PART I

Rethinking the Classics

1

The Legacy of Daniel Aaron

If a work of cultural history can be seen as analogous to the scientific works that establish what Thomas H. Kuhn calls "paradigms" in the sciences,[1] Daniel Aaron's pathbreaking *Writers on the Left: Episodes in American Literary Communism* (1961) is a leading contender among literary historical works published during the post-World War II era. Kuhn's *The Structure of Scientific Revolutions* (1962), appearing just one year after Aaron's book, may suggest several possible reasons for the endurance of Aaron's achievement. Anticipating the scientific paradigm theorized by Kuhn, *Writers on the Left* rethinks first principles as a consequence of the accumulation of challenges to older perceptions. Yet Aaron also offers a sufficiently open-ended argument to stimulate subsequent scholars to pursue additional literary problems within its broad framework.[2]

Thirty years later, there is no doubt that Aaron's 460-page volume was *the* pivotal text establishing US "literary radicalism" as a distinctive field in academic as well as popular scholarship. The classic, venerable status of this text can be easily demonstrated by the hundreds of references to it as an authoritative source in virtually all scholarship about US radical writers published since the 1960s in the United States, Britain, and France.[3] While many scholars, including myself, have tried to augment Aaron's work, there has never been another book seriously rivaling his achievement in overall scope, accuracy, and insight into the phenomenon of writers in the United States drawn to the far Left – first to left-wing socialism, then to the Communist movement – during the first five decades of this century.[4] This Morningside Books edition pays tribute to the stature of *Writers on the Left* as a historic treasure in twentieth-century US literary history that needs to remain permanently available to students, scholars, and general readers.

This chapter originally appeared as the "Introduction" to Daniel Aaron, *Writers on the Left: Episodes in American Literary Communism*, Morningside Books edn (New York: Columbia University Press, 1992).

At the present, teaching and scholarship about politically committed writers is of greater interest than ever before, despite conservative trends in the US national political climate since the election of Ronald Reagan in 1980. However, the field of "committed literature" looks rather different now than it did when Aaron was writing due to the recent emphasis on women writers, writers of color, mass culture, and the rise of a contemporary cultural theory (called "Cultural Studies") involving a Marxism infinitely more complex, various, and recondite than the one discussed in Aaron's book.[5] Nevertheless, it would be a mistake for students and younger scholars to see *Writers on the Left* as bound by the context in which it was produced, thereby reducing it to a foil that serves only to exemplify the "old," pre-enlightened mode of discussing culture and politics. It is crucial to recognize that Aaron accurately recreated the Left cultural movement in the United States as its major surviving participants themselves experienced it, and that by doing so he, in some important ways, transgressed the bounds of the conventional scholarship of his day. The task of a new generation of scholars is not to freeze his study but enlarge upon it by invoking new areas of knowledge and fresher evaluative categories. Toward this end, Aaron's work will no doubt be the source of some meanings different from those he originally produced, but the book will always be foundational in the historiography of studies of committed writers.

Genesis

Writers on the Left was not the first significant work on its subject. Walter Rideout's *The Radical Novel in the United States, 1900–1954*, a chronicle and typology of fictional texts and related debates, appeared in 1956, while Irving Howe and Lewis Coser's *The American Communist Party: A Critical History*, with biting chapters on Communist literary foibles, was published in 1957. Hitherto, there had been published a series of anticommunist tracts and Cold War prompted confessions relating to the subject of Marxism and literary intellectuals. One was Eugene Lyons's 1941 journalistic survey, *The Red Decade*, whose introduction was candidly titled, "In Defense of Red-Baiting." Another was Richard Crossman's 1950 anthology, *The God That Failed*, that featured two US writers among its six contributors.

Despite these and a few other writings about the US literary Left, it was Aaron's study that inaugurated the field as we know it today, with its characteristic strengths and weaknesses. Based on massive research, it is exceptionally readable and replete with reliable summaries. Aaron comprehensively reviews the knottiest debates in a lively, polished manner. His scholarly apparatus is substantial, yet it never retards the pace of the book. The tone is mature and balanced. Most important, Aaron's central thesis remains the basis of the bulk of the most productive scholarship in the field that has ensued. He argues convincingly that the Depression and the Communist Party did not *create* literary radicalism; it *focused* and *canalized* an indigenous tradition that had, and still has, its own roots and *raison d'être*.[6] Aaron's fascinating chapters on the first three decades of this century notwithstanding, *Writers on the Left* is ultimately about the unhappy marriage of Communism and the US cultural Left.[7] With the unraveling of the marriage in serious ways after 1939, the narrative begins to lose steam.

Aaron wrote the book while teaching English at Smith College, a position he had assumed in 1939. In 1971, he left Smith to join the Harvard English Department, serving also for a time as chair of Harvard's Committee on American Civilization. He initially came to his subject from a unique position, having more than merely armchair knowledge. Born in 1912 in Chicago, he graduated from the University of Michigan in 1933. In the late 1930s, as a graduate student at Harvard, he observed first-hand the pro-Communist intelligentsia active in the Harvard Teachers' Union . Some of these raised funds for the Republican cause in Spain, and a few met in a discussion group at his apartment where Communist Party intellectual Granville Hicks expostulated on the *Handbook of Marxism* (1935). According to a memoir published in the fiftieth anniversary issue of *Partisan Review*, Aaron's friend Hicks, then a "counsellor" at Harvard, invited him to join the Party but, although he considered himself decidedly to the left of the New Deal, the organization had no attraction for him because of its church-like qualities.[8] Twenty years later, partly because he had never been a Party member, Aaron was invited to write a book on the impact of Communism on writers for a series sponsored by the Ford Foundation. Although previously he had had no inclination to engage in such a study, he was nonetheless in an enviable situation to make use of personal contacts from his Harvard days – not only Hicks, but also Robert Gorham Davis, who had been in the Party while at Harvard and later came to teach at Smith; and Newton Arvin, a Party enthusiast during the 1930s who also taught at Smith. Aaron additionally developed a close association with Joseph Freeman, the fallen *New Masses* editor who served as Aaron's "Virgil" in his journey through the left-wing cultural world on both coasts.[9] No doubt Aaron's awareness that these participants in the events to be depicted in the book would be eventually reading it, if they were not already looking over his shoulder as he wrote, encouraged the "negotiated" character of the work that emerged.

More specifically, responsiveness to the perspectives of such diverse acquaintances as Mike Gold and Max Eastman probably accounts for the peculiarly non-partisan character of the paradigm Aaron established. On the one hand, *Writers on the Left* was praised by some reviewers, including the novelist Philip Bonosky writing in the Communist theoretical organ, for lacking the stridency one might expect in light of the controversiality of the subject. On the other hand, there were literary critics, including the one-time Trotskyist sympathizer William Phillips, who felt that Aaron's personal assessments were too weak, a view to which Aaron himself came to subscribe.[10]

Impact

Partly because of such broad sympathies on the part of its author, *Writers on the Left* became a pioneering study that effectively brought to life in its pages a number of the leading men (and I say "men" deliberately, because no women were featured) who initiated and guided the radical literary movement over five decades: Max Eastman, Floyd Dell, John Reed, Randolph Bourne, Joseph Freeman, John Dos Passos, Michael Gold, V. F. Calverton, Granville Hicks, and Malcolm Cowley. Aaron employed a complicated but lively structure inspired by John Dos Passos's *USA* trilogy that enabled him to shuttle among group narratives, representative figures, and inter-chapters. He combined biography and cultural history to present a general chronology of the rise and fall of the literary Left.

In 1968, James B. Gilbert, a historian once associated with the journal *Studies on the Left*, found it necessary to trace some of the same ground as *Writers on the Left* in order to present the context of *Partisan Review* in his *Writers and Partisans: A History of Literary Radicalism in America*. Gilbert used a similar historico-cultural narrative over several decades to establish the first cogent perspective on the evolution of the pro-modernist, anti-Stalinist communists who gathered around *Partisan Review* after it broke with the official Communist Party in 1936–37.[11]

The more specialized studies that followed Gilbert's book aimed to fill many other gaps that remained in the field; more recently there have been efforts to advance the serviceable but comparatively atheoretical methodology of Aaron and Gilbert. Starting in the 1980s, there also have been significant steps forward in the recovery of women's literary radicalism through the "rediscovery" of Josephine Herbst, and the growing recognition of the importance of Tillie Olsen and Meridel Le Sueur.[12] These last two writers are especially significant because, still active in politics and literature today, they openly embrace their roots in the Communist experience of the 1930s; hence they are living exemplars of the relevance and vitality of certain aspects of the Communist literary tradition as a usable past. Publishing projects by the Feminist Press, Monthly Review, and West End Press have brought back into circulation novels by Fielding Burke, Josephine Herbst, Myra Page, Josephine Johnson, and Tess Slesinger, and volumes of short fiction and reportage by Le Sueur and Mary Heaton Vorse. In 1987, a vibrant collection edited by Charlotte Nekola and Paula Rabinowitz, *Writing Red: An Anthology of American Women Writers, 1930–1940*, returned to print the work of fifty additional authors. There have been similar developments involving the publication of biographies of writers of color such as Richard Wright, W. E. B. Du Bois, Claude McKay, and Langston Hughes, but the task remains of reconstructing and assessing how a significant component of the African-American left-wing intelligentsia was shaped partly through an encounter with Communism.[13] In recent decades there have been new studies of Marxist writers outside of New York City – for example, in Hollywood and the Mid-West – but work done in other regions (such as the South, the Southwest, and the San Francisco Bay Area) remains largely unexplored.[14]

Aaron's book also succeeded in establishing the field as a meaningful and lively area of research at a politically significant moment – the early 1960s. The critical distance that allowed the author to stand above political partisanship, while rendering the main actors he portrayed sympathetic, could hardly have been more effective than at the inauguration of a new era of radicalization. Indeed, I myself was handed the book by a hard-bitten, cynical, older reporter at the *Washington Post*, where I was employed as a copy boy during the summer of 1965. She was dismayed at the SDS (Students for a Democratic Society) and anti-war buttons that I wore at work, and wanted to show me that this sort of radicalization had happened before, inevitably leading to a bad end. Instead, the book allowed me to see a role for myself as an aspiring writer in relation to the movements for social change then unfolding around me.

The widespread, favorable reception of the book was an indication that McCarthyism was in retreat as an intellectual force, and that a new mood of political tolerance was in birth. *Writers on the Left* was followed by reissues of anthologies of writings by Randolph Bourne and Malcolm Cowley;[15] memoirs by Edward Dahlberg, Max Eastman, Granville Hicks, Matthew Josephson, and Alfred Kazin;[16] selected writings from the *Masses*, *New Masses*, and *Anvil*;[17] and anthologies of writing during the Depression edited by Aaron and Robert Bendiner, Louis Filler, Jack Salzman, and Harvey Swados.[18] Reprints of radical novels by Jack Conroy, Edward Dahlberg, Daniel Fuchs, Michael Gold, Robert Cantwell, Tillie Olsen, Henry Roth, Tess Slesinger, Dalton Trumbo, Nathanael West, Richard Wright, Chester Himes, and others were published in years following the appearance of *Writers on the Left*.

Aaron's book had just the right tone to transmit the legacy of the literary Left as a usable past to the new generation at the beginning of the 1960s, although he was equally concerned with explaining it to veterans of the struggles of the 1930s. Aaron's book was one of the Fund for the Republic's series on "Communism in American Life," whose main purpose was to counteract the McCarthyite myth that Communism in the United States was a conspiracy by demonstrating, instead, that its attractiveness for intellectuals was due to their collective lapse in judgment. Aaron nonetheless had a genuine affection for many of the individuals discussed. If he consented to the mood of the late 1950s in judging those who considered themselves revolutionaries to be thoroughly misguided, he also drew back from Howe and Coser's conclusion that the Communist experience had to be assessed mainly in the negative, as having "exerted a profoundly destructive and corrupting influence upon American radicalism," resulting in "an enormous waste of potentially valuable human beings."[19]

Aaron also refused to endorse withdrawal and disenchantment as acceptable responses to the problems facing disillusioned left-wing literary intellectuals. The concluding paragraph of *Writers on the Left* admits no easy answer to the problems posed by the Communist experience: "We who precariously survive in the sixties can regret their inadequacies and failures, their romanticism, their capacity for self-deception, their shrillness, their self-righteousness. It is less easy to scorn their efforts, however blundering and ineffective, to change the world."[20] The phrase "change the world," drawn from Marx's Eleventh Thesis on Feuerbach, was also the title of Michael Gold's column in the *Daily Worker* and of a collection of his columns published by International Publishers in 1936. Aaron profoundly disagreed with Gold, but did not despise or caricature his efforts or those of his comrades.

Writers on the Left, in fact, is riven by a deep ambivalence. It was unquestionably anti-Soviet (in the sense that it opposed the policies and practices of the regime of the USSR), but this understandable anti-Stalinism was not marked by the shrill, smug self-righteousness of mainstream Cold War liberalism, honed to an art form by Sidney Hook. Aaron's anti-Stalinism, while anti-Leninist as well, was not anti-Marxist. Aaron saw the Communist Party as an intolerable straitjacket on writers; but he did not advocate anti-Communism as a more important concern for US intellectuals than anti-capitalism, or conclude that writers and left-wing politics are inherently a disastrous mix.

Through his consideration of the relatively independent behavior of Joseph Freeman, Aaron tended to deflate the myth that Communist Party members were nothing but mindless "soldiers of Stalin." Simultaneously, through his discussion of Granville Hicks, who seems to have been painfully gutted by the Communist experience, Aaron made a convincing case that excessive Soviet influence on US radicals was among the primary causes of the failure of the left-wing literary movement.

In the main, *Writers on the Left* developed what would become a more prominent genre in US scholarship, the social and political history of intellectuals. Yet also, perhaps in an inconsistent and intuitive way, Aaron's polyphonic approach pointed toward certain features of what we now call the "new" social history. Instead of restricting himself to quoting and discussing the most prominent writers or official pronouncements, Aaron presented opinions from a wide range of individuals (not just the "head-boys," as Josephine Herbst later complained, although they certainly were all men).[21] He drew from personal interviews, private letters, obscure publications, and political documents, as well as essays, fiction, and memoirs. Today, of course, it is easy to fault Aaron for his failure to pursue the categories of class, gender, race, and ethnicity; it would be harder to fault him for errors of fact, which are few.

As a result of Aaron's influence, the paradigm of US radical literary studies came to have three general features. First, the field has at its center the complex interaction between the indigenous traditions of US writers and Communism – both Communism as an ideal, and the narrower promulgation of "Stalinism" by the institutions of the Communist Party USA.[22] This is a valid approach because the Communist experience of the 1930s was in many respects the zenith of writers on the Left until the 1960s, at least from the perspective of numbers of Left writers and their production of critical and creative writings. A case has also been made by James B. Gilbert, myself, and several others for the importance of Trotskyist-influenced communism as an additionally fruitful arena of inquiry in quest of writers responsive to modernism and contemporary Marxist aesthetics – not to mention those searching for more democratic forms of communism. No one, however, has as yet been successful in making the argument for a substantial achievement in fiction, poetry, or literary criticism on the part of social democrats and anarchists, or other types of radicals in the 1930s or thereafter.[23]

A second feature of the paradigm is that the central literary form for Left writers is the novel – especially the "proletarian" novel.[24] In the United States the proletarian novel was the Communist Party's favored term for the radical novel in the early Depression, although a tradition of radical literature dealing with working-class activities lasted well beyond the 1930s. The proletarian novel has been the subject of more than ten dissertations, with several others in progress.[25] Studies of Marxist criticism, reportage and drama in the United States are significantly fewer, although hardly negligible.[26] The most serious absence has been the failure of scholars to devote appropriate attention to left-wing poetry, especially that written by such poets as Stanley Burnshaw, Joy Davidman, Sol Funaroff, Carlos Bulosan, Frank Marshall Davis, Aaron Kramer, Horace Gregory, Robert Hayden, Norman Macleod, Don Gordon, Isidor Schneider, and Genevieve Taggard.[27]

A third feature of the paradigm is that the field was for a long time isolated from the development of contemporary Marxist theory; conventional literary judgments prevailed, forming a consensus that the literary contributions by leftists were significant but modest, having sociological rather than "literary" value. With the exception of an occasional essay on Kenneth Burke by Fredric Jameson or Frank Lentriccia, commentary on Carlos Bulosan by E. San Juan, Jr., or Marxist-feminist insights by Deborah Rosenfelt and Elaine Hedges, a substantial encounter of contemporary Marxist aesthetics with US literary radicalism did not occur during the 1970s or early 1980s.[28] However, a dramatic new phase of reconsideration is under way, heralded by Cary Nelson's *Repression and Recovery* (1989), Paula Rabinowitz's *Labor and Desire* (1991), and James Bloom's *Left Letters: The Culture Wars of Mike Gold and Joseph Freeman* (1992), as well as books-in-progress by Constance Coiner, Barbara Foley, and Douglass Wixson.[29]

Assessment

Among the most striking features of *Writers on the Left* is the way that Aaron roots the leftist literary tradition in indigenous trends in US culture beginning with the pre-World War I literary rebellion championed by the *Masses*. While this approach has the disadvantage of limiting the amount of space that might otherwise have been devoted to later episodes and individuals, Aaron, by establishing a pre-Depression tradition, was able to specify the elements of dependency on the Russian Revolution and the Soviet Union that grew to a crescendo in the 1930s without reducing the complex experience of literary radicalism to simply the Soviet influence.

Also noteworthy is the method by which Aaron shifts back and forth between general historical chapters on matters such as the impact of the trial of Sacco and Vanzetti, and individual portraits of writers such as Mike Gold. But here he misjudged in imagining that his group of key actors constituted a genuine "cross-section of the literary Left Wing."[30] It is clear that women writers such as Josephine Herbst and Meridel Le Sueur should have been included among the major portraits. Moreover, it is surprising that Richard Wright, the subject of a later essay by Aaron, was not selected for scrutiny.[31] Admittedly, it would not be easy to decide which individuals to eliminate from the galaxy Aaron assembled to make room for additions. Nonetheless, despite the limitations of his choices from the vantage of gender, ethnicity, region, and even literary genre, Aaron's strategy works brilliantly on a technical level to convincingly depict writers who are representative of both conventional and distinctive trends within the Left tradition.

Moreover, Aaron's use of personal interviews, letters, manuscripts, ephemeral publications, and little known as well as major novels creates a rich texture enabling the reader to experience something of the "feel" of living through the famous debates and crises of the literary Left. This technique also creates a blend of many voices and perspectives anticipating certain aspects of what is now called the "new history of American Communism" in which pronouncements of the "tops" are contrasted with the practice of rank-and-file activists.[32]

How should contemporary scholars, students, and writers proceed to close the gap between Aaron's achievement and the research and theory of the past thirty years? Aaron's portrait of the cultural Left must be reconciled with the fact that subsequent scholars have discovered many individuals and episodes other than those included in *Writers on the Left*. While such recently reclaimed writers have yet to completely displace the canonical writers of the era, the case for expanding or otherwise transforming the canon is not so hopeless as it once was. In 1961, Aaron could remark with justification that "[Joseph] Kalar, Herman Spector, Martin Russak, Joseph Vogel, H. H. Lewis . . . [are] now virtually forgotten."[33] Yet in 1977, *Bastard in the Ragged Suit: Writings of Herman Spector* appeared; in 1985, *Joseph Kalar: Poet of Protest: An Anthology* was published; in 1989, Joseph Vogel's novel *Man's Courage* (1938) was reprinted; and in 1992, H. H. Lewis's complete works were among those being considered for reprinting by a university press. Works by writers who were barely more than footnotes in *Writers on the Left* – Alvah Bessie, Guy Endore, Claude McKay, Kenneth

Fearing, and Genevieve Taggard – have just reappeared or are about to be reissued. Other writers, not mentioned at all – such as William Attaway, Sanora Babb, Thomas Bell, Carlos Bulosan, Don West, Chester Himes, and John Sanford – have also had some of their works reissued. Still others, such as Ben Appel, Martha Dodd, Alexander Saxton, and H. T. Tsiang, are excellent candidates for revival.

Indeed, perhaps the greatest challenge to those of us who highly value *Writers on the Left* is to come to terms, at last, with the literary record or ranking of worthy works of the time.[34] This subject is worth a few brief observations, since this Morningside Books edition is likely to be used in university courses that engage literary as well as intellectual, political, and historical texts. And here is where there likely will be the greatest gap between the focus of Aaron's book and many of the interests of younger scholars and their students, for whom Max Eastman and Granville Hicks do not constitute the most inspiring models of politico-cultural resistance and rebellion. Can *Writers on the Left* prove useful for those whose examples of committed writers are likely to be Nadine Gordimer, Ngugi Wa Thiong'o, Ernesto Cardenal, or Toni Morrison?

Aaron's explicit literary judgments are few, although that fact in itself is a kind of judgment. In the final chapter, "Think Back on Us," he offers a summary of the impact of left politics on writing:

> The strongest writers of the thirties used politics and were not used by it. The party could not have dictated to a Dos Passos, a Hemingway, a Lewis, a Dreiser, a Steinbeck, a Wolfe, even if it had tried to do so. But the Left writer, in and out of the party, faced something more insidious than party pressure: his own compulsion to subordinate the problems of his craft and deeply felt intellectual concerns to political policy.[35]

Aaron's observation about self-imposed political pressures on art strikes me as the kind of insight that grows from extensive first-hand observation; in contrast, his list of "strongest" writers of the 1930s seems merely an expression of the conventional wisdom of the literary profession in the 1950s, a roster so "obvious" that it seems to need no defense.

Yet, it is important to note that, without exception, all the names on Aaron's list are of novelists, and the period emphasized is "The Thirties" – even though *Writers on the Left* covers all genres (except drama) during the years 1910–65. It is also ambiguous as to whether the adjective "strongest" refers to a writer's general achievement or to particular books. Leaving aside the omission of Faulkner, and the fact that the work of Steinbeck and Wolfe is no longer so universally lauded as it once was, it is worth considering that Lewis's novels written during the 1930s are *Ann Vickers* (1933), *Work of Art* (1934), *It Can't Happen Here* (1935), *The Prodigal Parents* (1938), and *Bethel Merriday* (1940). Hemingway published *Death in the Afternoon* (1932), *Winner Take Nothing* (1933), *Green Hills of Africa*

(1935), *To Have and Have Not* (1937), and *The Fifth Column and the First Forty-Nine Stories* (1938). Dreiser's only books of the 1930s are *Dawn* (1931) and *Tragic America* (1931). This raises the question as to whether many of the canonically important writers of the 1930s were already established and familiar prior to the Depression, due to work published in previous decades, and are thought to have an importance during the 1930s mainly because of their stature as well-known writers.

Moreover, even if we limit ourselves to the Thirties, and if we leave aside books written during that decade that were published in later years (Richard Wright's *Lawd Today* [1963], Meridel Le Sueur's *The Girl* [1978], and Tillie Olsen's *Yonnondio* [1974]), it is plausible to argue that other novels of the 1930s such as Grace Lumpkin's *The Wedding* (1939), Arna Bontemps's *Black Thunder* (1936), James T. Farrell's *Young Lonigan* (1932), Josephine Herbst's *Rope of Gold* (1939), Henry Roth's *Call It Sleep* (1934), and Nelson Algren's *Somebody in Boots* (1935) are equal in craft and vision to most of the novels written by Aaron's "strong" writers.

I don't think, however, that the final resolution of the conundrum of the "quality" left-wing literary practice will ultimately come through such "one-on-one" competition. It will be more fruitful to argue for a dramatic expansion and complication of our analysis of the relations between politics and literature, between "high" and "mass" culture, and between text and "value." In the case of the cultural Left, we must begin by deflating many conventional, arbitrary divisions. Writers on the Left moved freely among poetry, drama, reportage, fiction, screenwriting, and other literary forms. The career of Alfred Hayes, author of the song "Joe Hill," three volumes of poetry, *The Girl on the Via Flaminia* (1949), and six other volumes of prose fiction, as well as plays, screenplays, and television shows, is but one example of that breadth; his contribution looks much "stronger" if one is allowed to combine and cross genres. Moreover, if we treat as worthy of scholarly analysis not only conventional radical novels about strikes and political conversions, but also work of radicals who produced popular fiction, detective fiction, science fiction, historical fiction, biography, and children's literature, the impact of the Left will be seen as far more substantial and central to our culture. In the course of three years, the radical Guy Endore wrote *The Sword of God: The Life of Joan of Arc* (1931), a fictionalized biography; *The Werewolf of Paris* (1933), a pulp horror classic; and *Babouk* (1934), a revolutionary historical novel about the Haitian slave revolt.

There is also the question of the literary value assigned to texts that explore uncharted terrain, that attempt what other writers have never explored. Raymond Williams valorizes this kind of creative endeavor as that which involves "the reproduction and illustration of hitherto excluded and subordinated models; the embodiment and performance of known but excluded and subordinated experiences and relationships; the articulation and formation of latent, momentary, and newly possible consciousness."[36] Among the pre-1956 radical texts that admirably burst the bonds of conventional material and perspectives are H. T. Tsiang's charting of the Depression landscape of Manhattan from a Chinese-American perspective, *The Hanging on Union Square* (1935); Gordon Kahn's posthumously published 1950s novel focusing on a Chicano draft resister during the Korean War, *A Long Way from Home* (first published in 1989); Martha Dodd's subtle inquiry into the dynamics of resistance to a loyalty oath at a Southern university in *The Searching Light* (1955); and the efforts of Fielding Burke, Grace Lumpkin, and others to capture the dynamics of race and gender in the 1929 Gastonia strike.

Moreover, even if one accepts "The Thirties" as the high point of the experience chronicled in *Writers on the Left* (which may not be so evident once we learn more about Left writing during World War II and the witch-hunt era), "The Thirties" lived on long after the decade was over in the careers of those shaped by their experiences; in memories of the 1930s that motivated later writing projects; and in traditions generated by the Thirties that were embraced by younger writers. A consummate novel of the labor movement such as K. B. Gilden's *Between the Hills and the Sea* (1971) is hardly imaginable without the 1930s in the background, although the setting is 1945–56. John Sanford's *A Very Good Land to Fall With* (1987) is largely based on the reproduction of documents and remembered moments of the 1930s, on which the author meditates.

The paradigm established by *Writers on the Left*, for all its accomplishments, does not resolve such questions for us; but the open-endedness of the book will not shut off the debate either. It should be appropriated not as a Bible of literary criticism or theory but as a description of controversies, careers, and "episodes." Many young scholars may dispute Aaron's implied perspective on what constitutes significant cultural achievement, yet his book remains vital to the reconstruction process they will engage. It is a fundamental part of the scaffolding without which our subsequent research and theory will become detached and lose perspective. Fortunately, this new edition of Aaron's indispensable work comes at a moment when it can do the most good as a resource for a new generation's efforts to develop a relation to an older tradition of political commitment. Just as Aaron's memories, experiences, and personal associations of the 1930s were a "gift" to him when he set out to write this book in 1955, so his *Writers on the Left* is a profound gift to us as we set out to rethink and revise the legacy of literary radicalism in the 1990s.

Notes

1. The term has various meanings, but generally denotes constellations of beliefs establishing a consensus about means and ends, including exemplary "puzzle-solutions." See Thomas S. Kuhn, "Postscript – 1969," *The Structure of Scientific Revolutions*, second ed (Chicago: University of Chicago Press, 1970), pp. 174–210.

2. In what is still likely the most provocative consideration of Kuhn, "T. S. Kuhn's Theory of Science and Its Implications for History," *American Historical Review* 78, no. 2 (April 1973), David A. Hollinger argues against the facile conflation of the "paradigms" of scientific communities with the somewhat looser programs for research that characterize other professional communities, but suggests that certain works of humanistic scholarship do serve to authorize and structure such programs. On pp. 382 and 384, Hollinger cites as examples C. Van Woodward's *Origins of the New South* and Perry Miller's *The New England Mind*, and cavils against the unproblematic representation of history as a Kuhnian scientific community. See also the discussion of literary paradigms in Anthony Easthope's *Literary and Cultural Studies* (New York: Routledge, 1991), pp. 3–12.

3. While these are the main countries where I follow the scholarship on US literary radicalism, I have seen references to *Writers on the Left* in work from Germany and Italy, and there are no doubt many references in the scholarship of other countries as well.

4. Between 1987 and the present I have been researching a new kind of history of US writers and Communism (focusing on non-canonical figures and decades; mass culture; women and gay/lesbian writers; and Latino, Asian–American, Native American, and African-American aspects), and I have re-interviewed a number of the people with whom Aaron spoke, as well as some new ones who weren't talking in earlier decades. I have also re-examined many of the papers Aaron saw, plus reviewed many new deposits of archival material. I can testify that, on a factual level, there is very little to be contested in his remarkable book. In fact, I am amazed at how much he got right, considering the political climate when he undertook his research and the fact that much crucial scholarship had not yet been done. In the three decades since the publication of *Writers on the Left*, many dissertations, books, and essays have gone over similar terrain without displacing the centrality of Aaron's book.

5. A competent survey of this new methodology can be found in Patrick Brantlinger, *Crusoe's Footprints: Cultural Studies in Britain and America* (New York: Routledge, 1990).

6. This argument is stated in the beginning of the Preface to the first edition of *Writers on the Left: Episodes in American Literary Communism* (New York: Harcourt, Brace and World, 1961), pp. ix–xii.

7. On the cover of the first edition is the following description: "The impact of the idea of Communism on American writers of the past fifty years, both on those who accepted it and on those who did not."

8. Daniel Aaron, "Cambridge 1936–39," *Partisan Review* 50 (Double Anniversary issue, 1984–85): 833–7.

9. Letter from Aaron to Wald, July 25, 1989. Aaron later came to consider this a mixed blessing since Freeman, hoping to gain some degree of rehabilitation in intellectual life through Aaron's book, was understandably selective about the information he made available and the directions in which he pointed the young scholar.

10. The major reviews include: Anonymous, "The Fellows Who Traveled," *Time*, Feb. 2, 1962, pp. 64, 66; Philip Bonosky, "On Writers on the Left," *Political Affairs* (September 1962): 41–7; Robert Gorham Davis, "Social Chronicle of Literary Communism," *New Leader*, Dec. 11, 1961, pp. 27–30; Whitaker T. Deininger, "Literary Rebels," *Christian Century* 79 (March 7, 1962): 294–5; David Dempsey, "Ideological Hay Ride," *Saturday Review*, Dec. 9, 1961, pp. 21–2; Merle Fainsod, "Their Beacon Light Was Red," *New York Herald Tribune Books*, Nov. 12, 1961, p. 10; Harry Hansen, "When Authors Turn Left and Write," *Chicago Sunday Tribune*, Dec. 10, 1961, Part 4, p. 9; Irving Howe, "High Hopes That Led to Disillusion," *New York Times Book Review*, Nov. 12, 1961, pp. 1, 26; Bernard Kreissman, *Library Journal*, 86, (Dec. 1, 1961): 4185; Perry Miller, "Literary Communism," *Christian Science Monitor*, Nov. 22, 1961, p. 11; William Phillips, "What Happened in the 30s," reprinted in *A Sense of the Present* (New York: Chilmark, 1967), pp. 12–29; Robert Wheeler, "Some Aspects of American Communism," *The Yale Review* 51 (March 1962): 463–7. In his "Preface to the Galaxy Book Edition," Aaron states that he "didn't suffuse sufficiently enough or critically enough his own point of view into the book as a whole" (New York: Oxford, 1977), p. xii.

11. Numerous scholars have subsequently made important contributions to this area, including Thomas Bender, Alexander Bloom, Terry A. Cooney, Serge Guilbaut, Neil Jumonville, S. A. Longstaff, Mark Shechner, Harvey Teres, and Stephen Whitfield.

12. A few examples: Constance Coiner, "Literature of Resistance: The Intersection of Feminism and the Communist Left in Meridel Le Sueur and Tillie Olsen," in Lennard Davis and M. Bella Mirabella, eds, *Left Politics and the Literary Profession* (New York: Columbia University Press, 1990), pp. 16–185, and " 'Pessimism of the Mind, Optimism of the Will': Literature of Resistance," Ph.D.

Dissertation, UCLA, 1987; Elinor Langer, *Josephine Herbst: The Story She Could Never Tell* (Boston: Atlantic, 1984); Candida Ann Lacey, "Engendering Conflict: American Women and the Making of Proletarian Fiction," Ph.D. Dissertation, University of Sussex, 1986; Paula Rabinowitz, *Labor and Desire: Women's Revolutionary Fiction in Depression America* (Chapel Hill: University of North Carolina Press, 1991); Deborah Rosenfelt, "From the Thirties: Tillie Olsen and the Radical Tradition," *Feminist Studies* 7 (Fall 1981) 370–406; Joan Wood Samuelson, "Patterns of Survival: Four American Women Writers and the Proletarian Novel," Ph.D. Diss, Ohio State University, 1982.

13. The major study of the African-American cultural Left is Harold Cruse's *The Crisis of the Negro Intellectual: From Its Origins to the Present* (New York: William Morrow and Co., 1967), a powerful polemic that makes no claim to providing a balanced treatment of its targets, such as John O. Killens, Julian Mayfield, Lorraine Hansberry, and Paul Robeson. A number of provocative ideas can be found in Cedric J. Robinson, *Black Marxism* (London: Zed, 1983). Among the biographies of African-American writers are: Michel Fabre, *The Unfinished Quest of Richard Wright* (New York: William Morrow, 1973); Arnold Rampersad, *The Life of Langston Hughes*, 2 vols. (New York: Oxford University Press, 1986 and 1988); Wayne Cooper, *Claude McKay: Rebel Sojourner in the Harlem Renaissance* (Baton Rouge: Louisiana State University Press, 1987); and Manning Marable, *W. E. B. Du Bois: Black Radical Democrat* (Boston: G. K. Hall and Co., 1986).

14. The major study of the Hollywood Left is Larry Ceplair and Steven Englund, *The Inquisition in Hollywood* (Garden City, NY: Doubleday, 1980). See also Nancy Lynn Schwartz, *The Hollywood Writers' Wars* (New York: Knopf, 1982), Victor Navasky's *Naming Names* (New York: Viking, 1982), and Bernard F. Dick, *Radical Innocence: A Critical Study of the Hollywood Ten* (Lexington: The University of Kentucky Press, 1989). Douglass Wixson has published many essays on the Mid-West radical writers movement, and his forthcoming biography of Jack Conroy will be a major contribution to US cultural history. [Since published: *Worker-Writer in America: Jack Conroy and the Tradition of Midwestern Literary Radicalism, 1899–1900* (Urbana: University of Illinois Press, 1994) – A. W.] Robbie Lieberman's *"My Song Is My Weapon": People's Songs, American Communism, and the Politics of Culture* (Chicago: University of Illinois Press, 1989) is an insightful and well-researched study that also covers fresh terrain. Moreover, there are quite a few recent biographies of individual writers that cover neglected areas in considerable detail. Among the most thorough are Townsend Luddington, *John Dos Passos: A Twentieth-Century Odyssey* (New York: Dutton, 1980) and Janice R. MacKinnon and Stephen R. MacKinnon, *Agnes Smedley: The Life and Times of an American Radical* (Berkeley: University of California Press, 1986).

15. *The World of Randolph Bourne*, edited by Lillian Schlissel (New York: Dutton, 1965); Malcolm Cowley, *Think Back on Us: The Literary Record* (Carbondale: Southern Illinois University Press, 1972) and *Think Back on Us: The Social Record* (Carbondale: Southern Illinois University Press, 1972).

16. Edward Dahlberg, *The Confessions of Edward Dahlberg* (New York: Braziller, 1971); Max Eastman, *Love and Revolution: My Journey Through an Epoch* (New York: Random House, 1964); Granville Hicks, *Part of the Truth* (New York: Harcourt, 1965); Matthew Josephson, *Infidel in the Temple* (New York: Knopf, 1967); Alfred Kazin, *Starting Out in the Thirties* (New York: Atlantic, 1965).

17. Jack Conroy and Curt Johnson, eds, *Writers in Revolt: The Anvil Anthology, 1933–1940* (New York: Lawrence Hill and Co., 1973); Joseph North, ed., *New Masses: An Anthology of the Rebel Thirties* (New York: International, 1969); William L. O'Neill, ed., *Echoes of Revolt: The Masses, 1911–1917* (Chicago: Quadrangle, 1966).

18. Daniel Aaron and Robert Bendiner, eds, *The Strenuous Decade: A Social and Intellectual Record of the 1930s* (New York: Doubleday, 1970); Louis Filler, ed., *The Anxious Years: America in the 1930s* (New York: Capricorn, 1963); Jack Salzman with Barry Wallenstein, *Years of Protest; A Collection of American Writings in the 1930s* (New York: Bobbs-Merrill, 1967); Harvey Swados, ed., *The American Writer and the Great Depression* (New York: Bobbs-Merrill, 1966).

19. See the concluding chapter, "Toward a Theory of Stalinism," in Irving Howe and Lewis Coser, *The American Communist Party: A Critical History* (New York: Praeger, 1962), pp. 500–54.

20. Daniel Aaron, *Writers on the Left: Episodes in American Literary Communism* (New York: Oxford University Press, 1977), p. 396

21. "[Aaron's] heroes were the entrepreneurs of writing, the head-boys who have also been responsible for the rehashes." Herbst quoted by David Madden in his "Introduction" to a collection of scholarly essays on *Proletarian Writers of the Thirties* (Carbondale: Southern Illinois University Press, 1968), p. xxi.

22. See Aaron, *Writers on the Left*, OUP edn, p xvii.

23. Of course, there have been major studies of individual intellectuals such as Daniel Bell, John Dewey, Reinhold Niebuhr, and others. Among the most remarkable are Howard Brick, *Daniel Bell and the Decline of Intellectual Radicalism: Social Theory and Political Reconciliation in the 1940s* (Madison: University of Wisconsin Press, 1986) and Robert Westbrook, *John Dewey and American Democracy* (Ithaca, NY: Cornell University Press, 1991).

24. For the introduction of the category of "proletarian literature" into US writing, see Eric Homberger's fine chapter, "Proletarian Literature and the John Reed Clubs," in his *American Writers and Radical Politics, 1900–1939: Equivocal Commitments* (New York: St Martin's, 1986), pp. 119–40.

25. John Scott Bowman, The "The Proletarian Novel in America" (Pennsylvania State University, 1939); Cheryl Sue Davis, "A Rhetorical Study of Selected Proletarian Novels of the 1930s: Vehicles for Protest and Engines for Change" (University of Utah, 1976); William R. Day, "The Politics of Art: A Reading of Selected Proletarian Novels" (Drew University, 1983); Adam J. Fischer, "Formula for Utopia: The American Proletarian Novel, 1930–1959" (University of Massachusetts, 1974); Robert William Glenn, "Rhetoric and Poetics: The Case of Leftist Fiction and Criticism During the 1930s" (Northwestern University, 1971); Robert Haugh, "Sentimentalism in the American Proletarian Novel" (University of Michigan, 1948); Calvin Harris, "Twentieth-Century American Political Fiction: An Analysis of Proletarian Fiction" (University of Oregon, 1979); Kenneth Lee Ledbetter, "The Idea of a Proletarian Novel in America, 1927–29" (University of Illinois, 1963): John A. Penrod, "American Literature and the Great Depression" (University of Pennsylvania, 1954); John C. Suggs, "The Influence of Marxist Aesthetics on American Fiction" (University of Kansas, 1978); Joel Dudley Wingard, "Toward a Workers' America: The Theory and Practice of the American Proletarian Novel" (LSU, 1979).

26. A few of the major works are: Malcolm Goldstein, *The Political Stage: American Drama and the Great Depression* (New York: Oxford, 1974); David P. Peller, *Hope Among Us Yet: Social Criticism and Social Solace in Depression America* (Athens: University of Georgia Press, 1987); Richard Pells, *Radical Visions and American Dreams: Culture and Social Thought in the Depression Years* (New York: Harper and Row, 1973); Lawrence H. Schwartz, *Marxism and Culture: The CPUSA and Aesthetics in the 1930s* (Port Washington, NY: Kennikat Press, 1980); William Stott, *Documentary Expression and Thirties America* (New York: Oxford, 1973);

27. Cary Nelson's *Repression and Recovery: Modern American Poetry and the Politics of Cultural Memory, 1910–1945* (Madison: University of Wisconsin Press, 1989) may augur the beginning of a major revision of this neglected tradition. Jack Salzman and Leo Zanderer's *Social Poetry of the 1930s: A Selection* (New York: Burt Franklin and Co., 1978), remains a major source of key poems. One of the few long-time radical poets to receive significant attention is Thomas McGrath, although most of it came close to the time of his death. See Frederick C. Stern, ed., *The Revolutionary Poet in the United States: The Poetry of Thomas McGrath* (Columbia: University of Missouri Press, 1988).

28. See Fredric Jameson, "The Symbolic Inference; or, Kenneth Burke and Ideological Analysis," *Critical Inquiry* 4, no. 3 (Spring 1978): 507–23; Frank Lentricchia, *Criticism and Social Change* (Chicago: University of Chicago Press, 1983); E. San Juan, Jr., *Carlos Bulosan and the Imagination of the Class Struggle* (Quezon City: University of the Philippines Press, 1972); Rosenfelt; Elaine Hedges, "Introduction," *Ripening: Selected Work of Meridel Le Sueur, 1927–1980* (New York: Feminist Press, 1982). A fine book-length extension of the humane, liberal approach to judgments about the 1930s is Marcus Klein's *Foreigners: The Making of American Literature, 1900–1940* (Chicago: University of Chicago Press, 1981).

29. James Bloom, *Left Letters: The Culture Wars of Mike Gold and Joseph Freeman* (New York: Colombia University Press, 1992). For Nelson, see n. 27. For Rabinowitz, see n. 12. [Barbara Foley's work has since been published – *Radical Representations: Politics and Form in US Proletarian Fiction, 1929–1941* (Durham, NC: Duke University Press, 1993) – as has Wixson's, see n. 14 above – A. W.] One explanation for this bifurcation between the advance of Marxism in literary theory and, frankly, its tortoise-like progress in the study of US literary radicalism may lie partly in the European sources of contemporary theory. That is, the US specialists in Marxist aesthetics – spearheaded, of course, by Fredric Jameson – have drawn upon Lukács, the Frankfurt School, Althusser, and Eagleton, each of whom has a European frame of reference. As a consequence, the US disciples have until recently tended to discuss figures such as Balzac and Conrad, with the exception of a few recent books outside the 1930s, such as Carolyn Porter's *Seeing and Being: The Plight of the Participant Observer in Emerson, James, Adams, and Faulkner* (Middletown, Conn.: Wesleyan University Press, 1981) and June Howard's *Form and History in American Literary Naturalism* (Chapel Hill: University of North Carolina

Press, 1985). On the other hand, those engaged in US literary radicalism as their primary area of research have, until the 1980s (when veterans of the 1960s movements achieved tenture), suffered in part from the relative absence of senior Marxist literary theorists in the field of US literature to guide dissertations and encourage work.

30. Aaron, *Writers on the Left*, OUP edn, p. xviii.

31. Daniel Aaron, "Richard Wright and the Communist Party," *New Letters* 38, no. 2 (Winter 1971): 170–81.

32. Among the major books of this school are Paul Buhle, *Marxism in the USA* (London: Verso, 1980); Maurice Isserman, *Which Side Were You On? The Communist Party in World War II* (Middletown, Conn.: Wesleyan University Press, 1982); Robin Kelley, *Hammer and Hoe: Alabama Communists During the Great Depression* (Chapel Hill: University of North Carolina Press, 1990); and Mark Naison, *Communists in Harlem During the Depression* (Chicago: University of Illinois Press, 1983).

33. Aaron, *Writers on the Left*, OUP edn, p. 210.

34. According to his Preface to the 1977 Oxford reissue of *Writers on the Left*, Aaron had intended to write a follow-up book containing a review of literature of the 1930s. He also planned a work about his adventures in doing the research. The closest he came to the latter was an essay of general observations about memory and oral history, "The Treachery of Recollection: The Inner and Outer History," in Robert H. Bremmer, ed., *Essays on History and Literature* (Columbus: Ohio State University, 1966).

35. Aaron, *Writers on the Left*, OUP edn, pp. 392–3.

36. Raymond Williams, *Marxism and Literature* (New York: Oxford University Press, 1977), p. 212.

2

Alfred Kazin in Retrospect

Alfred Kazin's monumental study of the first forty years of US prose fiction, *On Native Grounds: An Interpretation of Modern American Prose Literature* (first edition, 1942; fortieth anniversary edition, New York: Harcourt, Brace, Jovanovich, 1982), has by now entered the twilight zone between "secondary" and "primary" literature. As secondary literature, it stood for several decades after its original publication in 1942 as an authoritative guide for students and scholars in search of the major twentieth-century US authors of the pre-World War II era. Moreover, Kazin's sensitive and erudite interpretations also provided a frame of reference for discussing the specifically "literary" qualities of these writers in historical, political, and social contexts.

Beyond this, Kazin's learned tome established the 27-year-old author as an influential arbiter of taste in leading New York literary publications. The book has served as the foundation of his reputation ever since; none of his subsequent books of criticism has garnered similar attention. Nevertheless, Kazin has been consistently in demand as a reviewer since the late 1930s. The first volume of his memoirs, *A Walker in the City* (1951), has independent stature as a Jewish-American autobiography of distinction.

At the same time as the high reputation of the book persists among the generation who cut their teeth on it in the 1940s and 1950s, *On Native Grounds* seems to have had minimal influence on the younger generation of scholars now ascending to full professorships in the teaching of US literature at the university level. Among the current group of graduate students in the field of US literature, the book may possibly have no influence at all. In sixteen years of teaching at the University of Michigan, I have never seen any faculty member other than myself use the work as either a required or recommended book for a course, nor have I seen it appear on a Ph.D. examinations list for US literature. The book has not been kept consistently in print, making it impossible for me

---

This chapter originally appeared in *Reviews in American History*, 20 (1992).

to count on its availablity for my seminars. The new *Columbia History of the American Novel* (1991), under the general editorship of Emory Elliot, contains not a single reference to *On Native Grounds* in its 905 pages – not even in its 25-page bibliography.

My own involvement with this text stems primarily from my research and writing on the politico-cultural circle known as "The New York Intellectuals"; and it is almost exclusively among the network of younger and middle-aged scholars tilling that particular vineyard that I have found knowledge of and interest in Kazin's book sustained. In 1981, the University of Chicago Press published a literary history covering virtually the same terrain as did Kazin, Marcus Klein's *Foreigners: The Making of American Literature, 1900–1940*. But *On Native Grounds* is never mentioned, nor did the reviews of Klein's book make the obvious comparison with Kazin's. Student reactions to Kazin's book in my courses have been surprisingly uninspired, despite my own enthusiasm for many of its conceptual features and sympathy for the humane, radical values demonstrated in the work. Some of these values shined again brightly in Kazin's 1983 attack on neo-conservatism, "Saving My Soul at the Plaza" (*New York Review of Books*, 31 March 1983, p. 40).

Yet Kazin's extraordinary synthesis is too rich and impressive, and too symptomatic of the thinking at a crucial moment in US cultural history, to simply vanish. Thus I believe that the next stage of appreciation of Kazin's book will have to come largely through its apprehension not as a secondary but as as a primary text; that is, not only as a sourcebook to be absorbed for its articulation of the critical consensus on "major writers, " but also as a canon-building ideological construction of selective "traditions" to be studied and criticized for its enduring assumptions as well as its blind-spots. That Kazin, in his 1982 "Preface to the Fortieth Anniversary Edition," could naively declare that his "last chapter . . . was no doubt written as a protest against ideology" (p. xii), clearly underscores the generation gap among scholars of US literature. Many of my younger colleagues would not hesitate to correct that statement to read that the last chapter is "a protest against certain ideologies on behalf of another."

Whether or not most of Kazin's periodizations, generic classifications, and judgments of "success" and "failure" will ultimately be vindicated and retained can not be determined at this early date in the major reconsideration of US culture now under way. Research and theory have taken off in such radically new directions during the past two decades that it is possible that, in the end, some parts of his argument will appear as quaint and dated as those old histories of nineteenth-century literature vaunting writers such as Henry Wadsworth Longfellow as a major voice and dismissing Herman Melville as a producer of lowbrow popular culture. In this essay, I can only make some tentative speculations about what in Kazin's book might be discussed in the evaluations to come, and what this might mean for our broader thinking about the contours and qualities of twentieth-century US literary practice.

To some extent the "problem" of Kazin's book mirrors the general problem of US literary studies. Most frequently one finds surveys and histories of a period, even those covering several decades, to feature only eight or ten "major books" by "major authors." The fact that Kazin, surveying about four decades, treats perhaps fifty authors with some degree of critical analysis, gives the book an exceptional claim to breadth and comprehensiveness. Indeed, reviewers at the time of its appearance, such as Peter Munro Jack in the *New York Times*, were quick to announce that Kazin "has apparently read every important book in American literature" (Nov. 22, 1942, p. 8). Yet the names of only six of the twenty-one winners of the Pulitzer Prize for the novel between 1917 and 1940 even appear in his index.

Of course, a few critics lamented the absence of a favorite writer here and there, and there was some questioning of the meaning of his omission of poetry and drama from his study. For example, writing in the *Nation* (Nov. 7, 1942, p. 483), Lionel Trilling lamented,

> I am sorry that the plan of Mr. Kazin's book forced him to exclude the poets. They would have made the picture both more cheerful and more instructive. Not that all our poets are exempt from the judgment of inadequacy. But many of our poets, pre-occupied as they are with form, hopeless of appealing to popular taste and of seeming to solve immediate situations, have been able to cultivate the inwardness and growth whose lack in the prose writers Mr. Kazin so often and so rightly deplores.

From these remarks, one can sense common elements in the literary orientations of Trilling and Kazin, despite differences in temperament that would create tensions later on. They share a belief that the object of criticism is for a cultivated individual to find like-minded cultivation in texts. This cultivation, especially in Trilling's case, tends to be associated primarily with works less accessible to popular consumption – what used to be called "highbrow" literature.

Thus Trilling had only one substantial disagreement with *On Native Grounds*: Kazin's undervaluation of the formalist critics. Trilling held that, despite their often reactionary political views, the formalists came closest to apprehending the authentic character of modern poetry. Neither Trilling, nor any of the other of Kazin's reviewers, including the left-wing (although by then ex-Communist) Granville Hicks, expressed the slightest concern about the absence of any discussion of prose fiction of the Harlem Renaissance (except one sentence on *Nigger Heaven* by the Euro-American Carl Van Vechten). Either Kazin was entirely unaware, or else he was simply dismissive, of the extraordinary novels and stories of Langston Hughes, Claude Mckay, Arna Bontemps, Jean Toomer, and Zora Neale Hurston. (In fact, the only reference in *On Native Grounds* to African-American literature during these four decades is Kazin's total disparagement of Richard Wright's *Native Son* as an example of bad writing resembling a slick crime story.) Nor was there any perturbance at Kazin's failure to seriously treat a single female author of the forty-year period other than Edith Wharton, Willa Cather, and Ellen Glasgow.

It is true that no scholar can possibly account for all books written in a decade or more, but in *On Native Grounds* we have the unacknowledged relegation of hundreds of fascinating texts of the period to the dustbin, apparently on the grounds that they are somehow subliterary. As a methodological contrast, one might examine the strategy of Maxwell Geismar's *Writers in Crisis: The American Novel 1925–1940*, published the same year; moreover, Geismar's title is nearly identical to that of Kazin's concluding section of his book, "Part III: The Literature of Crisis (1930–1940)." Geismar is, if anything, far narrower in his range of references than Kazin. Yet his decision to organize his argument around case studies of six novelists – Ring Lardner, Ernest Hemingway, John Dos Passos, William Faulkner, Thomas Wolfe, and John Steinbeck – militates against Kazin's illusion of a comprehensiveness that is, in actuality, never achieved.

Of course, in the 1990s it seems *de rigueur* to raise this sort of issue. Nowadays one has merely to invoke the categories of "race" and "gender" to justifiably precipitate the most profound doubts about the conception of "literary value" codified in conventional histories such as Kazin's. But it is also important to recognize that fifty years ago there were other writers and critics conscious of the areas of literary practice that *On Native Grounds* occludes from view. For example, the radical movement of African-American writers in the Depression was fixated on gaining recognition for the history and achievements of Black authors. This can be seen by the collectively written "Blueprint for Negro Writing" which appeared under Richard Wright's name in *New Challenge* in 1936, and in the efforts of Arna Bontemps, Sterling Brown, Langston Hughes, and others to anthologize key African-American texts. Josephine Herbst was acutely conscious of the relegation of female writers to, at best, second-rate versions of the leading males. Sensitivity to subsumption of her identity into trends represented by big name writers is evident from the time of her 1931 protest against critic Isidor Schneider's lumping her into the "Hemingway school" of literature (*Nation*, March 11, 1931), to her bitter letter of denunciation to David Madden (quoted in his Preface to the 1968 collection, *Proletarian Writers of the Thirties*) concerning literary histories that concentrate only on the "head-boys" of US literary radicalism.

In his neglect of these alternative perspectives, Kazin is at one with the mainstream of both commercial and academic culture. In fact, while commendably liberal and democratic, the literary judgments of *On Native Grounds* do not make for a heretical book in any profound sense. No author is given serious attention who was not already an established figure. Of course, the book had some opinions that would later seem dubious, such as the rather restrained enthusiasm for Faulkner. Also, Kazin's unusually sympathetic and subtle treatment of Theodore Dreiser now appears an exception in the context of the hostile literary winds to blow later in the 1940s. But there is one area in particular where Kazin's concessions to, or unwillingness to question, conventional literary discourse of the day seems to have gone much too far: his treatment of the literary Left, which is a crucial part of the book not only because the Left dominates the climactic chapter of *On Native Grounds*, but also because of Kazin's personal ties with the Left. From the vantage point of 1992, his assessment appears not only wrongheaded in important ways but also sometimes factually inaccurate. Kazin's depiction of Marxist-influenced novelists is certainly one of the major parts of the work that will have to be re-examined when *On Native Grounds* becomes the subject of the close scrutiny it deserves.

A paragraph on page 382 more or less sums up one aspect of the problem: a belief that 1930s literary-radicalism was a time-conditioned minor episode with no long-term future. Here Kazin argues that James T. Farrell outlived "other left-wing naturalists" only because of his self-confidence:

> Cantwell gave up after two novels; Dahlberg was exhausted by his own sensibility; Caldwell, as Kenneth Burke once said, became so repetitious that he seemed to be playing with his toes; Gold wrote nothing after *Jews Without Money*, which expressed all he had to say, except his *Daily Worker* twaddle; Schneider, Seaver, Rollins, Conroy, Burke, Lumpkin, were all unable to follow up on their early novels. Of the host of younger writers who seemed to promise so much to Marxist critics in the early thirties – the Tillie Lerners, the Arnold Armstrongs, the Ben Fields – only Richard Wright and Albert Maltz went on writing at all.

First of all, Kazin's assumption of a fundamental similarity of talent and literary objectives among all of these writers, which he groups under the label "left-wing naturalism," is only conceivable from Olympian heights. Second, his view that these sixteen figures, so diverse in style, theme, and personal situation, are really a bunch of "losers" is factually untrue in regard to later publications, as well as condescending. Third, his generic classification ("left-wing naturalism") is fallacious. To treat this last point briefly: Farrell was undoubtedly left-wing until the late 1940s, but throughout his career he consistently challenged "naturalism" as an appropriate label for the vision of his fiction. He was, as all serious Farrell scholars have contended, a critical realist, which makes sense considering his Marxist-pragmatist philosophical commitment, and this is probably the term most appropriate for the other novelists as well.

In my view, it is an indefensible method to offer a generalization about why certain novelists failed to continue producing at a rapid pace after a certain point without presenting the slightest bit of biographical or other factual evidence. Problems of economic survival, as well as psychological/personal difficulties, weigh differently on different individuals. Farrell, for example, was a famous man before he was thirty (as was Caldwell, the only other writer whose later productivity is acknowledged, and, for that matter, Kazin), which no doubt played a role in bolstering his confidence. Farrell was also unique in having the loyalty for years of an important publisher, James Henle's Vanguard Press.

Is it true that all the others gave up writing due to a dearth of talent? I do not know why Cantwell switched from fiction to history, biography, and journalism (his current biographer, Per Seyersted, may be able to explain this to us in time), although friends have speculated on his need to break completely with his radical past as a factor in his subsequent behavior. Dahlberg, however, did not "exhaust" himself, but continued doggedly to produce original (and cranky) work until his death in 1975. Even Gold is somewhat misrepresented here; I'm no enthusiast of his *Daily Worker* columns, but it's important to note that he is a decade older than almost everyone on the list and that an important part of his career was his avant-garde, sometimes "Futurist," playwriting during the 1920s. Moreover, after Gold turned forty in the mid-Depression, his battle with diabetes combined with his struggle to support a young family while remaining a public Communist Party member were singular factors that did not affect the younger Farrell or financially successful Caldwell.

Similar challenges can be made to the cruel characterization Kazin presents of most of the other writers on the list. Schneider, for example, was primarily a poet and critic, which he continued to be for a decade after the Depression, when he also published another novel. Rollins published regularly throughout the decade and into the next (he had a dual career as both a Marxist and detective writer) but died suddenly in 1950 just as Fawcett Press was preparing to reissue his works. Burke (Olive Tilford Dargon) and Lumpkin also continued publishing novels; in fact, each have books in print to this day.

Of the three other authors said to have stopped writing entirely, only one, Arnold Armstrong, may fit the bill. (This name was a pseudonym and no one has yet determined what became of the author.) Ben Field (Moe Bragin), however, continued publishing novels and stories up until his death a few years after the appearance of *Jacob's Son* (1971), and Tillie Lerner re-emerged as Tillie Olsen to become a major figure in the feminist literary movement, authoring in 1978 a book about non-prolific women writers called *Silences*.

Beyond this, it is worth noting that neither Nathanael West nor Henry Roth, both today regarded as major fiction writers of the 1930s, are mentioned in *On Native Grounds*. Nor is John Sanford (Julian Shapiro), a lifelong Marxist who steadily produced unusual novels in the 1930s and after, and whose five-volume "Scenes from the Life of an American Jew" may be the neglected left-wing masterpiece of his generation. The many other radical novelists who could have been placed on Kazin's list, instead of the group he selected, would also challenge his generalization in various ways: Ben Appel, Thomas Bell, Vera Caspary, Robert Coates, Guy Endore, Howard Fast, Martha Gellhorn, Josephine Johnson, Ruth McKenney, Leane Zugsmith, etc. To some extent the reason that the literary Left comes off looking so bad in this book is because Kazin never applies the rich and multifaceted method of analysis that he employs in his remarkable commentary on Hemingway and others. The Reds are bunched together and treated one-dimensionally. They are "artists in uniform," but unintelligently following the dictates of Depression violence rather than orders from Moscow.

Our understanding of some limitations of Kazin's method may also be enhanced by looking at his judgments about Marxist literary criticism of the period. In this instance, however, Kazin was well answered by one of his targets, Granville Hicks, in a book review in the March 1943 *Antioch Review*. After accurately observing that Kazin can "see only one aspect of the rise of revolutionary sentiment in the '30s – its narrowness and bitterness" (p. 27), Hicks offers a balanced perspective on the literary criticism of the Depression era Communist Party that still seems valid fifty years later:

> Though there was considerably more sense than Mr. Kazin admits – he obviously has not looked for it – there was a good deal of foolishness written in *The New Masses* and other left-wing periodicals. There was also a good deal of stupid sectarianism, but this, far more than Mr Kazin admits, was the sectarianism of strong feeling rather than the sectarianism of the party line. Against this latter sectarianism most of us struggled, and the cause for regret is not that we succumbed, as Mr Kazin would have it, but that we spent so much energy in resistance, and were so often distracted by irrelevant conflicts. (p. 28)

But here I must add that I am not convinced by Hicks's charge that, in the end, Kazin's work is quite "bookish" due to a foundation in "unanalyzed emotion" (Hicks, *Antioch Review*, p. 29). It does not read that way to me, especially in comparison to the large quantity of contemporary literary theory that "rigorously" interrogates linguistic and philosophical categories with little or no reference to biography and very often far less of an "empirical base" for its claims than Kazin employed.

What is more accurate, I think, is Hicks's criticism that Kazin, despite his social view of literary production, opts for the stance that literature can and should somehow rise above "extrinsic" factors and be true to itself "as a distinct element in human experience" (Kazin, *On Native Grounds*, p. 402). I have no quarrel with this as a literary attitude against pressures to conform; in fact, I would argue that it was precisely such an attitude that sustained James T. Farrell's productivity over the decades, even though Kazin treats him as one who succumbed to the extrinsic. On the other hand, Hicks makes the important observation that, when writers such as Dos Passos, Farrell, and Steinbeck also felt that they were writing as part of a larger effort to reform society, their work expressed certain unique features. Today, surely, we can go even further and affirm that, in fact, it is precisely the novels produced by these men under left-wing inspiration that scholars proclaim to be their greatest achievement.

Of course, it does not follow that the salutary effects of the Red Muse is evidenced in the case of every writer; the critical consensus of Sherwood Anderson scholars, for example, is that his Red period was his worst. Rather, literary practice is so diverse that, if Hicks is accurate that Kazin's loyalty is *au fond* to the claim that art needs to be true to itself, we must conclude that *On Native Grounds* offers little more than a vague platitude as an aesthetic guideline. Moreover, this is a viewpoint that functionally bears an ironic resemblance to one aspect of the Stalinist homily that "Art is a Weapon." Both views embody "general truths" so wide-ranging in possible interpretation and application that they have become empty clichés. Yet they can still be mobilized as substitutes for directly confronting the hard problems of cultural production and valorization.

Kazin is too quick to kill off the tradition of the left-wing novel. He is even more willing to demonize the Marxist critic, as in his hyperbolic proclamation that, "Wrapped in the vestments of his office, a Marxist critic could say *anything* [Kazin's emphasis]. And he usually did" (p. 418). But his theory of Depression culture as a whole is not without its recuperable aspects. For example, his oft-repeated argument about the peculiar literary "naturalism" of the Depression is that it was "the most intense literary 'equivalent' of contemporary disorder" (p. 371). Such a unique development of Eliot's idea of the "objective correlative" does little to salvage the naive use of "naturalism" as explanatory of literary style and motivation in the book. But it does provide an important link among many regions of Depression era culture that is likely to turn out to be a central theme of future studies of the decades that were painstakingly mapped for us in Kazin's pioneering but now somewhat dated masterwork.

To be more specific, Kazin attributes a general mentality to writers of the 1930s that exhibits a "surrender to naturalism" (characterized by a literal realism, mechanical prophecy, and disgust) and a "tropism toward Communism" (resulting in a coarsening and opportunism in literary standards). He then criticizes writers of the Thirties for following that course. This is an oversimplification tantamount to the creation of a "straw Marxism" against which he can easily counterpose a more sophisticated world-view. Moreover, Kazin's wholesale endorsement of Philip Rahv's notoriously exaggerated statement that "Proletarian literature was the literature of a party disguised as the literature of a class" (p. 293) is an example of the degree to which Kazin himself at times succumbs to a quality he later ascribed to major critics (Johnson, Goethe, Eliot, Trilling) in his 1962 essay on "The Function of Criticism Today":

> The critic who has the equipment to be a force, the critic who can set up standards for his age, must be a partisan of one kind of art and a bitter critic of another . . . . Such a critic will be not only unfair, he will pursue his prejudice to the point of absurdity, setting up a straw figure that will serve to bear all his dislikes, and even his hatred of a certain kind of art. (Kazin, *Contemporaries*, Boston: Little, Brown, and Co., 1962, p. 500)

Of course, some of the propositions underlying Kazin's premise about the "contagious naturalism" of the 1930s sound plausible. One of these is his assertion that writers exalt brutality and sentimentality because these qualities were necessary for surivival under Depression conditions. Yet without highly individualized qualifications, he ends up presenting generalities that belie the complex realities of individual texts. The "transformation of sensibility, of style, of the very nature of the American literary character" (*On Native Grounds*, p. 367) that Kazin insists ruptured the 1920s and 1930s may be challenged by our noting the many novelists who quite consciously tried to develop Twenties sensibilities in a Thirties context: William Rollins, Henry Roth, Nathanael West, James T. Farrell, and John Dos Passos, for starters. With poets – including the "proletarians" such as Kenneth Fearing, Edwin Rolfe, Horace Gregory, Alfred Hays, Muriel Rukeyser, Sol Funaroff, etc. – the bond between the culture characteristic of the Twenties and Thirties is even stronger.

Also plausible is Kazin's authoritative assertion that "the literal significance of the crisis had aroused a literature of literal realism." Yet this is hardly all that one finds in Fielding Burke's *Call Home the Heart* (1932) and Grace Lumpkin's *To Make My Bread* (1932), texts replete with regional themes and the delineation of character types that arise convincingly from the contested terrain of urban encroachment on rural tradition. Even in the case of a "classic" proletarian novel such as Mike Gold's *Jews Without Money* (1930), Kazin's categories only occlude from view the foundation of the narrative and vision in the warm folk culture of Eastern Europe. On the other hand, the "need to shock," that Kazin calls "the most intense literary 'equivalent' of contemporary disorder," is not exactly foreign to the Melville of "Benito Cereno" or the Hawthorne of "Ethan Brand," not to mention the novels of Norman Mailer at just about every point in his career.

As in the case of Georg Lukács's apologetics for Sir Walter Scott and his brief against Kafka's modernism, one feels compelled to admire the grandeur of the argument, although Kazin's rich textured sentences sometimes prevent clarity of meaning. The conclusion, however, simply can't be brooked. Indeed, many of Kazin's materialist-sounding interpretations of literary sensibility may be less an advance beyond the Stalinist Marxism of Depression critics, and more like a return to the pre-Marxist mechanical materialism of the "Progressive Historians" (although Kazin explicitly criticizes Parrington for being inattentive to art-specific issues).

Kazin also makes some leaps of faith based on thin documentation. To maintain the stereotype that Left writers "had little interest in literature and were even a little contemptuous of it," he offers a single quotation from Mike Gold to the effect that Jack Conroy's *The Disinherited* (1933) "cannot be regarded merely as literature" (p. 379). Kazin then jumps to the claim that

> For writers like these [Dahlberg, Farrell, Caldwell and Wright are named] the act of composition was truly . . . an escape from personality rather than an expression of it, a continual sacrifice of the writer's self in and through his book. The more intense the writer's disgust with the environment from which he sought release, the more ferocious his obsession with its details. (p. 379)

How does one justify such a harsh explanation of the writer's craft, style, and motivation without substantial biographical documentation?

Moreover, it is significant – although not conclusive – to note that the influential left-wing critics who promoted such writers in the early 1930s never themselves theorized artistic craft or motivation in ways similar to Kazin's argument in their major essays. Joseph Freeman, for example, a Communist critic, poet, and (later) novelist, wrote explicitly in his "Introduction" to the anthology *Proletarian Literature in the United States* (1935) that the category of "experience" is the litmus test for 1930s writers, emphasizing that it is only in class viewpoint that the proletarian artist differers from others. This leads Freeman to speculate about the "universal" elements in class-specific experience, and the transformation of "realism" into "metaphor" through time and technique. He also struggles with stages of development in class art, just as his colleague Granville Hicks struggled in his 1934 *New Masses* series on "Revolution and the Novel" to develop new formal typologies for what he called "collective" and "complex" novels of the Thirties. These are more ambitious efforts than Kazin attributes to the Left in his trivialization of their artistic drives as escapist compulsions. It is true that, sometimes, the answers of the Marxist critics to their own questions were botched; for example, Freeman is too quick to correlate categories of experience and perspectives to particular classes, and his prediction that the ultimate form emerging from the Thirties will be the "epic" doesn't mesh with the class basis of the ur-model in Greek slave society. Nevertheless, for Kazin to have refuted the left-wing literary tendency on the actual terrain of the debates of the 1930s would have given us a more lasting view of the Thirties than the one that is now unraveling. The version he codified in *On Native Grounds* probably survived as long as it did due to its compatibility with the anti-Communist cultural ethos that emerged during the Cold War (although Kazin himself opposed the excesses of that ethos). That version was given a new lease on life when Irving Howe and Lewis Coser endorsed and elaborated on it in their wittily influential chapter called "The Intellectuals Turn Left" in *The American Communist Party: A Critical History* (1957).

Today, many of the writers buried by Kazin, the victims of caricature or omission in his war against select ideologies, are rising from the dead. The new generation of scholars rethinking the Thirties has little use for the categories of "surrender" and "tropism." The genre of naturalism itself is being reinterpreted in fresh ways; for example, in June Howard's *Form and History in American Literary Naturalism* (1985), as an "immanent ideology" intended to accommodate specific historical conjunctures. Moreover, the assumption that the young writer was close to a *tabula rasa* before going Left in the Great Depression was never tenable in any event.

The latest theoretical studies, such as Cary Nelson's *Repression and Recovery: Modern American Poetry and the Politics of Cultural Memory, 1910–1945* (1989), Paula Rabinowitz's *Labor and Desire: Women's Revolutionary Fiction in Depression America*

(1991), and manuscripts in press by James Bloom [*Left Letters: The Culture Wars of Mike Gold and Joseph Freeman*, 1992] and Douglass Wixson [*Worker-Writer in America: Jack Conroy and the Tradition of Midwestern Literary Radicalism, 1899–1900*, 1994], feature the agency of the author and cultural syncretism of the text as main characteristics of Depression literature. The enthusiastic reactions of my own students to the recent reprints of Grace Lumpkin's *The Wedding*, William Attaway's *Blood on the Forge*, Josephine Johnson's *Now in November*, Joseph Vogel's *Man's Courage*, and Nelson Algren's *Somebody in Boots* – all books never mentioned by Kazin – convinces me even more that future generations will know and study a Thirties markedly different from the one indicted in *On Native Grounds*.

One cannot deny that the new interpretations are partly a product of contemporary preoccupations of the post-1960s generation of scholars. But it is equally fair to note the extent to which Kazin's book itself was a "presentist" response that erased some of the author's own enthusiasms of just a few years earlier. The mood of disillusionment and accommodation following the shock of the Hitler–Stalin Pact and growing recognition of the need for national unity in World War II are clearly in evidence. Kazin reveals in his 1982 Preface that, as he came to the conclusion of his book, he responded to his new perception of "the moral bankruptcy of many left-wing writers" with the view that, "The hope of justice in human affairs had become less important to me, less probable, than undeviating freedom" (p. xii).

Thus Kazin was semi-consciously drawn to the liberal effort to construct an "acceptable," de-clawed and de-fanged, version of the 1930s. On the one hand, such an attitude is suggested by his hailing Steinbeck's *The Grapes of Wrath* as the distinctive novel of this Depression trend – by virtue of its ability to dramatize "the inflictions of the crisis without mechanical violence and hatred" (p. 397). It is difficult for me to understand how he can seriously laud this work as one that towers in craft and vision over the scores of novels that he dimisses or omits. On the other hand, in its fixation on valorizing mostly establishment texts and figures, *On Native Grounds* writes off Josephine Herbst's impressive Depression trilogy, citing the "pedestrianism of [her] declining saga of the middle class" (p. 387). Yet Kazin's review of Herbst's third volume two years earlier, which used Hicks's category of "collective novel" and not "proletarian naturalism," hailed her "delicacy," "fullness" and "promise" (*New York Herald Tribune Books*, March 5, 1939, p. 7). Following Herbst's death in 1969, Kazin also characterized her in *The New York Review of Books* as "a natural writer, an expressive lyricist of human emotion and of landscape, a firm and canny observer in her novels of every human snare" (March 27, 1969, p. 20). Perhaps the first judgment was an "immature" enthusiasm, and the last colored by respect for a friendship that started only in 1950; but what makes the brief dismissal in 1942 any more "objective"?

More durable than Kazin's surface argument, characterizing Thirties left-wing culture as mostly a naturalist tropism, is his insight into a common substratum of sensibility linking a generation of "Marxists, tough-guy natural-ists, sociologists and documentary reporters" who exhibit an "obsession with society" (p. 286). If one traces out the careers of many writers beyond the Thirties – which Kazin was unable to do – one discovers an increasing amount of cross-fertilization among genres, especially between mass market and "high culture" regions. Most notably, left-wing novelists and playwrights went to Hollywood in the late 1930s and World War II years, and then many returned to fiction during the blacklist. There are also cross-overs from the Left to science fiction, pulp, detective, young adult, and children's literature. Kazin, of course, uses evidence of such links as reason to *ipso facto* disparage a writer; he clearly looks down on the "violent naturalism which slick broadway reporters and pro-letarian novelists now adopted with the same half-naive, half-cynical fatalism, a naturalism that embodied the discovery of Hollywood as well as the docks and logging camps, the tabloid murder along with the sharecroppers" (p. 290). Contemporary critics, in contrast, are more likely to find such links exciting; they provide yet another route to to the kind of rich inquiry into new cultural regions charactized by Janice Radway's *Reading the Romance* (1984) and Michael Denning's *Mechanic Accents* (1987). Ironically, *On Native Grounds* is likely to be reclaimed as a superior guide to the method of US literary analysis and judg-ment that locked most of the 1930s into an "unusable past" for many decades. It is also a good bet that scholars of the new generation will find many of Kazin's most recuperable conceptual values in areas quite different than the ones for which the book became famous and influential.

3

James T. Farrell in the 1930s:

The Athanasius of Union

Square[1]

Contested Legacy

From the moment that the 28-year-old Irish-American radical from Chicago first battled his way into US letters with *Young Lonigan: A Boyhood in Chicago Streets* (1932), the literary significance of James T. Farrell (1904–79) has been vigorously contested terrain. What should one make of this Proust-toting poet of Chicago's rough South Side Irish turf? How could this young proponent of John Dewey and Karl Marx declare himself to be more communist than the Communist Party?

In the 1990s, more than a dozen years after his death, Farrell's legacy still remains in dispute. Critics and scholars are still unable to fit his literary achievement and political convictions neatly into familiar categories, hierarchies, and binary oppositions; hence Farrell qualifies as a prime candidate for reconsideration as part of the fundamental rethinking of the contours of US cultural practice and values under way since the generation that rebelled in 1960s began addressing contemporary literary and historical scholarship in the 1980s.

In addition to the contemporary interest that may be attracted by the indeterminate status of Farrell's fiction between "high" and "mass" culture, the issues Farrell raised in his literary criticism of the 1930s also happen to address many of the tortuous debates of the most recent decades. Farrell, of course, was concerned largely with the validity of constructing a "proletarian" literary tendency and its relation to prior traditions,[2] while contemporary Cultural Studies addresses the "politics of identity" in terms of the construction of gender, "race," and ethnicity.[3] But the basic conundrum involving the application of social categories to cultural practice remains the same. Moreover,

---

This chapter originally appeared as the "Introduction" to *A Note on Literary Criticism*, Morningside Books edn (New York: Columbia University Press, 1993).

Farrell's refusal on Marxist grounds to reduce the category of aesthetic value to a relativistic functional aspect brings him into dialogue with a number of current debates.[4] And Farrell's adamant rejection of the political coding of literary form goes to the heart of the famous Brecht–Lukács debate over modernism.[5]

Today one would most likely discuss Farrell's distinctions between "use-value" and "aesthetic value" in terms of the "allogenetic" and "idiogenetic" aspects of art, or explore what he calls "carry-over value" in terms of "synchronic" and "diachronic" dynamics. Probably many contemporary theorists would also demand a more subtle interpretation of ideology than Farrell provides, and "hegemony," "reification," and "alienation" would be central categories. Farrell's confident judgments on the unchallengeable artistic superiority of Shakespeare, Dickens, and Dreiser would likely be rigorously interrogated, and his Enlightenment faith in reason would possibly be rejected as naive and one-sided.

Interest in Farrell's criticism has also emerged in two other arenas of scholarship. One consists of the numerous studies of "The New York Intellectuals," a group of influential ex-radical literati with whom Farrell was once associated; the other includes studies re-assessing the history of American Communism, especially those characterized by an extra-institutional, bottom-up approach. In the *Rise of the New York Intellectuals: Partisan Review and Its Circle, 1934–1945* (Madison: University of Wisconsin Press, 1986), Terry Cooney presents Farrell's *A Note on Literary Criticism* as "the most substantial consideration of Marxist aesthetics by an American Marxist during the thirties," which served as a necessary and decisive clarification of crucial literary issues (p. 83). A more recent book, James F. Murphy's *The Proletarian Moment: The Controversy Over Leftism in Literature* (Urbana and Chicago: University of Illinois Press, 1991), presents Farrell's work as the primary source of a long history of myths and distortions about the cultural practice of the literary Left in the United States.

In the late 1960s and early 1970s, a number of the texts discussed by Farrell in *A Note on Literary Criticism* were reprinted, including several paperbacks. These include Henry Dan Piper's collection of Malcolm Cowley's literary criticism, *Think Back on US: The Literary Record* (Carbondale: Southern Illinois University Press, 1967); Granville Hicks's *The Great Tradition* (New York: Quadrangle, 1969) and Jack Alan Robbins's edition of *Granville Hicks in the New Masses* (Port Washington, NY: Kennikat Press, 1974); Michael Folsom's edition of *Mike Gold: A Literary Anthology* (New York: International Publishers, 1972); and V. F. Calverton's *The Liberation of American Literature* (New York: Octagon Books, 1973). Morningside Books' new edition of *A Note on Literary Criticism*, the first complete reprinting since 1936 and its first appearance in paperback, will assist a new generation of students of literature in assessing the merit of Farrell's literary position.

The Young Manhood of James T. Farrell

As a one time University of Chicago student and literary expatriate in Paris, Farrell was exceptionally well-read in nineteenth- and twentieth-century philosophy, modern social psychology, and avant-garde literature.[6] Yet his first novel was packaged in a dust-jacket warning that its sale "is limited to physicians, surgeons, psychologists, sociologists, social workers, teachers and other persons having a professional interest in the psychology of adolescence."[7] Such a "notorious" introduction to the public helped create his popular image as a tough guy and literary brawler. The persona was reinforced by the frequent confusion of the author with his best-known character, Studs Lonigan, and was given popular form by an oft-reprinted publicity photograph of Farrell looking sullen and angry.[8] Thus Edmund Wilson probably reflected the sentiment of a large group of readers when he remarked upon the 1936 publication of *A Note on Literary Criticism* that "one is surprised, after reading Mr Farrell's novels, which derive so much of their effectiveness from the total immersion of the author in the lives of unreflecting and limited people, to discover behind them a mind capable of philosophical abstractions and analysis."[9]

The same year that *A Note* was issued, Farrell inaugurated his series of novels about the emergent consciousness of a revolutionary intellectual, Danny O'Neill, thereby marking a new direction in his fiction.[10] By the end of the Great Depression he had become, however, perhaps permanently typed as a novelist of greater "sociological value" than literary merit.[11] In Alfred Kazin's powerfully written cultural history, *On Native Grounds* (1942), Farrell was dubbed a "left-wing naturalist" and his work caricatured as exhibiting "an automatic style, a style rather like a sausage machine, and one whose success lay in the almost qualitative disgust with which Farrell recorded each detail."[12]

During the ensuing decades, many scholars labored to modify this image with arguments about the more complex dimensions of Farrell's literary projects and personality.[13] Nevertheless, when he died at seventy-five in 1979, the long *New York Times* obituary quoted street-tough passages from the character Studs Lonigan, and remarked upon Farrell's "rough-hewn look, with his big chest, his heavy bones, and his long arms."[14] From Farrell's list of more than fifty published books, only one other besides the Studs Lonigan trilogy was mentioned – *A World I Never Made* (1936), which had sparked a famous obscenity trial in New York in 1937.

Those who read more widely in Farrell's opus, and who knew him personally, understood his achievement – and saw his physical appearance[15] – as quite different from such popular representations. His technique remained constant – the minute reproduction of the thoughts and feelings of characters caught in the grip of institutions and emotions they can barely comprehend, let alone control, as long as they remain fragmented individuals.

But for his main characters Farrell ranged over the United States and Western Europe during the first fifty years of this century, choosing men and women from a variety of classes, cities, nationalities, and ethnicities. The foundation of his work was hundreds of short stories, increments of a vast patchwork that became interconnected novels, all of which was bounded at the outer edge by several volumes of criticism, poetry, journalism, reportage, and a *Baseball Diary* (1957).

The object of his literary project was to create a panorama of the life and times of his generation (and to some extent the generations just preceding it), through an examination of the growth and stultification of the human person- ality. During the period when he produced *A Note on Literary Criticism*, his vision of socio-psychological development was rooted in a classical Marxist under- standing of social formation, infused with notions from George Herbert Mead, John Dewey, and numerous other theorists.

Farrell's Marxism had evolved idiosyncratically in the late 1920s from his initial attraction to radicalism and socialism in Chicago. However, for a period of four or five years, roughly 1932 until mid 1936, it seemed compatible with support for the Communist Party of the United States (CP- USA). After 1936, Farrell, who was well-read in Lenin and admired the Irish radicals Jim Larkin and James Connolly, identified with various factions of the Trotskyist movement.[16] In 1948, he moved toward social democracy and later to the liberal and then finally to the center-right wing of the Democratic Party.[17] His self-identification as a Marxist faded during the early Cold War years, although Marx always remained for him a crucial figure, as did Lenin and Trotsky.

It would be foolish to claim that a particular brand of politics produces superior fiction and criticism, since this flies in the face of a vast amount of evi- dence to the contrary, not to mention the opinions of Marx, Engels, Lenin, and Trotsky themselves. Yet in the case of James T. Farrell, indications are strong that his writing during the 1930s and 1940s constitutes an achievement demanding reassessment and a more central role in US cultural history. While his political views were "revolutionary Marxist" during these decades, the superior quality of his fiction and criticism can more accurately be attributed to the surety of his literary vision. In contrast to such confidence, the end of the 1940s brought not only a political apostasy from revolutionary Marxism, but also the birth of a retarded child, the break-up of his second marriage, the death of his mother, a devastating fire that destroyed many of his manuscripts, and serious health problems. After that time, Farrell's work went in new direc- tions and he made distinct contributions in new arenas,[18] but to some extent both his fiction and his criticism of the last twenty-five years of his life were the afterglow of nearly two decades of activity as a left-wing fighter on "The Cultural Front."[19]

A Turning Point in the History of the US Cultural Left

A Note on Literary Criticism stands at the very center of Farrell's achievement during the 1930s and 1940s. Moreover, its appearance marked a critical turning point in the history of the US literary Left. Just as his early novels expanded and enriched the possibilities of fiction during the Great Depression, *A Note on Literary Criticism* clearly expanded the possibility for a Marxist cultural theory free of subordination to political expediency, which was the main problem with criticism promulgated by the organs of the CP-USA, despite the talent, intelligence, and sincerity of many of its authors. Moreover, both achievements, Farrell's fiction and his criticism, evolved in tandem in the 1930s, the latter as a necessary defense of the former. The rehabilitation of one will probably help facilitate the rehabilitation of the other. But central to the understanding of both is Farrell's complex association with the literary Left.

As early as his 1930 essay on "Plekhanov and Marx," one can see Farrell's sympathy for Marxism as a valuable instrument in his literary analysis as well as in his judgment that it can become dangerous when used as "a measuring rod."[20] His personal associations with members of the Communist movement can be documented at least as early as 1931; that year, while he was in Paris, *Young Lonigan* was submitted to Vanguard Press on his behalf by Walt Carmon, a Communist Party literary functionary who would soon depart to Moscow to edit the revolutionary English-language publication *International Literature*. And when Farrell and his first wife, Dorothy, returned to the United States to live in New York in 1932, they moved in with Frances Strauss, business manager of the *New Masses*, to which Farrell had contributed a book review in 1930.[21]

Farrell's political agreement with the CP-USA is evident through his public statements in the *Daily Worker* and elsewhere until 1936. His name did not appear on the famous list of intellectuals supporting Foster and Ford, the Communist Presidential and Vice Presidential candidates in 1932, but only because he was so little known that no one thought to ask him.[22] When John Dos Passos, Edmund Wilson, Lionel Trilling, and other writers publicly distanced themselves from the CP-USA after it disrupted a Socialist Party rally in Madison Square Garden in 1934, Farrell's name was noticeably absent from the round-robin letter of dissenters.[23]

Nevertheless, Farrell's agreement with the politics of the CP-USA was one thing; control over the shape, character, and direction of his fiction was another. This tension formed the "moment" in which *A Note on Literary Criticism* was forged. Doubts about literary theory and practice interacted with and rebounded against doubts about political theory and practice.

Contrary to the impression given by anticommunist polemicists, including Farrell himself in later years,[24] it was not the case that writers on the Left were marching in forced lock-step to orders given by the CP-USA or the Communist

Party of the Soviet Union. Max Eastman's catchphrase, "Writers in Uniform,"[25] may have had relevance to the zeal for political conformity desired by some CP-USA leaders and in the Soviet Union, but it does little to explain the complex situation of US radical writers who sought to put their skills as cultural workers in the service of social emancipation and invariably bridled at reviews in the *New Masses* and *Daily Worker* that pointed out political errors in their fiction and poetry. If writers rushed to impose the dramatic equivalent of political slogans on their fiction and poetry, it was more likely due, as Daniel Aaron observed, to the fact that "the Left writer, in and out of the party, faced something more insidious than party pressure: his own compulsion to subordinate the problems of his craft to political policy."[26]

Farrell was not alone in his resentment of attempts to judge his writing by a Marxist political yardstick. Indeed, in 1934, the *New Masses* sponsored an "Author's Field Day" in which virtually every one of the fourteen respondents rebuked the criticism they had received along the lines similar to Farrell's complaint that it was irrelevant.[27] Collectively they expressed many of the themes that Farrell would later elaborate in *A Note on Literary Criticism*.

The situation was more accurately a very fluid one in which several interrelated controversies were unfolding simultaneously. One entailed a historic battle to create a place for working-class life experience in US literature; indeed, to establish, as Joseph Freeman posed the issue in a fine essay that served as an introduction to *Proletarian Literature in the US* (1935), "what constitutes experience?"[28] With this Farrell had no quarrel; indeed, the interrogation of "experience" among the non-elite classes was a key to his whole artistic project and would later on add to tensions he had with the *Partisan Review* editors during their deradicalization in the 1940s.[29]

Another dynamic involved the Communist Party's running a cultural apparatus as an adjunct to its political strategy. This brought about the familiar host of problems that might be expected to accompany any such project: bureaucracy, cliquism, favoritism, pomposity, ignorance, sloppiness. Farrell, like most writers, was suspicious of the qualifications of many who passed judgment on him, whether directly in reviews, or by offering advice as to what the Left writer should do. Frequently he, like many others, felt that judgments were not being made on the basis of an author's chosen goals and objectives, but according to external or irrelevant criteria.

Farrell's singular contribution in *A Note on Literary Criticism* was not just the mouthing of such common grievances but his demonstrating a pattern to these problems and pointing to the gap between the critical excesses that appeared in the publications of the CP-USA and the authentic ideas of Marx. Behind this analysis, of course, was Farrell's own Trotskyist conception of the Stalinization of the CP-USA. This was a slow but steady process that had to some extent occurred as early as the expulsion of the pro-Trotsky and pro-Bukharin factions on orders from Moscow in 1928–29. But Farrell had only come to recognize this after 1934 when his literary grievances led him to associate increasingly with supporters of Trotsky in the United States.

By 1936 he had concluded that the evolving cultural orientation of the CP-USA was built on a combination of powerful half-truths and tragic self-deceptions. The inauthentic connection between professions of Marxist theory and judgments of literary quality was clearly evident after the CP-USA's 1935 Popular Front turn when the Party's emphasis on "revolutionary" and "proletarian" literature began to be displaced by calls for a people's "democratic" and "anti-fascist" culture. Farrell's book was effective because he identified associations among the distortions that suggested a deeper malaise beneath. His arguments could not easily be dismissed by writers grouped around the CP-USA. Many actually agreed with many of his charges – indeed, a few had made the same points themselves – but they could sense the implications of his overall synthesis. If Farrell's argument was accurate, the Communist cultural movement was not promoting Marxist values but instead promulgating dangerous heresies similar to those articulated by pre-Marxist and bourgeois critics.

The notion that Farrell had become by 1936 an "anti-Stalinist communist," and would remain so for another dozen years, seems nearly impossible for a post-McCarthy era generation to grasp. Reviewers of Farrell's time, however, understood that there were a range of Marxisms. *The Times Literary Supplement* observed that, "Mr Farrell . . . is himself a Marxist – a more orthodox Marxist, in his own view, than the majority of his comrades who write about the function of literature. He complains that there is an oversimplification of the issue in these writers, which derives from a pre-Marxist body of doctrine."[30] The *New York Times* reviewer understood that the book was aimed at "the Marxist pretenders" and "phony Marxism."[31] The *American Review* observed: "it is the purpose of Mr Farrell's book to point out the follies of those Marxian critics who have, in his view, deviated to the left . . . he appears to wear the mantle of orthodoxy in lonely grandeur, like an Athanasius of Union Square."[32]

However, if the meaning of communism has become obfuscated since the 1930s, so has the meaning of "Marxist orthodoxy." After all, were not the critics endorsed by the official Communists the "orthodox" ones and Farrell the "heretic"? The mid 1930s was, in fact, one of those complex moments in history when what was once thought of as orthodox became stigmatized as heretical. Although Farrell already professed a distaste for Plekhanov,[33] and was actually quite sympathetic to Sidney Hook's "instrumentalist Marxism," he was very close to the original thinking of Marx, Engels, and Lenin in literary matters. Indeed, *A Note on Literary Criticism* is brimming with authenticating quotations from the Marxist masters to the point where it has some features of a biblical exegesis. The critics who answered Farrell in the publications of the CP-USA could not seriously challenge his textual evidence; instead, they waivered between (falsely) calling Farrell an opponent of Marxism, and insisting (with a bit more justification) that he had unfairly ripped people's statements from their contexts.[34]

Farrell had also complicated the matter for those who wished to interpret his views by never referring to Stalin or Trotsky by name, or correlating literary policy to political policy, which he was nonetheless on the verge of repudiating publicly.[35] This was for three reasons. One was that his thinking about Stalin and Trotsky only crystallized as he was writing the book. A second reason he didn't want to wave the red flag of Trotsky was that by doing so he would be denied a hearing in the Communist press altogether. A third was that he still had doubts about making a break with the CP-USA cultural milieu, which would cost him many friendships and might also damage the career of his new companion, the actress Hortense Alden. Yet, just as Trotsky's monumental *History of the Russian Revolution* was implicitly a criticism of the degeneration of that Russian Revolution under Stalin's leadership, so *A Note On Literary Criticism* was implicitly an attack on the political party with which the leading Marxist critics of the day were allied.

The work itself elaborates themes that Farrell had enunciated not only in his contribution to the "Authors' Field Day," but also in his 1934 analysis of Edward Dahlberg, "In Search of the Image,"[36] in his 1935 address to the American Writers' Congress on "The Short Story,"[37] in numerous book reviews and private letters, and in essays against "leftism" that appeared in his "Theatre Chronicle" column in the 1934–36 *Partisan Review*.[38] In these latter writings Farrell consistently advocates techniques of indirection, fetishizes no particular school or tradition, advocates that the artist should render capitalist oppression concrete and eschew abstract denunciations, and pays detailed attention to the author's own aims and milieu.

Part of the vitality of *A Note on Literary Criticism* is its clarity and directness; it requires no plot summary nor explication of recondite arguments. The title, of course, seems at once overly modest and overly general. According to Farrell's diary, the work may have begun as a "note" but quickly evolved into a pamphlet and then a full-fledged book.[39] Possibly Farrell intended a pose of modesty, reinforced by his claim to amateurship – "in no sense do I consider myself a professional critic, let alone a professional Marxist" – to counter the arrogance of a number of his antagonists. But his modest title scarcely portends the powerful logic which he immediately enlists in his onslaught to hammer home his case. The choice of title may be justified, however, in the sense that the book is by no means as inclusive as the corrosive rhetoric implies; its brilliance lies in the agenda of knotty problems that are placed before the cultural Left and not in any definitive conclusions offered.

The book is also quite specifically about the practice of the cultural Left rather than "criticism" in general. The opening chapters, "The Duality of Literature," "Impressionism," and "Humanism, " strike one as a *pro forma* dispensing with niceties before getting to the heart of the matter, where Farrell maps out his common-sense distinctions between literature "as a branch of the fine arts" and "as an instrument of social influence," and then dispenses with

47

the major "bourgeois" schools of criticism before turning to what he regards as more serious matters. The slight treatment of Pater and Spingarn, and the literary humanists Babbit and More, are so simplified that they actually accomplish little more than the mapping out of Farrell's own orientation.[40]

It is worth noting, however, that his central clarifications are undertaken with traditional Marxist categories. Aesthetic and subjective values are contrasted to functional and objective use-values, an adaption of Marx's method in differentiating use-values and exchange-values in *Capital*. Farrell's conclusion that the two categories are not "absolutes" is just a more informal way of calling them "dialectically interconnected."[41]

Starting with the chapter titled "Left-wing Dualism," Farrell enters the fray of his time, quickly putting labels on chief critics associated with the Communist Party. He declares Mike Gold a revolutionary sentimentalist and Granville Hicks a mechanical determinist. Elsewhere, V. F. Calverton (who after 1934 was regarded as an opponent of the CP-USA) is charged with reducing aesthetics to craftsmanship. In the six chapters and conclusion that follow, Farrell reviews many of the central issues engaging left-wing literary debate: What is the "relative objective validity" of art in the sense of transcending immediate social meaning? How is art shaped simultaneously by past tradition as well as present economic factors? To what extent does art extend beyond its own epoch and acquire new meaning in the future? What is the relation between between categories of sociological description (such as "bourgeois" and "proletarian") and categories of evaluation? How does tradition function in literary development? What is the difference between literature as "social influence" and propaganda?

The appearance of the book by itself did not end Farrell's relations with the CP-USA cultural milieu, although its publication certainly put strain on the relationship. In the fall of 1936, Farrell made the decisive political break by joining the executive committee of the American Committee for the Defense of Leon Trotsky, which sought to expose the rigged nature of the Stalinist Moscow Purge Trials. His work on behalf of the Committee, which included an April 1937 visit to Mexico to observe the interrogation of Trotsky by John Dewey's Commission of Inquiry, cemented his relations with the Trotskyist movement and in late 1937 he lent his name to the relaunching of *Partisan Review* on an independent but quasi-Trotskyist political basis.

After the 1930s, Farrell continued to produce Marxist criticism that appeared in a wide range of publications. Many of these essays and reviews were collected in *The League of Frightened Philistines and Other Papers* (1945) and in *Literature and Morality* (1947), although many others have yet to be reprinted or anthologized. Some refer back directly to issues taken up in *A Note on Literary Criticism*, others extend the argument into areas of ideology, morality, and the social obligations of the novelist. Many more concern fresh issues such as film, Hollywood, psychoanalysis, and the re-evaluation of US and European classic literature from a Marxist perspective. Only when a major anthology of such writings is issued, along with the reprinting of key novels and short story collections from the 1930s and 1940s such as *Gas-House McGinty* (1933), *A World I Never Made* (1936), *The Short Stories of James T. Farrell* (1937), *Tommy Gallagher's Crusade* (1939), *Father and Son* (1940), and *My Days of Anger* (1943), will a new generation of students, scholars, and cultural workers be in a situation to judge the legacy of independent Marxism in US culture as epitomized by James T. Farrell more complexly and accurately than has been done to date.

Postscript

I knew James T. Farrell during the last six years of his life, from the time he was sixty-nine until his death at seventy-five. I was roughly the same age as was Farrell when he established himself as a writer. We corresponded, sometimes as often as once a week, and I visited his Upper East Side New York City apartment on many occasions as well as joined him in Cambridge, Massachusetts, and Tuscaloosa, Alabama, where he spoke to university audiences. He read over my 1974 doctoral dissertation[42] about his Marxist years, correcting all factual errors and reining in his temper when I made a political or literary judgment that he didn't like or share.

My political views were then, as they are now, not so different from those of Farrell during the 1930s and 1940s on the fundamental matter of inequality and exploitation in our society, despite the vast changes in domestic and international conditions since World War II and the collapse of the Soviet Union. By the time we met, of course, Farrell's political opinions bore certain resemblances to neo-conservatism, despite episodic declarations that he was still a "Jacobin," if no longer a Bolshevik.

Whether I reminded Farrell in some way of his younger self, or whether it was, as he said and wrote, that he simply found my scholarship "honest," we overcame many cultural as well as political gulfs. The relationship we cemented gave me confidence to persist in an area of scholarship – the human infrastructure and the knotty theoretical conundrums of the US cultural Left – that sometimes seems beyond redemption as a vital force in our national culture. Nevertheless, as I witness the debates of the early 1990s on the contemporary "Cultural Front," not only Right against Left but intra-Left and among those for whom the very terms "Left" and "Right" seem quaint, antiquated vestiges of bygone years and ancient wars, I recognize their similarity with pivotal issues raised in Farrell's book, and, indeed, with concerns raised throughout the entire course of his career.

I still believe there is a need for artists, writers, scholars, and other cultural workers to ally with the oppressed against the elite who hold power, with the colonized against the colonizers, and with the have-nots against the haves. In the 1930s and 1940s James T. Farrell added something distinctive to that radical tradition – an engagement as fierce as it was independent, as circumspect as it was militant. *A Note on Literary Criticism* is not merely a famous document of the Depression years; it is a landmark text in the tradition of the committed writer that remains a beacon and model for all whose eyes are still fixed on the prize.

Notes

1. Saint Athanasius (c. 297–373) was repeatedly sent into exile for his defense of orthodoxy against the widespread Christian heresies of Arius in fourth-century Alexandria.

2. The major text of the US proletarian literary movement was the anthology *Proletarian Literature in the US* (New York: International, 1935), edited by Joseph Freeman, Michael Gold, and Granville Hicks.

3. Among the many stimulating works of contemporary gender studies in literature is Elizabeth Meese's *(Ex)Tensions: Refiguring Feminist Criticism* (Urbana and Chicago: University of Illinois, 1990). An outstanding critque of theories of "race" and ethnicity in relation to culture is E. San Juan, Jr.'s *Racial Formations/Critical Transformations: Articulations of Power in Ethnic and Racial Studies in the United States* (Atlantic Highlands, NJ: Humanities Press, 1992). The most comprehensive collection of current cultural theory on the Left is Lawrence Grossberg, Cary Nelson, and Paula Treichler, eds, *Cultural Studies* (New York: Routledge, 1992). See also Stanley Aronowitz, *The Politics of Identity* (London: Routledge, 1992) for an impressive attempt to theorize gender and "race" in relation to class.

4. A sophisticated defense of the category of the aesthetic from a Marxist perspective can be found in Michael Sprinker's *Imaginary Relations: Aesthetics and Ideology in the Theory of Historical Materialism* (London: Verso, 1987). An assault on the category is the centerpiece of Tony Bennett's *Outside Literature* (London: Routledge, 1990).

5. See Eugene Lunn, *Marxism and Modernism: An Historical Study of Lukács, Brecht, Benjamin and Adorno* (Berkeley: University of California Press, 1983).

6. Farrell's parents were second-generation Irish-American working class, but, due to their poverty, he was raised by middle-class relatives.

7. A copy of the dust-jacket is reproduced in *Dictionary of Literary Biography Documentary Series*, Vol. 2 (Detroit: Gale Research Corporation, 1988), p. 63.

8. The Studs Lonigan Trilogy consists of *Young Lonigan: A Boyhood in Chicago Streets* (1932), *The Young Manhood of Studs Lonigan* (1934), *Judgment Day* (1935). The trilogy was issued as a unit in 1935.

9. Edmund Wilson, "Novelist Bites Critic," *Nation* 142 (June 24, 1936): 808.

10. The novels about Danny O'Neill, referred to by Farrell as the O'Neill–O'Flaherty Pentalogy, were: *A World I Never Made* (1936); *No Star is Lost* (1938); *Father and Son* (1940); *My Days of Anger* (1943); *The Face of Time* (1953).

11. See Halford E. Luccock, *American Mirror* (New York: Macmillan, 1940), p. 74.

12. Alfred Kazin, *On Native Grounds: An Interpretation of Modern American Prose Literature*, fortieth anniverary edition (New York: Harcourt, Brace, Jovanovich, 1982), p. 381. For a strong dissent from Kazin's treatment of the 1930s literary Left, in this otherwise monumental achievement, see Alan M. Wald, "In Retrospect: *On Native Grounds*," *Reviews in American History* 20 (1992): 276–88.

13. A fine survey of scholarship about Farrell can be found in Jack Salzman's "James T. Farrell: An Essay in Bibliography," *Resources in American Literary* VI, no. 2 (Autumn 1976): 131–63. An omnibus of mid-1970s scholarship about Farrell can be found in Jack Salzman and Dennis Flynn, Guest Editors, *Twentieth Century Literature: James T. Farrell Issue* 22, no. 1 (February 1976). Edgar Branch's *James T. Farrell* (New York: Twayne, 1971) is a basic sourcebook, along with Branch's *A Bibliography of James T. Farrell's Writings, 1921–57* (Philadelphia: University of Pennsylvania Press, 1959). Several of the more recent doctoral dissertations on Farrell are Peter A. Carino, "Plot in Studs Lonigan: The Failure of Manhood, the triumph of Artistry," University of Illinois, 1985; Matthew B. Lesser, "James T. Farrell as Literary Realist and Social Historian," University of New Mexico, 1985; Priscilla Hill, "Aesthetics and the Novel: A Study of the Relation of John Dewey's Philosophy and the Novels of James T. Farrell," Southern Illinois University, 1986.

14. Eric Pace, "James T. Farrell, Realistic Novelist, Dies; Author of Studs Lonigan Trilogy was 75," *New York Times*, August 23, 1979, II, p. 15.

15. Farrell was rather short, and, during the years I knew him, wore thick horn-rimmed glasses that gave him a blurry, fish-eyed look. Although he appeared serious and intense at times, such moments were often interrupted by eye-twinkling, mischievious grins. In contrast to the *New York Times* depiction of him as T. S. Eliot's "Sweeney," I thought Farrell as an elderly man appeared rather elfin.

16. He was primarily identified with the Socialist Workers Party (at times called Communist League of America, Workers Party of the US, and the *Appeal* group in the Socialist Party), led by James P. Cannon, from late 1936 to 1945, and then with the Workers Party, led by Max Shachtman, from 1945 to 1948.

17. A year before his death he joined Social Democrats USA.

18. *The Face of Time* (1953) is among his outstanding accomplishments, and *The Silence of History* (1963) received significant attention.

19. This was the title of his literary columns in the *Socialist Call*, while the Trotskyists were a faction in the Socialist Party, and *Partisan Review*, when the journal considered itself friendly to Trotskyism.

20. James T. Farrell, "Plekhanov and Marx," *New York Sun*, October 15, 1932, p. 19.

21. See Alan M. Wald, *James T. Farrell: The Revolutionary Socialist Years* (New York: New York University Press, 1978).

22. See the list of names in Daniel Aaron, *Writiers on the Left: Episodes in American Literary Communism* (New York: Columbia University Press, 1992), pp. 456–57, footnote 64.

23. See the discussion of the protest in Alan M. Wald, *The New York Intellectuals* (Chapel Hill: University of North Carolina Press, 1987), pp. 61–4.

24. An early example is his brief "The End of a Literary Decade," *American Mercury* 48 (1939): 408–15, unfortunately chosen as the concluding piece to the otherwise more balanced volume *Literature at the Barricades: The American Writer in the 1930s* (University, Alabama: University of Alabama Press, 1982), edited by Ralph F. Bogardus and Fred Hobson.

25. From the title of his book, *Artists in Uniform: A Study of Literature and Bureaucratism* (New York: Knopf, 1934).

26. Aaron, pp. 292–3.

27. "Book Supplement: Authors' Field Day, a Symposium on Marxist Criticism," *New Masses* 12 (July 3, 1934): 27–34.

28. Freeman et al., eds, p. 12.

29. See Wald, *James T. Farrell*, pp. 91–3.

30. W. Foxley Norris, "Marxist Criticism," *London Times Literary Supplement*, Aug. 15, 1936, p. 661.

31. Peter Munro Jack, "Marxist Books and Marxist Critics," *New York Times Book Review*, July 5, 1936, II, p. 2.

32. Geoffrey Stone, "A Critic of Marxian Critics," *American Review* 7 (September 1936): 468.

33. See Farrell, "Plekhanov and Marx," p. 19.

34. See Isidor Schneider, "Sectarianism on the Right," *New Masses* 19 (June 23, 1936): 23–5, and Granville Hicks, "In Defense of James T. Farrell," ibid. (July 14, 1936): 23–4.

35. V. F. Calverton must have been waxing ironic when he attacked Farrell for not referring to Trotsky's *Literature and Revolution* in "James T. Farrell and Leon Trotsky," *Modern Monthly* 10 (Oct. 1936):15–17

36. Reprinted in Farrell, *The League of Frightened Philistines* (New York: Vanguard, 1945), pp. 154–60.

37. Ibid., pp. 136–48.

38. At that time the journal was the organ of the New York chapter of the Communist-led John Reed Clubs. Farrell's allies wrote under the names Philip Rahv (Ivan Greenberg), Wallace Phelps (William Phillips), and Alan Calmer (Abe Stein). The first two evolved toward Trotskyism along with Farrell; the last remained with the CP-USA until 1939, and then disappeared from the literary and political scene.

39. See Cooney, p. 292, note 32.

40. In his review of the book, Edmund Wilson skipped the first chapters altogether. Other reviewers criticized Farrell's treatment of thinkers other than the Marxists – not only Pater and Spingarn but Plato, Spinoza, and Aquinas – as sketchy. They also faulted his neglect of I. A. Richards and Kenneth Burke. See Jack, p. 2; Norris, p. 661; and Stone, p. 468.

41. Farrell, *A Note on Literary Criticism*, p. 12.

42. "James T. Farrell: The Revolutionary Socialist Years," University of California at Berkeley, 1974.

4

Return of the Repressed

Premature Socialist-Feminists

Paula Rabinowitz, *Labor and Desire: Women's Revolutionary Fiction in Depression America.*
Chapel Hill: University of North Carolina Press, 1991. 222 pp.

The publication of Paula Rabinowitz's stunning new book about the theory and practice of 1930s fiction by left-wing women writers advances the study of US radical culture by a quantum leap. Through a complex, creative, and impressively researched sequence of theoretical propositions about narrative and genre, Rabinowitz offers a challenging method for reclaiming an entire "disappeared" generation of class-conscious women writers. Moreover, she practices what she preaches by providing readers with compelling interpretations of a range of novels from Agnes Smedley's *Daughter of Earth* (1929) to Mary McCarthy's *The Company She Keeps* (1942).

Rabinowitz's intervention into the "canon debate" ranks among the most courageous and circumspect to date, roughly analogous to recent books by Houston Baker, Jr., Cary Nelson, Ramón Saldívar, Hazel Carby, and a few others. Like these, *Labor and Desire* is not restricted simply to an indictment of literary histories (including, in this case, even those by feminist revisionists such as Sandra Gilbert and Susan Gubar) for their sorry silence about the cultural practice of Red women writers of the Depression era. More consequentially, the book also effectively demonstrates many of the ways in which the category of "gender" can enrich, complicate, and render more vital our understanding of cultural history through the subtleties and fresh perspectives its thoughtful application may illuminate. This is a "re-visioning" of scholarship on the 1930s

"Premature Socialist-Feminists" originally appeared in *In These Times*, March 25–31, 1992; "An Earlier 'Time of the Toad'" originally appeared in *Cineaste*, 20, no. 2 (Summer 1993); "The 'Radical Impressario' Revisited" originally appeared in *Journal of American History* (September 1993); and "Edwin Rolfe, *Presente!*" originally appeared in *Journal of English and Germanic Philology*, 91, no. 3 (July 1992).

inspired by the women novelists themselves, who rewrote both the male tradition of the "proletarian novel" and the female tradition of the "domestic realistic novel" to produce in letters a valuable history of female subjectivity during the Great Depression.

Yet this work is far more than just a gender study; Rabinowitz wrestles with the interaction of gender and class in a manner worthy of the legacy of the arduous labors of radical feminist theoreticians of recent decades. In a certain sense *Labor and Desire* is a testimony to the validity and vitality of that wing of the US New Left that kept the "light in the window" during the discouraging days of the Reagan–Bush era, seeking to advance the Marxist cultural tradition through a synthesis of what is best in the traditions of the Old and New Left.

The book has aspects of a personal testament even beyond the inaugurating story of the author's grandmother's Depression shame. Early chapters sparkle with the "shock of recognition" as Rabinowitz describes the nearly-lost legacy of women novelists who, within the limitations of their circumstances, anticipated many of the concerns of the contemporary socialist-feminist movement. The Epilogue resonates with themes of uncompromising defiance of the continuing outrages perpetrated by US capitalism and imperialism against women, people of color, and the subaltern classes domestically and internationally. At the same time, Rabinowitz expresses solidarity with the spirit of resistance within the broader movements that shattered the Stalinist monolith in Eastern Europe and that went down to a bloody defeat (temporarily, one hopes) in China. One could hardly find a scholarly book more timely for providing inspiration and guidance in the 1990s.

Methodologically, the crux of Rabinowitz's argument is a product of the intersection of rigorous empirical research into the actual writings of women in the 1930s, combined with participation in the ongoing dialogue among socialist-feminists (as well as contemporary Marxists and other feminist literary critics) about the complex interactions of class, gender, and cultural production. The result is an evocative trope of "labor and desire," representing the mutually shaping political, personal, and material demands flowing from one's position in class structure refracted through (and refracting) one's multifaceted socialization as female in a patriarchal system.

The argument, however, is pursued in concert with more conventional literary concerns. Indeed, *Labor and Desire* is powerful testimony that the new revisionists of the canon are not nihilists *vis-à-vis* traditional study; rather, they are out to expand and adjust what was been known through a broader contextualization and the unearthing of silenced voices. Take, for example, Rabinowitz's attitude toward those scholars who have shaped the study of US literary radicalism as we have known it – Daniel Aaron, Walter Rideout, and a few others (including myself). Her interest is not primarily in belaboring us for failing to introduce in books published ten, twenty, or thirty years ago the theories and texts to which she has devoted this book. Rather, she strives to show the advantages to all of our scholarship that will come about through the expansion, augmentation, rethinking and re-seeing that comes when gender serves as a category of knowledge to reconstruct literary history.

Moreover, it's worth noting that her book is one of the few to date that follows the salutary methodology of Paul Buhle's *Marxism in the USA* (1987). Like Buhle, Rabinowitz treats Left traditions, particularly Communism and Trotskyism in the 1930s, as a unit. She shifts back and forth among them when appropriate, although in literary matters the Communist movement rightly deserves to be at center-stage as the most influential.

Beyond this, Rabinowitz also builds cogently upon the observations of others about the influence of documentary and reportage strategies on radical fiction of the 1930s. She notes that the method of "documentary expression" was one that combined personal narrative with the exposition of class struggle, thereby connecting "traditionally feminine forms of writing to more conventionally masculine ones" (p. 2). Her observations on the refiguration of the traditional types of women's novels under the impact of the Great Depression and the Left are compelling as well.

Flowing from this rich convergence of theoretical work tested against numerous texts, and animated by a commitment to the reform of consciousness far beyond the walls of academe, are many strikingly original contributions for which Rabinowitz's book ought to be widely discussed. To me, one of several crucial features of the work is the way in which Rabinowitz proposes to resolve part of the riddle of the relations among political commitment, critical theory, and literary practice in the Red Decade. Scholars long ago demonstrated the tendency toward a mechanical correlation of changes in the Communist Party's political line and the literary policy promoted by its leading journals and critics. This is most famously evident in the switch from the "proletarian" (1928–34) to the "Popular Front" (1935–39) cultural perspective, which brought about corresponding changes in literary themes, styles, and forms, and even venues for organizing writers. Nevertheless, contemporary cultural workers have persisted in unearthing all sorts of remarkable and unparalleled novels and poems from both halves of the era that seem to offer far more than such a closed classificatory system suggests. Some of these writings have been coming back into print through the laudable efforts of the Feminist Press, Monthly Review, West End Press, and various university publishing houses.

In regard to left-wing women writers, Rabinowitz suggests that the reason for a discrepancy between official theory and actual practice flows from a failure to acknowledge the "masculinist" nature of the literary strategies and policies of the 1930s. Many male writers of the time, especially Communist Mike Gold, author of *Jews Without Money* (1930) and a *Daily Worker* columnist, tended to promote a "proletarian realism" in which all features of the category of the "proletariat" were male. Counterposed to this was an aesthetic associated with femininity and effeminacy, subjectivity, 1920s modernism, and middle-class decay. Later, Philip Rahv, in attacking Communist literary policy from a quasi-Trotstskyist perspective, established an influential methodology that correlated Party line to literary style, oblivious to the ways in which this model silenced the practice of women writers on the Left whose art was also shaped by female labor and desire. Rabinowitz shows that, once one introduces the issue of "gender" – especially female sexuality and maternity – into the equation, the simplistic approaches of Gold and Rahv to the decade break down and new categories are required.

Rabinowitz is generous not only in her manner of correcting previous scholarship by showing the costs of our blindspots, but also in the way she builds upon and gives credit to many of those whose work has facilitated her own insights, including Susan Sulieman and Deborah Rosenfelt. Her book is as much constructive as de(con)structive. In place of the mechanical schemes of Rahv and the influential literary typologies found in Walter Rideout's *The Radical Novel in the United States, 1900–1954* (1956), Rabinowitz argues for the rethinking of female revolutionary fiction as an independent genre, grouped around classifications such as "The Working-Class Female Subject" and "The Female Intellectual as Subject."

This enables her to present some breathtaking readings of texts such as Clara Weatherwax's long-traduced *Marching! Marching!* (winner of the *New Masses* – John Day Company proletarian novel prize for 1935), Meridel Le Sueur's *The Girl* (first published its entirety in 1978), Tillie Olsen's *Yonnondio* (issued in 1974 with previously unpublished chapters) under the first rubric; and Tess Slesinger's *The Unpossessed* (1934), Lauren Gilfillan's *I Went to Pitt College* (1934), Josephine Herbst's *Rope of Gold* (1939) and Mary McCarthy's *The Company She Keeps* (1942) under the second. Dispersed throughout the book are less-developed but equally provocative observations on works such as Agnes Smedley's *Daughter of Earth* (1929) and Fielding Burke's *Call Home the Heart* (1932) as well as lesser-known novels such as Bettinna Linn's *Flea Circus* (1936), Evelyn Scott's *Calendar of Sin* (1931), Bessie Breuer's *The Daughter* (1938), Myra Page's *The Gathering Storm* (1932), Ruth McKenney's *Jake Home* (1943), Josephine Johnson's *Jordanstown* (1937), Catherine Brody's *Nobody Starves* (1932), Mary Heaton Vorse's *Strike!* (1930), Grace Lumpkin's *To Make My Bread* (1932), Beatrice Bisno's *Tomorrow's Bread* (1938), and Gale Wilhelm's *We Too Are Drifting* (1935). A few novels by men, such as Thomas Bell's *All Brides Are Beautiful* (1936) and James T. Farrell's *The Young Manhood of Studs Lonigan* (1934) and *Judgment Day* (1936), also receive brief but incisive treatment. Many of her insights about genre theory, "minor literature," and the prefiguring in 1930s fiction of "postmodern materialist-feminist" critical concerns are on the cutting edge of current cultural debate.

A book that reaches so far beyond its peer scholarship is not without some risky and problematical features. The rhetoric of "labor and desire" is sometimes difficult to translate into clear analytical categories. More important,

Rabinowitz is up against an audience – scholars as well as cultural workers – unfamiliar with much of the material that she introduces on a relatively high level of sophistication. Since we still lack a collective biography of Red women authors, something analogous to a female version of Daniel Aaron's *Writers on the Left* (1961), there may be a hiatus before parts of her intended audience can catch up with her. Finally, a book as stimulating as this can only provoke readers to new inquiries. How might the intersection of "race" along with gender and class affect her models (a subject that will have to be explored in regard to later decades, since, as Rabinowitz observes, explicitly left-wing novels by women of color in the 1930s are few)? What about the factoring into her paradigms of other influential elements, such as regional, ethnic, and religious subcultures?

Such queries only confirm the richness of the major thrust and specific literary interpretations proffered in *Labor and Desire*. Rabinowitz herself makes an impressive case for the potential breadth, soundness, and contemporary relevance of her method in her concluding observations about Alice Walker's *Meridian* (1976), Nadine Gordimer's *Burger's Daughter* (1979), and Marge Piercy's *Vida* (1979). After finishing *Labor and Desire*, I read a neglected resistance novel of the McCarthyite witch-hunt, Martha Dodd's *The Searching Light* (1955), from the perspective of Rabinowitz's methodology. I came away feeling quite convinced that, in addition to everything else, she has also elaborated a viable theoretical apparatus that will be useful when we begin to extend our understanding of this generic tradition into the even more neglected decades (for the Left) of the 1940s and 1950s. *Labor and Desire* is both a grand summation and a bold leap forward. In sensitivity and insight, Rabinowitz outdistances all previous efforts to achieve a unity of radical generations, traditions, and methodologies.

An Earlier "Time of the Toad"

Greg Mitchell, *The Campaign of the Century: Upton Sinclair's Race for Governor of California and the Birth of Media Politics*. New York: Random House, 1992. 665 pp.

Greg Mitchell, an author and journalist currently assisting the preparation of an eight-part Public Broadcasting Service series on *The Great Depression*, has produced a generic hybrid of a book that is a fun read as well as highly informative about a significant moment in the development of contemporary relations between media and politics. *The Campaign of the Century* is a cross between an encyclopedia of anecdotes of famous people of the early 1930s and a non-fiction novel.

Mitchell employs a style reminiscent of the short segments used by Meredith Tax in her radical novel *Union Square* (1988), but his chronicle proceeds day-by-day from August to November 1934, rather than year-by-year from 1929 to

1939. With echoes of John Dos Passos's *USA* trilogy (1930–36), he presents a fascinating cast of real-life buffoons, crooks, operators, opportunists, and a few idealists to provide the reader with portraits of a cross-section of prominent and semi-prominent figures from the early Depression era. Snippets of their lives are used to dramatize the unscrupulous means by which socialist novelist Upton Sinclair (1878–1968) was defeated in a bid for governor of California after there were strong indications that he might win.

True, the world-famous socialist novelist had no practical political experience (he once organized a utopian commune that failed), and he was capable of making incredible gaffes in remarks to the press. But he won a landslide victory in the California Democratic gubernatorial primary on August 28, 1934, and his most formidable opponent was an undistinguished Republican Party hack. Moreover, Sinclair's program to "End Poverty in California" (widely known by the acronym EPIC) struck a responsive chord among much of the population at a time when the Great Depression was at its worst. Even President Roosevelt indicated that he might possibly support Sinclair, although he later sat out the election.

The focus of Mitchell's story is the construction of a Holy War to defeat Sinclair; the work is not particularly focused on Sinclair the man, his literary or overall political career, or the EPIC movement. The most famous of the anti-Sinclair gang were the Hollywood moguls, who made fraudulent "shorts" and newsreels about a likely invasion into California of free-loading "bums" and "foreigners," and who threatened to pull their lucrative businesses out of state if Sinclair won. They teamed up with the law firms, big corporations, and, of course, the bourgeois press. One unique element was turning the anti-Sinclair political strategy over to newfangled "public relations experts" and advertising specialists. Thus ensued a dirty campaign anticipating features of both the anti-Communist witch-hunt of the Cold War era and the scandal-mongering, sound-byte-oriented, simple-minded sloganeering of the 1992 US presidential election circus. An aspect that might have been more fully developed in Mitchell's book is that left-wing Hollywood writers and actors experienced a "lite" version of the political repression to come during the Blacklist era, when certain character-istic patterns of behavior (for example, tough talk followed by craven capitula-tion on the part of one famous "tough-guy" actor) were established. In the end, Sinclair was defeated, although he won 900,000 votes to Republican Frank Merriam's 1.1 million.

The strength of this delightful book is its lively style and the synthetic quality of its research. Mitchell has read widely in biographies, autobiographies, collec-tions of letters, unpublished archives, oral histories, and conventional histories, and he conducted around seventy-five personal interviews. His facility is impressive and effective in making interconnections among national, regional, and local political activists; Hollywood bosses, writers, and actors; journalists, editors, and novelists; and many others. Even the reader most informed about one or two areas, such as Hollywood and the New Deal, is likely to learn something new about the relation of these to other areas of life in the United States at that time.

On the other hand, for those already specializing in one or another subject – such as the political Left, Hollywood screenwriters, and Upton Sinclair himself – there is likely to be little that is fresh. Mitchell especially likes to tell outrageous anecdotes about eminent figures; for example, the drunken antics of novelist Sinclair Lewis, and the sexual escapades of humorist Dorothy Parker. This makes for entertaining reading, but appears in print elsewhere and is sometimes of dubious relevance to the main story other than to provide atmosphere.

Occasionally the specialized scholar may lose confidence in Mitchell's omniscience. For example, on page 394, he tells the famous story of radical playwright John Howard Lawson refusing to pay an assessment to Harry Cohn, President of Columbia Pictures, to support the Merriam campaign, which resulted in Lawson's dismissal. However, Mitchell adds the new fact that Lawson "had just joined the Communist Party." Surprised at this information, which is not confirmed by Lawson's (unpublished) autobiography and the available scholarship on Lawson, I checked his source, cited as Margaret Brenman-Gibson's *Clifford Odets: American Playwright* (New York: Atheneum, 1982). But Brenman-Gibson does not back this up; in fact, she says that it was only *after* the episode with Cohn that the Communist-sympathizer Lawson tried to resolve his conflicts "by turning to Marxist theory" (p. 286). On page 345 Mitchell makes the peculiar declaration that in 1934 former cartoonist Robert Minor was "America's most famous Communist writer. " But there is no question that Mike Gold (of *Jews Without Money* and the Thornton Wilder controversy fame) was then by far the "most famous" Communist writer, while Minor, never particularly well known for his writing, had become mainly an aide to Party chairman Earl Browder. Such a mistaken claim is possibly a result of Mitchell's desire to dramatize Minor's arrival in California to give a speech attacking Sinclair.

Neither the Lawson nor Minor infelicities are very important, but they are a result of a tendency toward hyperbole to fit a strategy of building tension in the book, which is sometimes achieved at the expense of communicating a genuine "feel" for the history of the cultural Left and perhaps other matters. In addition, the book's thesis, about the transformation of American politics in the 1934 campaign, is more declaimed than demonstrated through historical comparison or developed either theoretically or conceptually.

Still, *The Campaign of the Century* is effective popular history with a "progressive" political orientation. It even lends itself to production as a successful historical movie about an idealistic literary radical battling the corrupt establishment. The result could be something in the vein of *Reds* (Paramount 1981, written by Warren Beatty and Trevor Griffiths). Some of the men and women interviewed by Mitchell might turn out to be superb "witnesses" reminiscing about the event, in the way that Beatty and Griffiths used the "talking heads" of Henry Miller, Scott Nearing, et al. to reflect on Greenwich Village, World War I, and the Russian Revolution. However, sex-symbol Beatty, who plays John Reed as playboy-revolutionary in *Reds*, would never do as the puritanical "Uppie" Sinclair.

The "Radical Impressario" Revisited

Leonard Wilcox, *V. F. Calverton: Radical in the American Grain*. Philadelphia, Pa.: Temple University Press, 1992. 304 pp.

In his influential *Writers on the Left* (1961), Daniel Aaron dubbed the Baltimore-born Marxist man of letters Victor Francis Calverton (1901–40) "The Radical Impressario." Although Calverton (a pen name for George Goetz) wrote several volumes of literary criticism, fiction, history, sociology, and anthropology, Aaron judged him memorable mostly for his journal *Modern Quarterly* (later *Modern Monthly*), which in the 1920s and 1930s was "a kind of intellectual brokerage house for the revolution" (p. 322). In the first full-length book about Calverton, Leonard Wilcox aims to enlarge his reputation to that of intellectual fugleman for the Great Depression generation, and also a prophet for concerns that would preoccupy the post-World War II generations of radicalized intelligentsia.

This combination biography and cultural history is a fine addition to the important trend pioneered by Elinor Langer's *Josephine Herbst: The Story She Could Never Tell* (1984) in its recognition of the profound, indissoluble, and often painful link between the personal and political, even among those aspiring to a "scientific socialist" world-view. With maturity and subtlety, Wilcox explores the psychosexual drives of Calverton from adolescence to his complicated marital life to the self-destructive behavior precipitating his premature death.

Wilcox's book is also strong in its survey of the interlocking and multifaceted arenas of Calverton's interests, mapping the contours of his career with greater precision than ever before. Calverton's ideas about death, religion, and community are lucidly explicated, although the result is that his life takes on a distressingly neurotic cast undermining one's confidence in Calverton's judgment about intellectual matters. Also fresh are the details concerning the way in which Calverton sought to negotiate his dual role as editor of an "independent" revolutionary journal and publicist for A. J. Muste's American Workers' Party. To this, Wilcox adds fascinating facts about Calverton's frantic efforts to keep the journal financially afloat while pacifying several editors possessing large egos, such as Max Eastman, Edmund Wilson, and Sidney Hook.

Wilcox is less persuasive in his claims for a distinctively viable politico-intellectual accomplishment. He makes much of *Modern Monthly*'s beating out

Partisan Review by a few years in denouncing Stalinism from the Left, although I don't think this point was ever really in dispute. While Calverton had attractive human qualities (such as a healthy respect for debate and disagreement), his pragmatic radicalism, preoccupation with "Americanizing" socialism, and bohemian way of life are such familiar themes in the lives and work of so many others of his generation that one might be more inclined to believe that the "Age" set Calverton's agenda rather than vice versa (the book's thesis).

Wilcox's effort to link Calverton forward to post-World War II radical intellectual interests in Gramsci, C. Wright Mills, Frankfurt School Marxism, and Russell Jacoby's "Public Intellectuals" is a plausible move but declaimed more than demonstrated. For example, he affirms many times that Calverton wedded Freud and Marx, anticipating Paul Goodman, Norman O. Brown, and the Frankfurt Marxists. But he never systematically describes and assesses the fruits of that marriage, let alone makes a comparison with the work of the other figures mentioned. Quite superb on the "mode of production" of Calverton's lively magazine, Wilcox's main achievement lies in the sensitive and sophisticated research conducted into the private life of Calverton and his network of political, literary, and personal associations.

Edwin Rolfe, *Presente!*

Cary Nelson and Jefforson Hendricks, *Edwin Rolfe: A Biographical Essay and Guide to the Rolfe Archive at the University of Illinois at Urbana-Champaign.* Urbana: University of Illinois Library, 1990. 118 pp.

Scholars following the debate over the US literary canon as it concerns the subcategory of "writers on the Left" can only respond with enthusiasm and gratitude to the publication of the University of Illinois Library's catalogue of the archive of the Communist poet Edwin Rolfe (1909–54). What Cary Nelson and Jefferson Hendricks have accomplished with the Rolfe papers, until now mostly in possession of Rolfe's widow and invisible to scholars, needs to be duplicated with the papers and biographies of hundreds of other forgotten left-wing writers. Only then will we have the empirical basis for fully theorizing what really happened in US literature from the 1920s to the 1950s.

There is a dramatic contrast between the Edwin Rolfe who comes through in this description of his papers (and in Nelson's fascinating 65-page biographical essay that is largely based on these papers), and the image – or non-image – of Rolfe in conventional studies. In the latter Rolfe is usually a name-in-passing mentioned almost exclusively in connection with his participation in the Abraham Lincoln Brigades in Spain. But to raise the Rolfe archive from the depths also brings brings to the surface part of a lost legacy of a literary generation far too neglected. In fact, a huge percentage of the writers, publications, and literary activities mentioned in the University of Illinois publication, which together comprise an intense subculture that nurtured the work of Rolfe and many others, will be unfamiliar to all but a handful of specialists. Students whose curiosity is piqued may find it nearly impossible to gain additional information about many of the writers, organizations, and publications in any extant histories, and several of the journals mentioned in the booklet may be impossible to locate.

A second corrective to the history of the literary Left offered by the Rolfe archive is that it may help refute the conventional view of literary Communism as mainly a Great Depression phenomenon. Rolfe himself became a Communist in the mid 1920s, and, in fact, underwent a period of disillusionment and separated from the movement around the turn of the decade. Then, after rejoining the movement in 1931, his commitment remained steadfast until his death during the McCarthyite witch-hunt while he was fighting his black-listing in Hollywood. In each phase Rolfe formulated his writing in response to a significantly changed set of political and personal circumstances.

A third "revision" of the conventional view of the Left that one can deduce from this archive is that attempts to treat left-wing writing generically, no matter how well-intended, as "political," "radical," "revolutionary," "proletarian," or whatever, only transform the cultural practice from something broad and diverse into something much narrower – and probably less interesting. In the case of Rolfe, one learns that, even though his political views remained more consistent than those of most of his contemporaries throughout his entire life (his disagreements with the Communist Party were mostly over literary matters and always kept internal), the canonical labels can only explain a small part of his project.

He began with writings that resembled what is usually regarded as the Whitman trend within modernism. But the University of Illinois archive reveals that he ended, like so many other Communists seeking to earn a living in Cold War America, by producing detective and science fiction. While this phenomenon of dual or multiple careers has received no attention from scholars, the fact is that "radical" or even "Communist" writers for the most part, unless independently wealthy, had to produce the kind of literature that could be sold: pulp, romance, children's, science fiction, detective, horror, Westerns, and so forth. Of course, this was often augmented by lyric verse for small press publications and "occasional" poetry for leftist periodicals.

The publication of this description of Rolfe's papers and biography is such a signal event for the reconstruction of the authentic history of twentieth-century US literature that my first impulse is merely to sing its praises. Yet the study of this topic cannot go forward without searching dialogue and friendly criticism; therefore, I also feel obligated to look at certain problem areas.

The first of these is that, whatever the chosen social and political commitments of a writer, the matrix of artistic drive and literary sensibility reside largely in personal life. Toward that end, the biographical elements of Nelson's essay admirably serve to reconstruct the economic constraints that haunted Rolfe's struggle to be a writer throughout his entire life. He describes a large number of Rolfe's work experiences and records the details of his and his wife Mary's financial resources. This data include useful economic figures about payment received for publishing in Party organs and for journalistic assignments. But the nature of the Fishman family subculture (Rolfe was born Solomon Fishman but began using pseudonyms in high school) is confusing because, while his father is described only as a "socialist" and a "union organizer," there are other indications that the family itself may have actually been part of the Communist subculture. (The two movements should not be confused because, after 1919, Communists and Socialists were usually quite hostile.) If true, then a Communist home and cultural upbringing would be a fairly important fact to consider in assessing the character of Rolfe's political commitment; such a background would possibly place him in a network of writers who were also from Communist families, such as Aaron Kramer and Martha Millet.

A second concern is the way in which Nelson depicts, or fails to depict, Rolfe's relation to the politics of Stalinism. While Nelson is admirably free of Cold war prejudices that reduce members and associates of the Communist Party to only the most negative features of the movement, he seems to have the attitude that delusions about Soviet Communism as authentic democratic socialism were entirely understandable in light of the time in which Rolfe lived and wrote.

One immediate problem for me is that there were other left-wing writers of the era who saw things quite differently. How do Rolfe's writings on Spain, for example, compare to those of George Orwell? My own sense is that Rolfe's view of Spain may well exhibit regurgitated Party-line positions, quite different from the critical-minded consciousness that many of us would like to promote on the Left and that were held in some circles outside the Communist Party milieu at that time.

The issue of Rolfe's political sophistication is somewhat related to a third area of concern. While Nelson tends to evade the knotty problem of political Stalinism, he explicitly seeks to redeem Rolfe as a writer not "in uniform" (Max Eastman's phrase for Communist writers who judged art by narrow political criteria of the immediate line). In this case, Nelson has documentary evidence that Rolfe regarded himself in opposition to unnamed "vulgar" Marxist critics in the Party; that he silently supported Albert Maltz's 1948 protest against the "Art as a Weapon" orientation; and that his own writings were eventually undervalued by the Communist press. Moreover, in describing the important role that Rolfe played in the early stages of *Partisan Review* magazine, Nelson astutely observes that the history of the magazine has come to reflect the version promoted by the "victors" – the circle around Philip Rahv and William Phillips who publicly took the magazine out of the Communist Party orbit in late 1937.

Here I would suggest that it is more appropriate to demystify the notion of a homogenous lock-step Communist literary movement altogether than to make any great claims for Rolfe's signal independence. The fact is that all writers are quarrelsome and opinionated about literary matters, and young as well as leading writers around the Communist movement behaved as subjectively, ego-centrically, and in as a refractory manner as most other writers; the main difference, however, is that all of this happened within the general conventions, structures, and tropes of Stalinism. Rolfe confirms rather than stands in contrast to this diversity, and this diversity was in turn variously limited by constraints of the Communist institutions through which the Left writers tried to function.

Based on my own reading of Rolfe's literary criticism, I think it may be a lost cause to claim for him noteworthy achievements or perspectives in that area. I cannot make much sense of his 1935 *Partisan Review* essay on "Revolutionary Poetry"; and his 1934 criticism of James T. Farrell's short stories, for failing to show a way out for the working class, is an example of the sectarianism that marred much of the cultural criticism of the time. (Farrell's excellent personal letter of rebuttal is reprinted in full in this booklet.)

None of these challenges to the image of Rolfe in Nelson's essay is meant to deny the essential decency as a human being and the devotion to literary craft that shine forth in Rolfe's life and much of his writing. Whatever his failings as a political thinker and his limitations as a literary critic, Rolfe is a figure from whom we may be able to learn far more than from many of his antagonists who might have been more "politically correct" about a certain international question or more subtle in critical exegesis. In fact, it is precisely in this area of learning from Rolfe that Nelson makes his most outstanding contribution, a contribution that flows logically from his recent extraordinary book *Poetry and Repression* (1989).

What Nelson offers is a plausible view of Rolfe's artistic project as the articulation of "agency within historical necessity." This is strategically formulated in each of Rolfe's three books, *To My Contemporaries* (1936), *First Love and Other Poems* (1951), and *Permit Me Refuge* (1955). Under changing conditions from the 1920s to the 1950s, the dual themes of "witness" and "resistance" are always present. And after looking at a number of Nelson's examples, I can only agree that, so long as one takes into account the deformations due to the tragic premises of Stalinism, Nelson is justified in his conclusion that "to recover Rolfe's work is to recover poetry's critical role."

PART II

New Approaches

5

Culture and Commitment:

US Communist Writers

Reconsidered

Introduction: Class War Against the Literary Canon

After Walter Lowenfels, the Lost Generation poet turned Communist journalist, was arrested by Federal agents in 1953 for violating the Smith Act, he protested that the charges against him were inadequate: "A large part of my adult life has been spent trying to overthrow not only the government but the universe."[1] In the strategy session before his trial, Lowenfels, sequestered with the eight other defendants, was asked to give his opinion: "Comrades, I have made many mistakes during my years in the Party. Some were left sectarian; others were right opportunist. During this trial of ours, I want to be sure all my errors are straight down the middle." The decision was unanimous that perhaps the best contribution Walter might make to the defense would be to keep to writing his poetry.

During the trial itself, Walter was astonished at the verbiage of the stool-pigeons and informers, who transformed Marxist thought and terminology into a "long-drawn-out gobbledegook of 'proletariat,' 'cadres,' etc." He predicted to his Communist co-defendants: "This jury is going to find us guilty of having endured boredom and convict us of talking nonsense." And so it did.

When higher courts later overturned his conviction, Walter was disappointed that the grounds were "for lack of evidence." Did the learned judges not know Emerson's dictum that one must "Beware of poets; they leave nothing unchanged; they overturn everything"?

These excerpts from letters of Walter Lowenfels, published in Robert Grover's *The Portable Walter* (1968), ought to remind one how partisan and irresponsible it is to reduce the hundreds of poets, fiction writers, and critics drawn

This chapter originally appeared in Michael Brown et al., eds, *New Studies in the Culture and Politics of US Communism* (New York: Monthly Review Press, 1993).

to the US Communist movement throughout its seventy-year history to tools, dupes, acolytes, or other mere instruments of "the Party line." As these quotations suggest, imaginative writers, whether Communists or vegetarians, are primarily engaged in recreating human experience through language and situating themselves in relation to traditions among contemporaries and earlier generations of writers. Whatever their political delusions and human flaws, left-wing artists possess other distinctive characteristics that make them unique and complex.

Indeed, the very fact that so many of the most extraordinary US writers felt, for longer or shorter amounts of time, that the ideals of Communism and the organized Communist movement held out the best hope for humanity ought to be understood as an augmentation, complication, and enrichment of their literary lives. The choice of Marxist commitment, no matter how ill-founded in inaccurate information about the Soviet Union, ought not to be perverted into a means of dismissing their cultural contributions.

The additional fact that so many of the Communist writers who once appeared in the *Daily Worker, New Masses, Dynamo, Rebel Poet, Anvil, International Literature, Directions, Harlem Quarterly, Jewish Life, California Quarterly, Contemporary Reader, Mainstream*, and other publications are entirely absent from extant literary histories, anthologies, and the lists of publishing houses should by no means be taken as a sign of the "inferiority" of their writings. Increasing evidence shows that the authentic history of twentieth-century US literary practice has yet to be written, especially in regard to the Left.[2]

The 1990s, the first decade when the implosion of Stalinist societies in Eastern Europe may finally strike the overdue death blow to Cold War mythologies of "Communist monolithism," is probably an appropriate occasion to start reversing the disgraceful and unfair treatment accorded the study of the varying impact of US Communism on writers. In terms of scholarly advances, there has not been a more propitious moment in the past twenty-five years. A quarter of a century ago, coming out of the McCarthyite witch-hunt era, several new books appeared analyzing the impact of Communism that were widely discussed.

The authors of those new books, Walter Rideout, who published *The Radical Novel in the United States, 1900–1954* in 1956, and Daniel Aaron, who published *Writers on the Left: Episodes in American Literary Communism* in 1961, did not write as militant partisans of a revolutionary new social order; rather, they depicted Communist writers as people of goodwill naively deceived by utopian illusions. Although dated by the scholars' failure to predict the spectacular rebirth of literary Marxism in the West and in the Third World in the 1960s and after, such an approach was a vast improvement over the earlier view that Communists of any kind were lemming-like agents of an international conspiracy.[3]

Even though Aaron and Rideout conducted their research in the 1950s, their work was an indication of the breakdown and invalidation of McCarthyite versions of the literary Left. Rideout argued for a modest although genuine contribution on the part of the radical novel to US literary history, and Aaron expressedly honored the writers and their good intentions. Thus, while the Communist novelist Philip Bonosky wrote a harsh critique of Rideout for the Party's theoretical journal *Political Affairs*,[4] the editor of the Party-sponsored literary review *Mainstream*, Charles Humboldt, praised the same book as a "singularly fair study."[5] A few years later, Bonosky was more generous with Aaron's work, and Philip Stevenson, a Communist novelist, playwright, and screenwriter who played a major part in sustaining the journal *California Quarterly*, hailed *Writers on the Left* as "heroic."[6] The concluding sentences to Aaron's book even appear as the epigraph to the International Publishers 1969 anthology of the *New Masses* edited by Joseph North.[7]

Nevertheless, subsequent books and dissertations on Communist writers that have appeared in the last decades have been accorded far less attention than Aaron and Rideout by scholars as well as left-wing cultural workers. Three decades after publication, their two books remain the *loci classicus* for scholarship on the Communist literary Left, although there are signs that the situation is changing in the early 1990s with the appearance of new research by Cary Nelson, Paula Rabinowitz, Constance Coiner, and several others.[8] To some extent this apparent lack of continuing impact may be due to the exceptional quality and success of the first two books, which are unusually rich and accurate, giving the appearance of having exhausted the subject far more than actually was the case. The fault may also lie with some of the subsequent scholars, who, with some exceptions, tended to recycle old material about a dozen or so top male, mostly white, figures, neglecting the hundreds who made up the infrastructure of a politico-cultural movement unparalleled in US history, with the one possible exception of the Black Arts movement in the 1960s.[9]

Still, it is surprising that, even though we have been living through more than two decades of sustained assaults against the dominant literary canon in the universities – assaults that have resulted in real though inadequate changes in the literary representation of women and people of color – the situation in regard to the study of Communist writers has stagnated until just recently. Although some radical novels reissued in paperback in the 1960s and 1970s are no longer in print, new ones are becoming available for the first time.[10] Moreover, a few of the literary histories that are being updated in so many areas are now for the first time presenting fresh material about the literary Left.[11]

Thus it appears that, in the wake of all the "culture wars" of recent decades, a new war is beginning to be waged, a second front has been opened, against the literary canon, and it is one that needs to be in part a "class" war. This is because, even though Communist-influenced fiction-writers and poets did pioneer issues of importance to women and people of color in their writings, if not always in their critical theorizations, it was specifically the promotion of class culture, and culture viewed through the prism of class, that was understood as the hallmark of the Communist effort.

Conversely, as in so many other areas of politico-cultural repression in the United States, the silencing and distortion of the Communist literary tradition has turned out really to be a means of silencing the larger radical and working-class tradition in literature. As has been well-documented by now, the ideology of "anticommunism" in the United States has little to do with genuine opposition to the brutal and authoritarian policies of the Stalin and post-Stalin regimes.[12] It is more often a means of discrediting the entire effort of the Left by tainting all radicals with the crimes of the Soviet ruling group, real or fabricated – although today we must recognize that most of those crimes were real.

One result of this kind of anticommunist ideology in literary studies is the disempowerment of the population of ordinary people who are denied a genuine history of their own cultural activities through access to authors who wrote about strikes, rebellions, mass movements, the work experience, famous political trials, the tribulations of political commitment, as well as about love, sex, the family, nature, and war from a class-conscious, internationalist, socialist-feminist, and anti-racist point of view. Instead, the population is often exclusively presented with literary role models that inculcate notions of culture that distort visions of possibilities for social transformation.

If many institutions today teach the outstanding African-American novelists Toni Morrison and Alice Walker alongside Saul Bellow and Henry James, it is not simply because the professors on their own discovered "literary merit" outside the traditional canon. It is partly because students took over campus buildings; African-Americans rebelled in the streets; and the colonies of the West rose up arms in hand. Something analogous may have to happen before the Red tradition also gets a foot in the door of academia.

At present, so far as any writers from the Communist tradition go, Walter Lowenfels, the Marxist poet with whose reminiscences I began these remarks, is one of the lucky ones. In the decades prior to his death, he was able to get a number of books into print, and he became something of an entrepreneur in the promotion of counter-literary anthologies that might be characterized as "prematurely anti-canon." These include *Poets of Today* (1964), *Where is Vietnam?* (1967), *In a Time of Revolution: Poems from Our Third World* (1969), *The Writing on the Wall* (1969), and *For Neruda, For Chile* (1975).

But in my estimate there are several hundred US Communist-influenced novelists and poets of real merit who have received *no* critical attention, and whose names never appear in literary histories except sometimes in those long lists of endorsers of various Writers' Congresses and other Communist causes catalogued for us in Eugene Lyons's conspiracy fantasy *The Red Decade* (1941). The most comprehensive source I have been able to locate on their activities is, in fact, not the multi-volume *Dictionary of Literary Biography* but the national and local files of the FBI.

In the remainder of this essay I will suggest several new angles of approach for recognizing this important legacy. The underlying premise is that one must abandon the view that a writer drawn to the Communist movement necessarily demonstrates certain stylistic or thematic qualities demanded by the political character of Stalinism as a movement. The meaning of the Communist experience is less a matter of literary form or content than of commitment to racial equality, anti-fascism, anti-capitalism, national independence of colonies, and similar values, even though all of these attitudes were variously qualified by the erroneous belief that the Soviet Union was a living example of socialism that must be preserved and defended. A new generation of scholars must put less emphasis on the claim that Communism "created" a literary/cultural movement, although there were certainly efforts in that direction, and more on the view that Communist institutions, ideology, and committed cadres "gave voice" in variously effective ways (some beneficial and prophetic; other deleterious and retrograde) to a large number of diverse writers radicalized by the inequities of capitalism.

Part 1: Communist Writers in Perspective

The new perspectives suggested in this essay are based on substantially fresh empirical research that includes not only the examination of previously unexplored archives, oral histories, and unanalyzed literary texts, but also interviews with participants who have not been sought out previously or who have not spoken up earlier. This includes officers of the John Reed Clubs, League of American Writers, and the National Council for the Arts, Sciences and Professions; editors of *Dynamo*, the *New Masses, Mainstream, California Quarterly, Jewish Life*, and many similar pro-Communist publications; numerous left-wing novelists, critics, and poets; and surviving Reds in Hollywood. This research has convinced me of the importance of reconsidering the centrality of the Communist experience in US cultural history.

There are many reasons why it is crucial to recognize that "Communism," by which I mean official Communist Party "communism," and not the other more heterodox varieties of Marxism to which I myself am more partial, is at the center of what one might call cultural "commitment" from the 1920s until the New Left of the 1960s. One is that the Communist cultural movement was the largest and most coherent expression of twentieth-century rebellion by workers, women, people of color, and committed intellectuals prior to the 1960s. It touched the lives of millions – not only the perhaps one million who passed directly through membership, but the many millions influenced by Communist ideas in literary publications, trade unions, civil rights and peace organizations, and elsewhere.

But to defend Communism as central to the legacy of the committed is also to present ourselves with a host of problems, the most important of which is the wholly mistaken view of the Soviet Union as an authentic socialist society that was doing the best it could under Stalin to abolish inequality, achieve a genuine democracy, and protect the interests of the poor and oppressed throughout the world. For those who really want to learn the lessons of the past, this flaw in the otherwise insightful and humane vision of the pro-Communist writers cannot be ignored or even minimized.

Indeed, "flaw" is hardly a sufficiently strong adjective. Stalin and his policies were virtually deified in the official declarations of the US Party up until 1956, as any reading of *The Communist* and *Political Affairs* will demonstrate.[13] Afterwards, it was mainly pronouncements from abroad – the 1956 Khrushchev revelations – that precipitated a partial re-evaluation. Ideologically, then, in terms of formal adherence to policy, the CP-USA was dogmatically Stalinist. But this characterization of official program has turned out to have less importance for the local practice of Communist cultural workers and even the individual consciousness of pro-Party writers than I, as one trained in textual analysis and theoretical critique, had previously imagined.

The "tragic" side of the Communist literary movement is that, from the per-spective of the movement's creative potential, a tremendous amount of energy by devoted and intelligent people was canalized into promoting literary prac-tice in order to bolster a political orientation based on such a mistaken premise. On the other hand, the counterpart to trivializing this real "flaw" is very often to try to *reduce* the whole complex experience *to* the flaw; that is, to sneer at those who failed to see Stalinism for the system of bureaucratic tyranny that it was. This reduction violates the historical record because, so far as I can tell, for the most part, the people involved and their dreams were superb, and many of their writings explore fresh terrain with insight and power unmatched by more famil-iar texts.

As the poet and critic Stanley Burnshaw wrote in a letter years after he had abandoned Communism: "I'm bitterly anti-Soviet, but I still believe I behaved as I'd want to behave during my Thirties period, for we were all moved by what Michael Gold described as the passionate view of the future's powerful beauty."[14] Novelist Guy Endore, in his UCLA Oral History interview, held a similar view: "The truth about the Communist Party was that it was a dedicated group of people who wanted to improve the world. . . . [The members were] for the most part very decent people who gave of their time and of their money and contributed everything they could to this movement, which was not going to benefit them in any way."[15]

For a less familiar approach than personal testimony, one might turn to the vividly dramatized view of that shared dream for "a better world" appearing in Ben Barzman's 1960 Marxist science fiction classic, *Echo X*. Here the familiar twin-planets motif is used to contrast our own post-holocaust and Cold War world with one in which the "pre-mature anti-fascists" had won out in the 1930s, saving the Spanish Republic and preventing World War II.

Part 2: Obfuscation of the Left Cultural Tradition

In my view, two major constraints have limited scholarship on US Communist writers up to the present moment. The first is the experience of the McCarthyite witch-hunt that forced a generation of writers to conceal, dissemble, and even to actually forget what they had gone through. The second has been the limitations of liberal thought as manifest in politics and literary criticism.

In regard to the former situation, even as late as the 1980s, writers significantly influenced by Communism omit that fact when submitting their own autobiographical statements for publication. In regard to the latter, the critics who created the "field" of US literary radicalism were, as were many who followed them, still prisoners of literary categories that occluded from vision vast amounts of literary practice. This is usually writing by women, people of color, radicals, people from the non-elite classes, people who wrote in what were stigmatized as more popular forms, and also people from many regions, especially outside big northern and West Coast urban centers. The field was designed in such a way that what these others wrote didn't fit; much of this creative practice wasn't even "seen."

The prevailing approach was not to pursue in open-ended manner the question "what kinds of writing did people sympathetic to Communism produce?" Instead, many scholars, perhaps precipitously, created special categories – helped by the fact that certain Communist critics themselves wanted to create special categories – of proletarian novels and revolutionary poetry for the early 1930s, and radical novels and social poetry for the Popular Front.[16] This was an advance that, in the absence of further inquiry, eventually transformed into a barrier.

Moreover, scholars almost always declared that this Communist literary phenomenon for all practical purposes came to a halt at the time of the Hitler–Stalin Pact when several key academic Party members, such as Granville Hicks and Robert Gorham Davis, resigned, and a few fellow-traveling critics, such as Malcolm Cowley, disassociated themselves. However, whatever moral blow the Hitler–Stalin Pact was to the Communist movement at that time and retrospectively, the majority of Left writers remained willing to work closely with the Communists. For example, the League of American Writers' membership lists indicate that seven-eighths of these weathered the year-and-a-half long crisis.[17] That is one of the reasons why a new study of literary Communism should not be limited to a 1930s act of nostalgia, but should go all the way up to the early 1970s and the experience of *American Dialogue.*

The research I have undertaken to date confirms the work of those younger historians of US Communism – such as Paul Buhle, Mark Naison, Robin Kelley, and Maurice Isserman – who see the Party as a war of a good many voices, but with the political and (I now add) literary orientations from Moscow (which tended to be narrowly functionalist in demanding political conformity) ultimately hegemonic.[18] While I have my own Marxist political opinions, I agree with the argument that in interpreting the reality of US Communism there has been much too much emphasis on what was said in Central Committee directives or (in regard to writers) by a few select Party critics. What actually happens in a trade union or in the pages of a novel is usually far more dependent on matters such as the personalities and abilities of those who are the human agents, and the context in which those agents are active.

It is true that one can document that Michael Gold offered many simplistic and half-baked judgments in his "Change the World" column, as his own comrades sometimes protested. One can show that John Howard Lawson and V. J. Jerome liked to review manuscripts by Party members prior to publication and that they would not hesitate to insist that material that might be interpreted as "defeatist" or that might possibly militate against class unity be altered or held back from print. But one can also show that Gold upheld some important values in difficult times, and that the majority of Communist writers either ignored or bypassed the informal supervision of Party institutions such as Lawson's "Writers' Clinic" in Hollywood. Moreover, almost every Communist critic progressively evolved in one way or another to embrace the argument of Leon Trotsky's *Literature and Revolution* (1923): that a Marxist political party should encourage literary practice, especially by workers, but not try to lead a partisan literary movement with a "line" in the way one tries to lead trade union and other struggles.

An important weakness of much scholarship on the Communist literary Left is that non-membership among sympathetic writers is sometimes taken as a sign of superior talent, morality, and intellect to those who joined. This means that considerable effort has been devoted to attempts (often futile) to determine who did or didn't have the equivalent of a "card." If a writer turns out to have had one, then a scholar who is sympathetic to the writer (for example, to Meridel Le Sueur, Edwin Rolfe, or Thomas McGrath) must prove that the writer was really a "maverick" or earned the ire of some higher-up Stalinist "official." If no "card" can be produced, then the critic's task of humanizing the writer becomes easier.

This approach fails to take into account many subtleties, such as the evidence that artistic autonomy often survived official membership and that some writers in the broader Communist "movement" beyond the Party might have had opportunist reasons for staying at arm's length. In fact, the typical pattern seems to be that numerous writers considered themselves devoted Communists in one way or another, but, due to their desire to spend all their spare moments writing, rather than going to meetings, they simply could not find the time or a good reason to join up. Stanley Burnshaw wrote that "I was never a party member. [But the] matter is not of importance. What counts is the attitude, the public position."[19] Thus the non-member Burnshaw considered himself a Communist by his own account up until the 1952 Doctors' Plot, which is at least twenty years. The situation is much the same in regard to many others who retrospectively claimed that they were not actually Party "members" – Kenneth Fearing, Ralph Ellison, Josephine Herbst, Nelson Algren, Jack Conroy, James T. Farrell, Irwin Shaw, and so forth.

Due to McCarthyism, which virtually forced writers to find some way to claim that they had never been Party members, or, if they had been, to say that the Party had abused them, the public statements of writers themselves are often unreliable. In his autobiography, *The House on Jefferson Street* (1971), Horace Gregory first introduces his association with Communism in the following manner: "At this time (circa 1929–1931) I was moving closer to the Communist orbit."[20] But back in February 1935, in the pages of a *New Masses* debate with Meridel Le Sueur, he wrote: "Ever since I left college (that is, 1923), my political interests have centered in the work of the Communist Party. Ever since 1924 my poetry has contained social implications that can be resolved only by the success of the Communist Party in America."[21]

Another problem with the "membership fixation" is that it doesn't respond to the reality of political repression. Writers, like union activists, might be fired or blacklisted if they could be pegged as a Party member. So it became possible and often desirable to be a member in practice with no material evidence. That is, one didn't have a card, one didn't pay dues in the regular manner, and one's name didn't appear on a list of members. Moreover, one's presence at a branch, unit, club, or fraction meeting of the Party was proof of nothing definite because it was known that sometimes non-members were present at such times (as a recruitment technique, or to facilitate collaboration on some project) and people didn't go around the room identifying themselves as "in" or "out." The entire Hollywood branch of the Party was organized in this manner. Similarly, the diverse African-American writers drawn to the Left in New York, Chicago, and at Howard University in Washington, DC, cannot be put into clear-cut boxes by virtue of membership or not; they constituted a kind of continuum of relationships to Communist ideology and organizations with all sorts of complex interactions. Terms such as "unorganized Communists" or "non-Party Bolsheviks," used on occasion by the activists of the Left themselves, are never used by the scholars, who are fixated on "card-carrying members" who are most often seen as dour "hacks," and "fellow-travelers" who are depicted as "dupes," cynics, or "innocent" liberals.

Unfortunately, such problems as the inability to explain how one might be significantly influenced by Communist thought but not in a formal sense a member have caused large-scale confusion among academics and thus produced a cliché-ridden simplification in cultural history of this major phenomenon. The major biographer of Sherwood Anderson, apparently uncertain about how to explain that Anderson said he was a Communist but didn't join, ended up with the following formulation: "Whether or not [Theodore] Dreiser or Anderson joined the Party, which neither ever did, whether or not they went to the Soviet Union, which Dreiser did and Anderson did not . . . as Anderson knew full well, the Party wasn't terribly interested in the likes of them."[22] This statement suggests that, even though Anderson claimed to be a Communist, he was farther away from this source of all evil than was Dreiser, who dirtied his hands by visiting the USSR but at least refused to commit the unpardonable sin of signing a card. However, this familiar trope of anticommunism does violence to the facts, for Dreiser *did* join the Party; his letter of application is a public Party document that reads:

> These historic years have deepened my conviction that widespread membership in the Communist movements will greatly strengthen the American people, together with the anti-fascist forces throughout the world, in completely stamping out fascism and achieving new heights of world democracy, economic progress and free culture. Belief in the greatness and dignity of man has been the guiding principle of my life and work. The logic of my life and work leads me therefore to apply for membership in the Communist Party.[23]

A different type of confusion exists about the politics of Mari Sandoz, a prolific author of Western US literature such as *Old Jules* (1935), *Slogum House* (1937), and *Cheyenne Autumn* (1953). Her biographer writes only the following of her views:

> Mari was not a pessimist; she was, more than she realized, an idealist. She believed that although there were ills, people, once aware of them, could cure them, but she did not approve of some of the cures offered. Many writers, discouraged by the government's failure to solve the country's problems, became communists, but the extreme left never attracted Mari. She read the proletarian novels of the 1920s and '30s (some of her ideas in *Capital City* may have come from them), but she believed as strongly as her father in democracy.[24]

Nevertheless, Sandoz's name appears as a member of the Communist-initiated-and-led League of American Writers in the mid-1930s. In and of itself, that might not be significant, but in 1982 *Colorado Heritage* published a memoir of Sandoz by a close literary friend, Caroline Bancroft. This sketchy memoir starts by attributing symbolic significance to Sandoz's red hair: "its color represented her firebrand political bias." The memoir then recounts Sandoz's sympathy for the Foundation for Soviet–American Friendship during World War II. Finally Bancroft recalls that "by 1950 I had become completely disillusioned with the Soviets and was definitely anti-Communist . . . . But she had grown to admire the Communist system more and more and was berating me sharply for my shift . . . . (I do not know if Mari was ever a card-carrying member of the Communist party, but there were a number of years when I was suspicious.)"[25]

The primary research on Sandoz's politics was apparently never thoroughly done, and it may be impossible to determine the full truth at this late date; but it is evident that Sandoz cannot be boxed into pristine alternative categories of "card-carrying member" or "democrat." However, it would be unfair to attribute such misrepresentations as these references to Dreiser and Sandoz to poor or sloppy scholarship on an individual basis; it is a generalized phenomenon that many literary scholars have trouble talking accurately and with subtlety about the relation to Communism of a whole generation, major and minor figures.

Part 3: Agenda for Research

Where to begin in terms of rectifying this situation? Here are some of the areas that require fuller research and theorization.

1. *Jewish-Americans.* What is taught today in Judaic Studies Programs and English Literature Departments as the "Jewish-American literary tradition" is still a tiny portion of a huge body of literature, a surprising amount of which was pioneered by Communist-influenced writers. Some of the early studies of Jewish-American literature such as Judd Teller's *Strangers and Natives* (1968) and Bernard Sherman's *The Invention of the Jew* (1969) offer a few pages on Communists Isidor Schneider and Mike Gold. Moreover, Henry Roth has received substantial scholarship, although none of it deals substantively with the fact that Roth spent twenty years as a Party member and another fifteen years as a self-proclaimed independent "Titoist."[26] However, ever since Irving Malin's *Jews and Americans* (1965), almost all the attention has gone to Saul Bellow, Bernard Malamud, and Philip Roth. The most recent book, Mark Shechner's *After the Revolution* (1987), is being hailed by some as the greatest work ever on Jewish-American literature, even though Jewish Communist writers are never mentioned. In the past few years Louis Harap has published a three-volume work about Jewish-American writers that is enormously helpful, but, since he casts his net so wide, a great deal more depth and detail needs to be filled in by successors.[27]

What is ignored is that, especially in the 1930s, although before and after as well, there existed major groups of Jewish-American Communist poets and novelists who wrote in English (not to mention those who wrote in Yiddish) and very often on Jewish subjects. At least three Jewish pro-Communist women poets won the Yale Younger Poets Award and had their works published by Yale University Press: Muriel Rukeyser, Joy Davidman (also author of the Jewish pro-letarian novel *Anya* in 1940), and Eve Merriam (an extraordinarily prolific writer in many genres). Norman Rosten, the Jewish-American leftist author of what might be regarded as the major epic poem of the 1930s, *The Fourth Decade* (1943), also won that prize.

A beginning list of Jewish-American fiction and poetry writers on the Left should also include Martin Abzug, Nelson Algren (born Nelson Abraham), Benjamin Appel, Nathan Asch, Ben Barzman, Alexander Bergman, Alvah Bessie, Beatrice Bisno, William Blake (born Blech), Michael Blankfort, Maxwell Bodenheim (born Bodenheimer), Stanley Burnshaw, Laura Caspary, Lester Cohen, Edward Dahlberg, Guy Endore (born Samuel Goldstein), Howard Fast, Kenneth Fearing, Joseph Freeman, Ben Field (born Moe Bragin), Sol Funaroff, Robert Gessner, Michael Gold, Albert Halper, Alfred Hayes, Maurice Hindus, V. J. Jerome (born Jerome Isaac Romaine), Gordon Kahn, Aaron Kramer, Melvin Levy, Walter Lowenfels, A. B. Magil, Albert Maltz, Martha Millet, Arthur Miller (author of an anti-racist novel and collection of short fiction), Tillie Olsen (born Tillie Lerner), George Oppen, Sam Ornitz, Abraham Polonsky, Naomi Replansky, Edwin Rolfe (born Sol Fishman), Sam Ross (born Sam Rosen), John Sanford (born Julian Shapiro), Edwin Seaver, Isidor Schneider, Budd Schulberg, Edith Segal, George Sklar, Tess Slesinger, Herman Spector, Joseph Vogel, Len Zinberg (better known as "Ed Lacy") Leane Zugsmith, and Louis Zukofsky.

These names hardly exhaust the field. Jewish-American Communist writers had their own publication, *Jewish Life*, later called *Jewish Currents* as it became increasingly independent, which started in November 1946 and contains fascinating material excluded from the version of Jewish-American literature propagated by the universities. One revealing document is a polemic against US anti-Semitism by John Howard Lawson.[28] Lawson, whose family name was Levy, is a figure rarely treated as Jewish in any of the canonical studies of the cultural Left, although he wrote on specifically Jewish themes as in *Success Story* (1932). In fact, six of the "Hollywood Ten" were Jewish, and, long before synagogues burst forth in vigorous debate about Philip Roth's *Portnoy's Complaint* (1969), they were thrown into turmoil by *Bride of the Sabbath* (1952), written by Samuel Ornitz while serving his prison sentence.

2. *African-Americans.* A second area that deserves serious and fresh attention is the profound interconnection between Communism and African-American cultural theory and practice. There is no doubt that the Communist effort to defend the Black nation thesis in the early 1930s rebounded against powerful themes of African-American cultural autonomy, pride, and resistance evident in much radical Black writing. Much is known about the Communist associations of Paul Robeson, W. E. B. Du Bois, Langston Hughes, Countee Cullen, and Richard Wright, all highly influential figures; but less about Lorraine Hansberry, Margaret Walker, Alice Childress, Shirley Graham, Margaret Burroughs, Arna Bontemps, Ralph Ellison, Sterling Brown, Robert Hayden, John O. Killens, Julian Mayfield, Lance Jeffers, William Attaway, Willard Motley, Chester Himes, Nat Turner Ward, Lonne Elder III, and many others.

3. *The premature socialist-feminists.* A third area of importance that is just beginning to receive discussion is that of women writers attracted to

Communism. I have already mentioned Sandoz, but Meridel Le Sueur and Tillie Olsen are the figures who have received the most attention, while Anna Louise Strong and Agnes Smedley, both of whom wrote novels, have just recently been the subject of full-length books.[29] Josephine Herbst is featured not only in a fine 1984 biography by Elinor Langer, *Josephine Herbst: The Story She Could Never Tell*, but in a half-dozen doctoral dissertations.

Yet little has been written in regard to the US cultural Left about the complex case of Christina Stead. She was an Australian by birth, but spent the 1930s and 1940s active in the Communist cultural Left in New York and Hollywood. Well-known leftists Ruth McKenney, Grace Lumpkin, and Dorothy Myra Page wrote novels, but have lapsed into obscurity. So has Leane Zugsmith, who claimed not to be a Party member but was a Communist ideologically. Laura Caspary has been pegged as a prolific "romantic mystery writer"; but her numerous novels dramatize many concerns and perspectives reflective of her years as a member and then a friend of the Communist Party.

Sanora Babb, Beatrice Bisno, Bessie Breuer, Catherine Brody, Henrietta Buckmaster, Fielding Burke (a pseudonym for Olive Tilford Dargon), Olga Cabral, Joy Davidman, Martha Dodd, Martha Gellhorn, Josephine Johnson, Jean Karsavina, Margaret Larkin, Gerda Lerner, Irene Paull, Ruth Suckow, Caroline Slade, Evelyn Scott, Janet Stevenson, Genevieve Taggard, Frances Winwar, and Helen Yglesias are all intriguing left-wing women fiction writers and poets who have for the most part been "disappeared."

4. *Writers in popular genres.* To my knowledge, despite the highly apt tools available to Marxists, we have not even made a rudimentary beginning of an examination of the major contributions of leftist writers to the historical novel (for example, William Blake and Howard Fast) and to the radical farm novel (for example, Ruth Suckow and Paul Corey) in the United States. In addition, the topics of Communist producers of mass culture, detective fiction, horror fiction, pulp fiction, children's fiction, and science fiction have received no attention beyond the famous instances of Dashiell Hammet's Party membership and the Hollywood Ten case. Yet this is the primary site of cultural production by the Left after the Depression.

Howard Fast, a best-selling historical novelist from the 1930s to the present, published much detective fiction (often as "E. V. Cunningham") and a fair amount of science fiction. A prolific Communist journalist, Mike Quin, is well-known on the Left for his classic *The Big Strike* (1947), about the 1934 Longshore strike, but under the name "Robert Finnegan" he was developing a reputation as a pulp novelist when he died prematurely in 1947. His books *The Lying Ladies* and *The Bandaged Nude* appeared in 1946 and *Many a Monster* was published posthumously in 1948.

Robert Carse, a leftist known mainly for sea stories, turned to pulp fiction in *Drums of Empire* (1959), set during the Haitian slave revolt with Toussaint L'Ouverture among the characters. Although the dust-jacket reads "The fire of revolution made them enemies . . . the flame of desire made them lovers," the plot concerns a white man won over to fight on the side of the Black rebels. Margaret Larkin (married to Albert Maltz) wrote a non-fiction mystery thriller, *Seven Shares in a Gold Mine* (1959). Guy Endore wrote not only mystery thrillers such as *Methinks The Lady* (1945) and *Detour at Midnight* (1959), but also the most famous werewolf novel in the English Language – *The Werewolf of Paris* (1933), which has been compared to Stoker's *Dracula* and Shelley's *Frankenstein.*

Kenneth Fearing wrote numerous successful detective novels. Edwin Rolfe wrote at least one. So did Abraham Polonsky. William Lindsay Gresham wrote *Nightmare Alley* (1946) and *Limbo Tower* (1949). The core of the group of major science fiction writers known as the "Futurians," such as Frederik Pohl, also held membership in the Flatbush chapter of the Young Communist League.

5. *Writers Treating "Race" and Cultural Difference.* A fifth area never discussed is the contemporary ways in which many Communist writers, in contrast to some critics and theoreticians, depicted issues of cultural difference. For example, the Communist movement was an important avenue of expression for the forgotten Chinese-American writer H. T. Tsiang and the great Filipino writer Carlos Bulosan. In the Depression era, Japanese-American Communists in Los Angeles organized the Japanese Proletarian Art League. The group published a monthly magazine called *Proletarian Art,* which lasted from December 1928 until January 1932, when the Los Angeles Red Squad raided a party meeting, arresting forty-five Japanese-Americans and deporting most of the writers.

The contemporary issue of representing "cultural difference" is among the most recurring concerns in Communist cultural activities. For example, there are representations of Native American Indians in left-wing novels by Robert Gessner *(Broken Arrow,* 1933), Robert Cantwell *(The Land of Plenty,* 1934), and Howard Fast *(The Last Frontier,* 1944), and there is significant use of Native American Indian cultures in the radical modernist poetry of Norman MacLeod and Thomas McGrath. Franklin Folsom, who was for five years the full-time Executive Secretary of the League of American Writers, wrote *Red Power on the Rio Grande: The Native American Revolution of 1680* (1973); Alfonso Oritz wrote for the book-jacket, "For the first time, I feel that someone is writing about my [Pueblo] people."

Daniel James, a descendant of Jesse James and a Communist political activist and screenwriter in the 1940s, gained a national reputation before his death when he published under the pseudonym "Danny Santiago" the novel *Famous All Over Town* (1983) depicting the world through the eyes of a fourteen-year-old Chicano. There are also dramatizations of Mexican-American miners struggles in Phillip Stevenson's unfinished series of novels called "The Seed, " published under the name Lars Lawrence: *Morning, Noon and Night* (1954), *Out of the Dust* (1956), *Old Father Antic* (1961), and *The Hoax* (1961). Gordan Kahn's post-humously published *A Long Way from Home* (1989), written in the early 1950s, depicts a Chicano draft resister during the Korean War.

There are representations by Jewish-Americans of African-Americans as major characters in novels by Len Zinberg (*Walk Hard – Talk Loud*, 1940), John Sanford (*The People from Heaven*, 1943), Benjamin Appel (*The Dark Stain*, 1943), Howard Fast (*Freedom Road*, 1944), David Alman (*The Well of Compassion*, 1948), Earl Conrad (*Gulf Stream North*, 1954), and the poetry of Aaron Kramer (*Denmark Vesey*, 1952), as well as the work of many others. There are also Black dialect poems by Sol Funaroff. One scholar of African-American fiction called Scott Nearing's 1931 Communist novel *Free Born* "the first revolutionary novel of Negro life."[30] There is a representation of the Jew as midwife to radicalism in Alexander Saxton's *The Grand Crossing* (1943).

Surely a provocative case is that of Jewish-American Communist Guy Endore's 1934 *Babouk*, just republished by Monthly Review Press. After *The Werewolf of Paris*, Endore obtained a publisher's contract to write a romance in the period of the slave trade. Arriving in Haiti to do primary research, he became entranced by the tales of African resistance. Soon he found himself, in his own words, "becoming Black."[31] The result was a startlingly original novel about the anti-slavery resistance of captive African-Americans that gives voice to a colonial subject in a manner far-outdistancing most works of its day.

Conclusion: Recovering the Radical Tradition

As another decade passes, with the 1980s becoming the 1990s, it becomes more, not less, urgent to come to terms with the Communist foundation of the Left movement in this country. Even as the problematic of the Cold War disintegrates, nothing fundamental has changed in regard to the need to profoundly transform and restructure US capitalism. Moreover, there still remains no more attractive, meaningful, and creative life for a young person in this society today than to devote himself or herself to "being all that he or she can be" by remaking the United States through organizing the unorganized, battling to extirpate the filth of racism and anti-Semitism, democratizing wealth, fighting for the extension of the rights of women and gay people, defending the environment, and, most of all, spreading the internationalist ideas of self-determination in the Middle East, Africa, Latin America, and Asia. Without doubt, the recent experiences of social change in every part of the globe during the 1970s and 1980s have made every aspect of this effort infinitely more complex. But on moral and practical grounds, there can hardly be a more meaningful life than that of what used to be called a "Red."

However, in order to build upon the Red tradition effectively, to truly overcome the grave errors and yet still draw sustenance from the real glories, one must know the past. Here the Left must be reminded of the lesson taught to us so well by the feminist historians and historians of people of color: If one does not represent oneself, whether in regard to Red writers or Red trade unionists or Red political parties or Red student activists, others will do the representation for one. Moreover, despite some substantial achievements, for the past twenty-five years the "others" have been doing a seriously inadequate job. Just as Marx argued that the overthrow of capitalism and the construction of socialism must be carried out and administered by the producers themselves – not any self-proclaimed surrogates making decisions for others "for their own good" – so the telling of the story of the literary left remains the long overdue and the urgent task of Left cultural workers themselves.

Notes

1. These and all the following quotations from Lowenfels appear in Robert Grover, ed., *The Portable Walter* (New York: International, 1968), pp. 34–9.

2. It would take many pages to list the materials that have arisen in the "canon debate" of the past twenty years. However, to gain some insight into the new approaches to US literature and an awareness of some of the writers who are in the process of rehabilitation, one might examine Emory Eliot et al., eds, *Columbia Literary History of the United States* (New York: Columbia University Press, 1988), and Paul Lauter et al., *The Heath Anthology of American Literature*, two vols. (Lexington, Mass.: D. C. Heath and Co, 1990).

3. This image was partly created by Eugene Lyons, whose view is explicitly stated in his opening chapter of *The Red Decade* called "In Defense of Red-Baiting": "During the Red Decade we are confronted, in the main, with a horde of part-time pseudo-rebels who have neither courage nor convictions, but only a muddy emotionalism and a mental fog which made them an easy prey for the arbiters of a political racket" (New York: Bobbs-Merrill, 1941, p. 16). The tropes of vulgar Red-baiting were reinforced by the title and some of the writings in Richard Crossman's anthology *The God That Failed* (New York: Harper & Row, 1950) and Whitaker Chambers' *Witness* (Chicago: Henry Regnery).

4. Philip Bonosky, "The 'Thirties' in American Culture," *Political Affairs* 38, no. 5 (May 1959): 27–40.

5. Charles Humboldt, "Fiction on the Left," *Mainstream* 10, no. 3 (March 1957): 48.

6. Philip Bonosky, "On *Writers on the Left*," *Political Affairs* (September 1962): 41–7; and unpublished review of *Writers on the Left*, Philip Stevenson papers, Wisconsin State Historical Society.

7. By mistake, Professor Aaron's words are attributed to the working-class novelist Jack Conroy.

8. Cary Nelson, *Repression and Recovery: Modern American Poetry and the Politics of Cultural Memory, 1910–1945* (Madison: University of Wisconsin Press, 1989); Paula Rabinowitz: *Labor and Desire: Women's Revolutionary Fiction in Depression America* (Chapel Hill: University of North Carolina Press, 1991); Constance Coiner, "Literature of Resistance: The Intersection of Feminism and the Communist Left in Meridel Le Sueur and Tillie Olsen," in Lennard Davis and M. Bella Mirabella, eds, *Left Politics and the Literary Profession* (New York: Columbia University Press, 1990).

9. The main departure in focus was James B. Gilbert's *Writers and Partisans: A History of Literary Radicalism in America* (New York: John Wiley and Sons, 1968), integrating the history of *Partisan Review* into the larger story of the cultural Left. Richard Pells presented a striking synthesis in *Radical Visions and American Dreams* (New York: Harper & Row, 1973), but his literary material consists of brief discussions of relatively familiar figures. References to female creative writers in Pells' study come to one out of 424 pages; the book contains no mention at all of the major women writers such as Herbst, Lumpkin, Page, McKenney, or Slesinger. Pells provides no consideration of writers of color other than a few pages on Richard Wright and some brief references to Langston Hughes. Marcus Klein's *Foreigners: The Making of American Literature, 1900–1940* (Chicago: University of Chicago Press, 1979) treats many more women writers in passing and takes a fresh look at a number of neglected literary anthologies. Yet Klein's work is nearly as limited as Pells' in regard to writers of color, treating in detail only the well-known figures of Mike Gold, Nathanael West, and Richard Wright.

Among the many impressive unpublished dissertations on the literary Left, there is a common pattern of focusing chapters on the same group of texts most familiar within the category of radical writing. This might be justified if there were conclusive evidence that this relative handful were the richest works of the hundreds that qualify for the genres discussed; but I don't see evidence that such judgments are being made through rigorous first-hand comparisons with a broad sample. For example, Cheryl Davis's "A Rhetorical Study of Selected Proletarian Novels of the 1930s" (University of Utah, 1976) discusses mainly the widely-known novels by Conroy, Cantwell, Gold, and Roth; Calvin Harris's "Twentieth-Century American Political Fiction: An Analysis of Proletarian Fiction" (University of Oregon, 1979), treats the most famous novels by Dos Passos, Steinbeck, Conroy, Lumpkin, Herbst, and Cantwell; K. L. Ledbetter's "The Idea of a Proletarian Novel in America, 1927–1939" (University of Illinois, 1963) focuses on Gold, Roth and Fuchs; and Joel Wingard's "Toward a Workers' America: The Theory and Practice of the American Proletarian Novel" (Louisiana State University, 1979) treats the most frequently cited novels of Gold, Conroy, Cantwell, and Farrell. Of course, the discussions of the writers in these works have many virtues and are not repetitive in other ways. But it is surprising how few of them refer to earlier scholarly studies other than Aaron and Rideout. Some useful observations on the treatment of radical women writers in anthologies is presented in Paula Rabinowitz's "Women and US Literary Radicalism," in Charlotte Nekola and Paula Rabinowitz, eds, *Writing Red: An Anthology of American Women Writers, 1930–1940* (New York: Feminist Press, 1987), pp. 1–16.

10. As I write, it is no longer possible to obtain for classroom use the paperback reprints once available of James T. Farrell's Studs Lonigan Trilogy; Josephine Herbst's *Pity is Not Enough* and *The Executioner Waits*; and Grace Lumpkin's *The Wedding* (although a hardback is available and inexpensive). However, there are new paperback editions with useful introductions of William Attaway's *Blood on the Forge* (New York: Monthly Review, 1987), Fielding Burke's *Call Home the Heart* (New York: Feminist Press, 1983), Jesus Colon's *A Puerto Rican in New York* (New York: International, 1982), Alice Childress's *Like One of the Family* (Boston: Beacon, 1986), Guy Endore's *Babouk* (New York: Monthly Review, 1991), Josephine Herbst's *Rope of Gold* (New York: Feminist Press, 1984), Myra Page's *Daughter of the Hills* (New York: Feminist Press, 1986), Tess Slesinger's *The Unpossessed* (New York: Feminist Press, 1984), Joseph Vogel's *Man's Courage* (New York: Syracuse University Press, 1989).

Moreover, West End Press (Albuquerque, New Mexico) has reprinted many writings by Don West in *In a Land of Plenty* (1982), and collected numerous writings by Meridel Le Sueur in *I Hear Men Talking* (1984), *Harvest Song* (1990), and *The Girl* (1982). At the present time, Omnigraphics, Inc. (Detroit, Mich.), is in the process of issuing hardback reprints of Nathan Asch's *Pay Day*, Louis Adamic's *Grandsons*, Daniel Fuch's *Homage to Blenholt*, Albert Halper's *Union Square*, and Clara Weatherwax's *Marching! Marching!*

In addition, Volume 2 of the new *Heath Anthology of American Literature* has short excerpts from Michael Gold, Albert Maltz, Lillian Hellman, Clifford Odets, Meridel Le Sueur, and several writers of color who were variously drawn to Communism.

11. An example of the current crossroads in scholarship on the literary Left can be seen in a comparison of several chapters of *The Columbia Literary History of the United States*. In a section called "Literary Scenes and Literary Movements, 1910–45," Daniel Aaron devotes the last dozen pages to presenting the Left cultural movement as he saw it in *Writers on the Left*. Complementing this, Elaine Showalter considers a number of left-wing women writers in a segment called "Women Writers Between the Wars," and Cary Nelson discusses quite a few neglected radical poets in "The Diversity of American Poetry."

12. See the landmark volume edited by Ralph Miliband, John Saville, and Marcel Liebman, *Socialist Register 1984: The Uses of Anti-Communism* (London: Merlin, 1984), especially "Reflections on Anti-Communism" by Miliband and Liebman, pp. 1–22.

13. At the time of Stalin's death, Party leaders tried to outdo each other in presenting the most disgusting accolades to this bloody tyrant. He was characterized by William Z. Foster, Elizabeth Gurley Flynn, and Pettis Perry as "the best loved man on earth, enshrined in the hearts of people everywhere, to whose well-being his life was selflessly devoted." See "On the Loss of Stalin," *Political Affairs* 32, no. 3 (April 1953): 4.

14. Undated letter to Elinor Langer, Stanley Burnshaw papers, National Humanities Center.

15. Oral History of Guy Endore, UCLA Library.

16. Granville Hicks was among the more aggressive Communist critics in promoting categories. Among the most creative were those of "Complex and Collective Novels" in his series on "Revolution and the Novel" that ran in seven issues of the *New Masses* in April and May 1934. The

series is reprinted in Jack Alan Robbins, ed., *Granville Hicks in the New Masses* (Port Washington, NY: Kennikat Press, 1974), pp. 19–66. The most influential scholarly theorist of categories of the radical novel is Walter Rideout, who in *The Radical Novel in the United States, 1900–1954* argued that most works written by leftists "can be fitted fairly easily on the basis of content or subject matter into four main groups: 1) those centered around a strike; 2) those concerned with the development of an individual's class-consciousness and his conversion to communism; 3) those dealing with the "bottom dogs," the lowest layer of society; and 4) those describing the decay of the middle class" (Cambridge, Mass: Harvard University Press, 1956), p. 171.

17. The papers of the League are at the University of California at Berkeley library.

18. See Paul Buhle, *Marxism in the USA* (London: Verso, 1987); Maurice Isserman, *Which Side Were You On? The Communist Party in World War II* (Middletown, Conn.: Wesleyan University Press, 1982); Robin Kelley, *Hammer and Hoe: Alabama Communists During the Great Depression* (Chapel Hill: University of North Carolina Press, 1990); and Mark Naison, *Communists in Harlem During the Depression* (Chicago: University of Illinois Press, 1983).

19. Undated letter to Elinor Langer, Stanley Burnshaw papers, National Humanities Center.

20. Horace Gregory, *The House on Jefferson Street* (New York: Holt, Rinehart and Winston, 1971), p. 182

21. Horace Gregory, "One Writer's Position," *New Masses*, February 12, 1935, pp. 21–2.

22. Kim Townsend, *Sherwood Anderson* (Boston: Houghton Miflin, 1987), p. 272.

23. The letter appears in Philip Bart et al., eds, *Highlights of a Fighting History: 60 Years of the Communist Party USA* (New York: International, 1979), p. 486. The letter is dated July 1945.

24. Helen Winter Stauffer, *Mari Sandoz: Story Catcher of the Plains*, 1982, pp. 127–8.

25. Caroline Bancroft, "Two Women Writers," *Colorado Heritage*, 1 (1982): 103, 108.

26. Wald interview with Henry Roth, New Mexico, 1989.

27. See Greenwood Press's *Creative Awakening, In the Mainstream,* and *Dramatic Encounters* (all Westport, Conn., 1987).

28. John Howard Lawson, "The Politics of Anti-Semitism," *Jewish Life* (September 1950): 10–13.

29. Tracy B. Strong and Helene Keysar, *Right in Her Soul: The Life of Anna Louise Strong* (New York: Random House, 1983) and Janice R. MacKinnon and Stephen R. MacKinnon, *Agnes Smedley: The Life and Times of an American Radical* (Berkeley: University of California Press, 1988).

30. Hugh M. Gloster, *Negro Voices in American Fiction* (Chapel Hill: University of North Carolina Press, 1948), p. 197.

31. Undated letter, Guy Endore papers, UCLA.

6

Communist Writers Fight Back

in Cold War Amerika

Among the many "disappeared" subjects from the historiography of left-wing writers is a consideration of the forms of literary resistance to Cold War repression in the United States. Apart from discussions of the Hollywood blacklist, almost nothing has been written about the poets, fiction writers, and literary critics who were members of, or close to, the US Communist Party (CP-USA) during the McCarthyite witch-hunt years.[1] My own attraction to the subject is recent, stemming from the conclusions of research in related and somewhat better-documented areas.

As I neared the end of the research for my book *The New York Intellectuals* (1987), I realized that the project of creating a radical cultural tradition based solely on an anti-Stalinist Left had been destroyed by the behavior of the one-time so-called "Trotskyist Intellectuals" during the Cold War. This became the conclusion of that book, although the extent of the wreckage to that tradition was not so evident when I commenced primary research a decade earlier. Nevertheless, I was forced to recognize that, in the Cold War years, these one-time revolutionary socialists, led by the pugnacious Sidney Hook and the more gentlemanly Lionel Trilling, used the knowledge of Stalinism they had gained from the Trotskyist movement to rationalize warfare against the entire Left by the forces of reaction. Their toleration and tacit complicity in political persecution was conducted largely under liberal ideology, a move that became integral to advancing their own careers. Thus one of the most promising alternatives to the Stalinist trend on the Left was not merely obliterated as a force in the Cold War United States, but, even worse, it became incorporated into the apparatus of cultural domination. Under the misnomer of the "New Liberalism," these apologists for imperialism and class oppression became elevated to seats of power and privilege, in some cases rather disproportionate to their authentic talents and achievements.[2]

This chapter is to appear in Philip Goldstein, ed., *Styles of Cultural Activism: From Theory and Pedagogy to Women, Indians, and Communism* (Newark: University of Delaware Press, 1994).

The second factor motivating a new look at radical resistance culture to the Cold War is more directly the result of my conducting new primary research over the past few years that went far beyond the hitherto circumscribed boundaries of what the pro-Communist cultural movement was thought to be in the canonical studies of that period. Although I initially began this new research with the idea of exploring only the literary criticism of a dozen or so Marxist critics who had suffered neglect due to fixation by unsympathetic scholars on the easy targets presented by the literary criticism of Mike Gold and V. J. Jerome, I soon discovered that I had compiled a list of neglected Communist-influenced writers of interest of somewhere between three and four hundred.

The composition of the group is itself noteworthy. At least half of these writers were Jewish (keeping in mind that John Howard Lawson's family name was Levy, Guy Endore's was Goldstein, Lester Cole and Earl Conrad were both born Cohen, John Sanford was born Julian Shapiro, and Nelson Algren's birth name was Abraham – although he actively cultivated the nickname Swede). Many were neglected women writers who promoted prematurely socialist-feminist ideas – such as Laura Caspary, Frances Winwar, Joy Davidman, Sanora Babb, Wilma Shore, Eve Merriam, Josephine Johnson, Dorothy Page – to name others besides the more familiar Tillie Olsen, Meridel Le Sueur, Josephine Herbst, and Agnes Smedley. Quite a few were writers of color. A dozen were identifiable as gay, lesbian, and bisexual. And the preponderance were connected with the production of literature hitherto consigned to the once-scorned area of mass culture – pulp, romance, horror, science fiction, detective, children's, and the popular.

It is not possible for this short essay to even begin to summarize the ways in which this material has challenged most of the conceptions of the Communist cultural movement that I had inherited from previous studies, and from my own earlier work on the canonical twenty or so "official" Communist writers. Instead, my more modest goal is to suggest some of the ways in which I have been forced to rethink Communist cultural activity that took place in the Cold War years – cultural activity that I would characterize as part of the conscious resistance to the dominant ideology and its culture. To minimize misunderstanding of the argument, here is a summary of my three underlying premises.

The first is that nothing I have uncovered in my research has led me to challenge the notion that the CP-USA was "Stalinist" in its official political positions and in its general approach to cultural issues. In this sense I have no quarrel with the basic Trotskyist approach to Stalinist politics. This view holds that the policies called "Stalinism" are a set of political ideas and practices formulated by the Soviet ruling elite to express the outlook and interests, first of all, *not* of the working class of any particular country, but of the ruling group of the Soviet Union. This is the case regardless of the social categories one chooses to apply to the new ruling group – a class, caste, new class, class fraction, Bonapartist parasitic layer, or whatever.

The second premise is that everything that I have uncovered during the past three years convinces me that these official "Stalinist" positions were far removed from the heart and soul of much of the cultural practice of writers around the Party. However one might choose to describe the situation of writers in the Soviet Union, the US writers were in no simple way "artists in uniform."[3] The conformity to literary doctrines that existed in the Party – and the manifestation was much more in theory than practice – came mainly from inner conviction, as deluded as those convictions might have been about the reality of political freedom in the USSR. In this sense the work of the "new historians" of American Communism – Paul Buhle, Maurice Isserman, Mark Naison, Robin Kelley, et al. – who emphasize rank-and-file agency and autonomy, has been vindicated for me in cultural activities far beyond what I have read in studies of other arenas, such as the unions.[4]

The third premise is that the assessment of Communist cultural praxis that I have come to embrace has no pretense to "academic objectivity" or "neutrality," which in truth should be labeled "pseudo-objectivity." I remain convinced that, even if the Cold War is fully over today, and Soviet Stalinism has truly self-destructed, US capitalism and imperialism remain an absolute horror for the poor and the people of color of the world, and ultimately hazardous to the health of the rest of us. Therefore, the construction of an effective oppositional movement in the United States remains the most rewarding, and the most stimulating, task for radical cultural workers. That is why I choose to assess the experience of Communist writers during the Cold War era from the perspective of learning lessons, finding ancestors, and resurrecting models of cultural practice that can contribute to the development of a seriously organized, pluralistic, democratic, and culturally rich left-wing movement.

Endless Repression

When one speaks of Communist writers fighting back during the Cold War, the first point that needs to be made is that, for Communists, there are no precise dates enclosing this experience. The meaning of the domestic Cold War is the intensification of the anti-radical witch-hunt and the persecution of Communists and other radicals, at least those who did not themselves embrace anti-communism. This was manifest first of all in job discrimination, but there also were cases where it reached the point of imprisonment if writers did not agree to become informers by "naming names" of others who might be construed as "Communists" in some fashion. However, the persecution of Communists actually began with the founding of the Party in 1919. So far as writers are concerned, fear of being identified as a Communist is a constant sub-theme of the cultural movement from the onset, and one must acknowledge the courage of writers such as Mike Gold, Granville Hicks, V. J. Jerome, A. B. Magil, Meridel

Le Sueur, Ruth McKenney, Jesus Colon, and others who cut themselves off from the possibility of leading a "normal" worklife because they openly acknowledged their Party membership.

Moreover, the legacy of anticommunism lives on to the present, as evidenced by the recent controversy over Carl Bernstein's decision to violate his parents' wishes and mention their brief period of Party membership in his book *Loyalties* (1988). Even today in the 1990s, it is clear that, in addition to institutionalized Red-baiting publications such as *Commentary* and *New Criterion*, a new group of ex-radical writers is trying to make a living off this vile occupation.[5]

In fact, because of the fear of this unwarranted and often opportunistic kind of persecution, probably some things about the Communist cultural movement will never be known. There are writers and scholars, some minor and some world-famous, who will not speak candidly to this day about their CP-USA associations and activities. Many of those who have written about the experience have either purposefully, or as the result of self-delusion because of years of secrecy, misrepresented the nature of their association.[6] Misrepresentation of the relationship is especially easy, because virtually no writers fall simply into one of the two basic categories that cultural historians have allowed, "Party hack" or innocent "fellow-traveler." Rather, they fall along a continuum of complex relations with Party institutions and ideology. Given the inherited pejorative definitions of a "Communist" writer, it is no wonder that so many writers once influenced by the CP-USA, but not out to make a career as "professional anti-Communists," will use every opportunity available to insist that they weren't "really" Communists. Separation of their subjects from the allegedly orthodox "hacks" is also the *sine qua non* for many scholars wishing to rehabilitate worthy CP-USA writers from obscurity.[7] The widespread use of pseudonyms, and the massive destruction of primary materials during the witch-hunt (not only letters and records, but rare periodicals that will never be recovered) significantly complicate accurate reconstruction. Nevertheless, although for Communists the Cold War at some level actually began in 1919 and persists to the present, I think it is possible to focus on a particularly intense "moment" of that phenomenon. Anti-Communist harassment heated up dramatically in the late 1940s with the end of the World War II alliance; and it continued with unabated intensity into the mid 1950s with the Korean War and the ascendancy of Joe McCarthy in the national security business.

Reconstructing the Cold War Left

The first and clearest way to trace Communist cultural activity in the Cold War years is through a series of publications. During the 1930s, cultural workers associated with the CP-USA produced as many as forty or fifty publications throughout most regions of the country which covered almost every conceivable arena of culture (film, theater, modernist poetry, proletarian literature, regional literature, left-wing pulp and romance, Black culture, Japanese-American culture, and so forth). Regrettably, several of these serials have vanished entirely and exist in no known collections. However, during the World War II years, I believe that only the *New Masses*, *Directions*, *Jewish Life*, *Negro Quarterly*, the cultural pages of *Daily Worker* and *People's World*, and the *Hollywood Quarterly* were around as CP-led cultural publications, and almost all of these are available.

Then, in 1946, the decisive event for the left-wing cultural movement in the Cold War years occurred: the beginning of the demise of the *New Masses*. No doubt the purge of Earl Browder for "revisionism" in late 1945 was a major blow, because Browder had always paid special attention to the *New Masses* and played a role in its professional reorganization from a monthly to a weekly in 1932. Then came the bitter break with two of the *New Masses*' central editors in early 1946. These were the novelist and humorist Ruth McKenney, and her husband, the labor writer Bruce Minton (a pseudonym for Richard Bransten), accused of ultra-leftism.[8]

Of course, the official explanation of the CP-USA, as expressed by Party functionaries such as Joe North and James Allen, was that the Cold War atmosphere of the late 1940s destroyed the magazine.[9] Nevertheless, it should be recognized that, even as the magazine stumbled through the last two years of its existence, one finds a remarkable store of talent. There was fiction, poetry, reviews, and literary debates by such skilled writers as Thomas McGrath, Sanora Babb, Guy Endore (author of the classic horror novel, *Werewolf of Paris*), Alvah Bessie, Albert Maltz, John Sanford, Isidor Schneider, Millen Brand, Frederic Ewen, Eve Merriam, Richard Boyer, Aaron Kramer, Carlos Bulosan, Dalton Trumbo, Meridel Le Sueur, José Yglesias, Horace Cayton, Alfred Kreymborg, and much work published under pseudonyms by Arthur Miller and others.

In early 1947, the same year the *New Masses* was terminated, a literary quarterly called *Mainstream* was launched by the Party. This was preceded by a voluminous debate among Party writers as to whether it should be a coalition magazine, a view propounded by Albert Maltz, or one led clearly by Marxists, the perspective that won out and was promulgated by Dalton Trumbo in letters that were sometimes twenty pages long and single-spaced.[10] This magazine lasted only a year, four issues, edited by Samuel Sillen, a New York University English professor who resigned his faculty position in anticipation of the anti-Communist purge. The patterns by which *Mainstream* organized creative literature and cultural criticism set the tone for New York-based official Communist cultural efforts over the next decade.

First, the editorial committee was in the hands of strong Party supporters, such as Jerome, Lawson, Fast, Gold, Le Sueur, and Theodore Ward (the African-American playwright). Second, *Mainstream* regularly presented a small quantity of international Left superstars such as Roger Garaudy, Anna Seghers, and Nicolas Guillen. Third, the magazine offered work by leading figures of the 1930s literary Left such as Lawson, Trumbo, Thomas Bell, Langston Hughes, and Ben Field. Fourth, the magazine served as a sort of training ground for figures who would come to prominence in the late 1940s and 1950s such as Eve Merriam, Thomas McGrath, Stefan Heym (who fled to East Germany during the Cold War, only to subsequently emerge as a leading dissident), and Lance Jeffers. Fifth, the magazine published a small amount of writing by lesser-known Communist literary figures such as Martha Millet, Edwin Rolfe, and Milton Blau. Finally, the magazine was in advance of its time in terms of race and gender balance, and would still probably compare favorably to many literary publications today.

By 1948, however, diminishing resources forced the weekly *New Masses* and quarterly *Mainstream* to blend into a monthly *Masses & Mainstream*. Nevertheless, it was the features of *Mainstream* that seemed to predominate. Sillen remained editor, although now the sophisticated and sensitive Charles Humboldt (a pseudonym for Clarence Weinstock) was brought on board as an associate editor; he would play the major role in the magazine after Sillen's abrupt departure following the Khrushchev revelations in 1956. The size and format were closer to *Mainstream*, and the news reportage characteristic of the *New Masses* was dramatically reduced to mainly editorials.

However, the basic categories established by *Mainstream* remained steady throughout the first eight years of *Masses & Mainstream*. For example, the secondary editors were strong Party figures such as Herbert Aptheker and the African-American writer Lloyd Brown. International Left superstars now included Picasso, Hans Eisler, Georg Lukács, Pablo Neruda, Louis Aragon, Martin Anderson Nexo, Nazim Hikmet, Ilya Ehrenburg, Julius Fuchik, Ting Ling, Jack Lindsay, and Jack Beeching. Figures from the 1920s and 1930s included Lawson, Gold, Kreymborg, Maltz, Walter Lowenfels, Robert Morss Lovett, and Rockwell Kent. New left-wing writers getting their start included Lorraine Hansberry, Warren Miller (*The Cool World*, 1959), Ira Wallach (*Muscle Beach*, 1959), George Hitchcock (who was older but just beginning to publish), Yuri Suhl, Ring Lardner, Jr., Abraham Polonsky, Curtis Zahn, and Gene Frumkin. Lesser-known Communist writers included Philip Bonosky, Barbara Giles, Sidney Finkelstein, Morris Schappes, Edith Segal, A. B. Magil, Joseph Bernstein (a translator), Franklin Folsom, Louis Harap, Ettore Rella, Louis Lerman, and Aaron Kramer. Women writers and writers of color included Martha Dodd, Alice Childress, Margaret Larkin Maltz, Sanora Babb, Eda Lou Walton, Naomi Replansky, W. E. B. Du Bois, José Yglesias, Lorraine Hansberry, Lance Jeffers, Shirley Graham, Carlos Bulosan, Louis Burnham, and Jesus Colon.

Meanwhile, the West Coast Communist cultural movement, which had its own history of literary journals and even conferences, launched a "coalition" journal in the autumn of 1951, *California Quarterly*. However, perhaps mindful of New York criticisms of the dangers of a Popular Front orientation in this era, the board was heavily weighted toward pro-Communists such as Philip Stevenson (the novelist, playwright, and screenwriter who was the guiding figure), Sanora Babb, Tom McGrath, and Wilma Shore. A small literary journal, *Writers' Workshop*, was also launched by the San Francisco Workers' School, edited by the novelist (now UCLA historian) Alexander Saxton.

The inaugurating issue of *California Quarterly* carried only creative writing, including a long poem by E. P. Thompson. Lasting until 1955, when it merged with *Coastlines*, a journal that blended Left traditions with new poetic trends, *California Quarterly* published only a few of the *Masses & Mainstream* writers. Instead, Stevenson featured work by figures such as Ray Bradbury, B. Traven, John O. Killens, Norman Rosten, Edward Huebsch (author of *The Last Summer of Mata Hari*, 1979), Lawrence Lipton (most famous for *The Holy Barbarians*, 1959), Esther McCoy (the architectural specialist), Winfield Townley Scott, Babbette Deutsch, Gene Frumkin, Phelps Putnam, George Abbe, and Don Gordon. (Of this last list, only Don Gordon, in his Oral History just before his death in 1989, acknowledged Party membership. Huebsch, also dead, was named in hearings as a Communist and blacklisted. Rosten will say only that he was graylisted. Putnam considered himself an independent communist close to F. O. Matthiessen. Frumkin was attracted to some Communist Party writers but found that he was incapable of sharing their belief in the USSR.[11])

In these years there were, of course, cultural articles in *Political Affairs*, but these were more of a negative polemical character chastising deviations. There were also cultural pages worth noting occasionally in the *Daily Worker* and West Coast *People's World*. Here materials ranged from the horrendous assault on Albert Maltz for challenging the slogan "Art is a Weapon," to thoughtful debates about the relation of culture to working-class life.[12]

The African-American publications *Freedom* and *New Freedom*, eventually to become *Freedomways*, are also valuable sources for studying the radical cultural resistance of the times, as well as the aforementioned *Jewish Life*. Moreover, on the East Coast in the 1950s radical writers connected with the National Council of the Arts, Sciences and Professions published *Contemporary Reader*, and similar figures later on produced the *Promethean Review*. In addition, during the Cold War years the Communist Party-sponsored publishing house, International Publishers, produced major book-length studies of aesthetics by Sidney Finkelstein (*Art and Society* 1947) and Louis Harap (*Social Roots of the Arts* 1949), although both works came under sharp criticism from Jerome, Sillen, and Lawson for allegedly echoing the looseness of the Browder era. International Publishers also produced poetry and fiction by Meridel Le Sueur (*Salute to Spring*, 1940), Thomas McGrath (*Longshot O'Leary's Garland of Practical Poesie*, 1949), Aaron Kramer (*The Golden Trumpet*, 1948), and Milton Blau (*Brief Journey*, 1949), and international figures such as Neruda and Fuchik. *Masses & Mainstream* had its own book series that brought out original novels such as Lloyd Brown's *Iron City* (1951), Philip Bonosky's *Burning Valley* (1953), W. E. B. Du Bois's "The Black Flame" Trilogy (*The Ordeal of Mansart*, 1957; *Mansart Builds a School*, 1959; and *Worlds of Color*, 1961), and V. J. Jerome's *A Lantern for Jeremy* (1951), along with some fairly undistinguished cultural pamphlets by Lawson, Sillen, Jerome, and Fast. Still, Sillen's small book *Women Against Slavery* (1955) anticipates feminist scholarship of decades to come, while Lawson's *Film in the Battle of Ideas* (1953) contains nuggets of important truths among the Stalinist orthodoxies. Moreover, Brown's *Iron City* is a unique literary answer to African-American anti-Communist novels by apostates such as Chester Himes, Richard Wright, and Ralph Ellison.

A review of the cultural activities by Communists during the witch-hunt years is a book-length project, but a few benchmarks can be quickly noted: Philip Stevenson's four-volume novelistic tribute to the struggles of Chicano mine workers in the Southwest, *Morning, Noon and Night* (1954), *Out of This Dust* (1956), *Old Father Antic* (1961), and *The Hoax* (1961); the many extraordinary works of Jewish-American culture such as Sam Ross's *Sidewalks are Free* (1950) and Samuel Ornitz's *Bride of the Sabbath* (1951, written while Ornitz was in prison); the novels textualizing first-hand witch-hunt experiences such as Bessie's *The UnAmericans* (1957), Dodd's *The Searching Light* (1955), Polonsky's *Season of Fear* (1956), Carl Marzani's *The Survivor* (1958), and Haakon Chevalier's *The Man Who Would Be God* (1959); the hundreds of children's stories by leftists (a circle of whom were known in New York as "The Loose-Enders") in one of the few industries where no witch-hunt occurred; the reappearance of Walter Lowenfels on the poetry scene, a result of his Smith Act trial; radical science fiction by Ben Barzman, Chandler Davis, Fredrik Pohl, Henry Myers, and many others; the books about McCarthyite repression by foreign left-wing visitors to the United States, such as James Aldridge's *Goodbye America* (1979) and Christina Stead's posthumous *I'm Dying Laughing* (1986), the latter of which is a *roman-à-clef* about the aforementioned *New Masses* editors, Ruth McKenney and Bruce Minton.

Literary Retrospectives

Not only is much of the literature of the time neglected, so are some of the most recent literary re-creations of the witch-hunt period, as well as reissues of texts that came out in those years that fell into oblivion. Among the most searing of these works for its direct focus on gender and race is Dorothy Doyle's *Journey Through Jess* (1989).[13] Two others demanding critical evaluation for understanding this era are the reprint of Myra Page's *Daughter of the Hills*, 1986 (originally called *With Sun in Our Blood*, 1950), and John Sanford's *A Walk in the Fire* (1989).

Page's novel might be characterized as an example of "premature socialist-feminism" because of the ways an underlying feminist sensibility disrupts its more conventional surface formulae. Because of the time and circumstances of its creation, this is a novel that could not fully anticipate contemporary feminist programs, exemplified, for example, by Marge Piercy's *Woman On the Edge of Time* (1976). Yet *Daughter* provides more than simply the depiction of a "strong woman" or the "respect for women's work" that one might expect to constitute the outer limits of women's literature of her generation. The text must be apprehended, first of all, as a product of female bonding. Myra Page, a Communist Party novelist with a Ph.D, met a woman from a mountain mining camp named Dolly Hawkins at Commonwealth College (a southern workers' school) in the 1930s. After hearing Hawkins's story, Page proposed that she become her literary voice. Page, no doubt, conceived of this relationship mainly in terms of an intellectual serving the working class by rendering a worker's life experience accessible to broader audiences, but the experience depicted is distinctly female.

Daughter recreates the world-view of a Tennessee mountain woman in a mining camp in the decades leading up to World War I. As part of its mode of faithfulness to the depiction of characters who were part of the dominant culture of that setting, Page interprets the world of Dorothy Hawkins through Christian structures, which valorize heterosexual monogamy and sexual fidelity as unchallengeable marks of virtue. Nevertheless, despite the absence of a modern socialist-feminist theoretical consciousness from the world-view of the main character (which is not necessarily the same as that of the author), the plot operates to significantly undercut the conventional appropriation of the dominant values. For example, Christianity is progressively re-functioned into a radical political praxis roughly equivalent to what we now call Liberation Theology by having Dolly Hawkins reformulate Christian tropes along class lines to promote class interests.

More important is the novel's inversion of the dominant paradigm of the nuclear family as an institution in which the male yields productive labor and the female carries out unpaid domestic labor. While Dolly Hawkins repeatedly articulates narrow-minded homilies to imply that these traditional roles are not only recuperable but even the foundation of class struggle praxis, the plot unconsciously (or maybe semi-consciously) becomes a battleground for meanings suggesting alternative strategies for survival.

At first, the opening movement of Page's novel appears to redeem conventional marriage by contrasting Dolly's experience to that of her mother. We learn that Jim Hawkins, Dolly's father, was a working-class hero and a courageous union leader, but also sexually undisciplined. He spent the family's small funds on a mistress and eventually threw away his life when he became the victim of one of her jealous rival suitors. Our introduction to Dolly takes us through the stages of her progressive transcendence of her terror of love – because she believes that love might make her vulnerable to a repetition of her mother's victimization. Gradually her fear of love is overcome by the charm and sincerity of the folksinger John, who wanders into the mining camp and becomes her husband.

Yet this new relationship is never truly tested in a way comparable to her mother's experience. Initially, John is depicted as a devoted husband resisting and scorning the advances of Sally, a neighborhood flirt who reincarnates the temptation offered by Jim Hawkins's mistress. Yet before long John loses his leg in a mining accident, seriously limiting his ability to duplicate Jim Hawkins's behavior. Moreover, as Dolly rises to become a local union figure modeled after Mother Jones, John first tries to prevent her from fulfilling this goal by demanding her attention whenever she is away from home; his death is a prerequisite to her finding her true calling. The final scene depicts Dolly's brother married to the local school teacher, a woman who works outside the home, and who is also giving books to influence the son Dolly had with John.

Hence the socialist-feminism of this novel released during the Cold War is "premature" in that the critique of patriarchy from a class-conscious point of view is nearly invisible in superficial features of the narrative, yet strongly suggested by the underlying events of the plot. Elements of this subtext can be constructed so as to point toward the need for a female-centered community as the transitional stage to an egalitarian future.

John Sanford's *A Walk in the Fire* also has a complex relation to the Cold War radical cultural resistance. A recent production, written in 1988 and published in late 1989, the novel is based on notes and documentation created during the late 1940s and early 1950s that are in many instances reproduced verbatim. The "notes" came about primarily because, for reasons of self-protection, Sanford and his wife, the screenwriter Marguerite (Maggie) Roberts, wanted a record of all events around the time of their summons to testify before the House Committee on Un-American Activities (HUAC), a subcommittee of which was convened in Los Angeles in 1951. At the same time Sanford also recorded notes of his and Maggie's meetings with her studio officials and the negotiations surrounding the officials' attempt to void their contract guaranteeing several thousand dollars a week. In addition, a third group of notes used in the novel covers meetings that Sanford held on the East Coast with prospective publishers of books-in-progress; Sanford had already abandoned screenwriting and was in these years devoted to producing fiction full-time.

The second source of Sanford's 1950s documentation consists of letters Sanford received from these same publishers, who at first were anxious to obtain rights to the manuscript of his novel *A Man Without Shoes* (eventually published in 1951). However, the publishers then proceeded to reject the novel when he refused to cut the politically suggestive historical episodes that provide a background to the plot in the style of Dos Passos's *USA* trilogy. Eventually Sanford published *A Man Without Shoes* on his own. He used $7000 of Maggie's money, but he sold less than two hundred copies. He then reproduces for us in the book his correspondence with blacklisted Communist novelists Albert Maltz and Dalton Trumbo about the strengths and weaknesses of *A Man Without Shoes*.

A Walk in the Fire is a bold experimental text, although eminently accessible to a broad readership. Moreover, the experiments are brilliantly chosen to express the *Zeitgeist* and historical setting, synchronic as well as diachronic. The novel is first of all structured as scenes rather than chapters, reflective of the professional screenwriting occupation of Maggie, Sanford, and most of the other characters in the book.

The autobiographical figure of Sanford in the novel, called John Sanford (or sometimes "Julian Shapiro," his birth name), is always referred to by the narrator as "you" rather than by the conventional "he" or "I." Among other things, this may acknowledge the intricacy involved in the effort of a writer to depict in 1988 his consciousness back in 1946–51. Besides, the narrative is frequently disrupted by prose poems about different episodes in US history that the author believes bear a relationship to the events of the novel, or that influences his own perception of the events because they depict the behavior of people in analogous situations at earlier moments in history. Finally, there is a surprisingly successful method of footnoting in the novel that adds new and updated information about various people and events that it would have been inappropriate to mention, or that would have simply not been known at the moment depicted in the narrative.

Beyond this, the important issue of the personal and political motives of the unfriendly witnesses of HUAC is brilliantly probed by the narrator's decision to focus on the respective attitudes and behavior of husband and wife. On the one hand, the sacrifice of John and Maggie is considerable. By refusing to name names for HUAC and knowingly going on the blacklist, they are forfeiting not only an income that is rather large for its time, but the sole means of sustenance for the married couple as well as for John's father, an attorney supported by Maggie's income after he abandoned his law practice for health reasons. Yet John and Maggie are not true-believing fanatical purists. To the contrary, Maggie had quit the CP-USA years earlier in disgust because she saw some Party members behave like other non-leftist screenwriters when it came to hogging credits. John, on the other hand, is considered such a loose cannon that the Party leaders won't allow him to be a member of the Writers' Unit, assigning him instead to a unit of housewives. In addition, the Sanfords seem to detest all but four or five members of the Party, and the two of them live in virtual isolation on a ranch where they keep racehorses. Nevertheless, they resist, John taking the Fifth Amendment and Maggie the "diminished Fifth," where people state only facts about themselves but invoke the Fifth Amendment for all other responses.

The explanation for such intransigent behavior is not rendered completely clear in the novel; but the ambiguity of motive works well in this book, because there really are no simple explanations for such complex acts. John, who was then and remains to this day his own brand of ideological Communist, insists that the motivation for his becoming an unfriendly witness stemmed from a desire to take the side of the underdog, as have many admirable figures in US history. Yet there are ways in which he is the weaker of the pair. In fact, until the very end John is not quite certain as to how the two of them will respond to their summons by the Committee, although informing on others is out of the question. Maggie, however, holds politics that are more along the lines of simply desiring to act "decent." She feels that, because she didn't like the idea of other people naming her as a "Red," she herself should refrain from giving any names. Yet this somewhat pragmatic attitude renders her far more confident than John about the ability to stand firm and to refuse to fink for a big paycheck.

Thus the characters are complicated in that they embody several contradictions. One is the superficial politico-organizational commitment of John and Maggie suggested by their posh living conditions in contrast to the more substantial degree of conviction suggested by their heavy financial sacrifice. Another is the highly moral and ideological stance of John that seems weaker when contrasted with the common sense and pragmatic attitude of Maggie. These ambiguities create a sense of the human texture – not always logically explainable – of so many (actually, the majority) of those attacked directly by the HUAC and who refused to capitulate.

One more tension of special significance in this book, which is the fourth volume of a serial that Sanford calls "Scenes from the Life of an American Jew," concerns the representation of Jewish identity by left-wing Jewish-American writers. There are a number of episodes referring to Jewish culture and customs, such as Sanford attending a family funeral; Sanford's recollection that he felt nothing on the day the State of Israel was declared; Sanford aggressively charging anti-Semitism when the HUAC interrogator repeatedly calls him by his birth name, Shapiro; and so forth. Yet for the most part the book is devoid of what one would traditionally call "positive" Jewish ethnic identity. In my view, this approach is authentic in regard to the prevailing attitudes of the Old Left. Much of the response to Jewish identity of radicals of Sanford's generation was to incorporate a Jewish consciousness into an internationalist perspective. There also was a strong commitment, exhibited by Sanford in many places, to identify with the struggle of African-Americans as the group most under attack by US racism, one to be defended in the interest of all potential targets of prejudice.

Conclusion

A concluding question remains: How does one proceed to assess the significance of the resistance led by writers with Communist beliefs during the Cold War years?

What must be recognized first is that, at that time, despite a few quiet and other more notorious defections, Communist writers, whatever their other failings, acted with a heroism unparalleled by any other group of writers in US cultural history. They produced an enviable and admirable steady stream of collaborative left-wing journals and volumes of path-breaking fiction and poetry; they campaigned against racism, for the Bill of Rights, and for the rights of labor; and they put their livelihoods on the line rather than betray their comrades and other potential victims of McCarthyism. It is inspiring to this day to read the dignified testimony of Philip Stevenson, Annette Rubinstein, Morris Schappes, John Sanford, Louis Harap, Sam Ornitz, and so many others before the witch-hunt committees. It is generally not remembered that investigating committees were formed in almost every area in which a writer or scholar might work. If someone named a person as perhaps having once been a Communist, that person could be called and asked to name others as a condition of maintaining his or her job or even avoiding jail.

One can quarrel about whether invoking the First or Fifth Amendment was the most effective strategy for the "unfriendly" (uncooperative) witnesses. But the fact remains that, unlike name-namers such as Elia Kazan, and unlike those responsible for or who were taken in by the misnamed "American Committee for Cultural Freedom," the Communist writers, led at the outset and to the bitter end by the heroic John Howard Lawson, made it unambiguously clear that they would not bend to the bottom line of the form of repression characteristic of liberal capitalism – crawl in the mud or lose your paycheck.

Of course, if one applies to Lawson and the others the yardstick of revolutionary internationalist politics according to Lenin, Luxemburg, and Trotsky, one finds they deified Stalin as a great revolutionary leader and thinker; they denied the political, and specifically anti-Semitic, murderous persecution of writers and many others in the Soviet Union and Eastern bloc countries; they slandered Trotskyists in the United States as agents of fascism and did not support their basic democratic rights; they touted a bureaucratic-centralist political party as democratic-centralist; they repudiated Stalin only when preceded by Khrushchev; and so on.

Still, except for the earlier Communist-led cultural movements of the 1930s and World War II years, there has existed no other organized cultural movement in the United States as strong and effective as the Cold War resistance – and as sincerely devoted to the rights of labor, people of color, and anti-imperialism, all within the blinders of the CP-USA version of Marxism. Should delusions about the USSR, and adherence to strategies premised on that delusion, be cause for one to negate that sincerity? I think not, although their disastrous mistakes should certainly cause one to critically review the pro-Communist writers' various political policies and practices. In contrast, all wings of the more "politically correct" Trotskyist movement and the anti-Stalinist Left lost the small but exciting cultural movement they had inspired in the 1930s with almost the first shot of World War II; and, so far, no one has made a case that the post-World War I Social Democratic movement *ever* even had a vibrant and distinctive cultural movement of which to speak. Up until the rise of the comparatively heterogeneous New Left, there is nothing comparable; and the

New Left cultural movement itself might appear deficient in relation to the Communist movement when its own history has been written and its own problems seriously theorized.

In sum, the Communist cultural movement of the Cold War era, like its predecessors in the 1930s and 1940s, was profoundly flawed. But perhaps we must either critically embrace the Communist cultural legacy of the era as a kind of foundation from which to extrapolate lessons, or else act as if there was virtually no honorable or noteworthy achievement of left-wing (or other) writers at all during the one period when political repression was at its height after World War II. No doubt there are those who would rather take the side of "nothing" than taint their hands through the slightest contact with those blind to the bloody rule of Stalin. However, to retrospectively choose allegiance to a movement during the Cold War that never existed runs the danger of promoting purism that is likely to be a rationale for sectarian abstention. It is ignorant of genuine artistic practice as well, for, as I have tried to suggest, there is much to admire in the left-wing cultural work of and about the Cold War era. Many of the writings will be particularly striking in the context of the 1990s because they anticipate contemporary cultural debates about canon, gender, cultural difference, Eurocentrism, and "race." Moreover, in its original Cold War context, a good deal of the literature explores with unusual craft areas of human experience neglected by the reigning literary culture.

Finally, by accepting as one's heritage the "really existing" Left experience, we can see concretely the dangers that flow from two features that continually reappear whenever radical movements seek expression through cultural practice on a large scale. One is the tendency to sustain optimism and combativity by unrealistically idealizing historical or contemporaneous struggles; the other is to align judgments on cultural practice with the political strategies of the radical movements. Those who write off the 1950s legacy as totally alien because of its Communist leadership are perhaps the most likely to repeat exactly these errors, should they ever achieve comparable political influence. This is because they do not recognize that many aspects of the problems are *not* Stalinist-specific in origin but inherent to the project of building a resistance culture.

In the end, people have to honestly ask themselves whether or not they are merely posturing when they reject *in toto* what did exist in favor of a non-existent politico-cultural movement that would not have the profound flaws of what came to pass. Will rectification of a Left cultural tradition come through wholesale denial of the mixed record of the past, or through a sympathetic understanding, flaws and all, and its critical acceptance? Utopias are indeed a necessary part of the construction of a vision that will guide people to future liberation, but while fixing on what might have been, they should not simultaneously join in the unwarranted disparagement of achievements that have actually transpired.

Notes

1. Even in this instance, little of the scholarship contains literary analysis. See Larry Ceplair and Steven Englund, *The Inquisition in Hollywood* (New York: Anchor Press, 1979); Bernard F. Dick, *Radical Innocence: A Critical Study of the Hollywood Ten* (Lexington: University of Kentucky Press, 1989); and Victor Navasky, *Naming Names* (New York: Viking, 1980).

2. Arguably Sidney Hook's major scholarly achievements were in the 1930s, *Toward an Understanding of Karl Marx* (1933) and *From Hegel to Marx* (1936), written under the inspiration of revolutionary Marxism, whereas his 1950s work was more in the vein of journalistic polemics. It is true that Lionel Trilling came into his own in the Cold War climate, but, in general, the reputation of the 1950s work of the New York Intellectuals seems to be wearing thinner than one would have been led to believe a few decades ago.

3. The phrase comes from Max Eastman's popular book about writers in the USSR, *Artists in Uniform* (1934).

4. See Paul Buhle, *Marxism in the USA* (London: Verso, 1987); Maurice Isserman, *Which Side Were You On? The Communist Party in World War II* (Middletown, Conn.: Wesleyan University Press, 1982); Mark Naison, *Communists in Harlem During the Depression* (Urbana: University of Illinois Press, 1983); Robin Kelley, *Hammer and Hoe: Alabama Communists During the Great Depression* (Chapel Hill: University of North Carolina Press, 1990).

5. David Horowitz is the most notable of these.

6. Among the autobiographies in which CP-USA associations are acknowledged but significantly diminished are Horace Gregory's *The House on Jefferson Street* (1971) and Laura Caspary's *The Secrets of Grown-Ups* (1979).

7. See my discussion of this in the case of Edwin Rolfe in *Journal of English and Germanic Philology* 91, no. 3 (July 1992): 464–7. [See Chapter 4, pp. 60–63 in this volume – A.W.]

8. See Matthew Josephson's memoir of these writers in *Infidel in the Temple* (New York: Knopf, 1967).

9. See Joseph North, ed., *New Masses: An Anthology of the Rebel Thirties* (New York: International, 1969), p. 32.

10. See the relevant correspondence in the Trumbo papers, Wisconsin State Historical Society, and Maltz papers, Boston University.

11. See Oral History of Don Gordon at UCLA; Wald interview with Gene Frumkin, Albuquerque, New Mexico, Dec. 1990.

12. Information about the Maltz controversy is contained in Navasky, *Naming Names* (New York: Viking, 1982), Daniel Aaron, *Writers on the Left* (New York: Harcourt, Brace and World, 1961; reprinted New York: Columbia University Press, 1992), and Jack Salzman, *Albert Maltz* (Boston: Twayne Publishers, 1978).

13. See review by Wald in the August 16,1989 issue of the *Guardian*.

7

The 1930s Left in US

Literature Reconsidered

The "Other" Thirties

On January 7, 1968, a 56-year-old man, over six feet tall and heavy with dark features, collapsed and died of a heart attack in a laundromat near St Nicholas Place in New York City. The ensuing investigation revealed that the man who died had several identities. One was that of a famous mystery writer, "Ed Lacy," whose works had sold over 28 million copies and were printed in twelve countries. Books by Lacy first appeared during the Cold War era, with raunchy pulp fiction titles such as *The Woman Aroused* (1951), *Sin in Their Blood* (1952), *Strip for Violence* (1953), *Enter Without Desire* (1954), and *Go for the Body* (1954). However, in 1957 Lacy made literary history with *Room to Swing*, winner of the Mystery Writers of America's "Edgar Award" for the best novel of the year.

Room to Swing is noteworthy for introducing the African-American detective Toussaint Marcus Moore, declared by the *New York Times* to be "the first Negro private eye."[1] The entry on Lacy in John Reilly's authoritative reference book, *Twentieth-Century Crime and Mystery Writers*, states that, "Before the civil rights movement made it fashionable, Ed Lacy made blacks a part of mystery fiction."[2] In fact, some readers and editors thought Lacy himself was Black. His work appears in *Best Short Stories by Afro-American Writers, 1925–1950*. This collects fiction from the *Baltimore Afro-American* that depicts new types of African-American characters beyond conventional stereotypes.[3]

But the man who died had been known in an earlier time, in the pre-McCarthy years, by another name, his birth name, Leonard S. (or "Len") Zinberg. Zinberg was not African-American but Jewish-American. He was not in those years a detective pulp writer but spent the late 1930s writing a power-

---

This chapter was originally presented at the April 30–May 2, 1992, Youngstown State University Conference on "The Thirties," and a version will appear in Bill Mullen and Sherry Linkon, eds, *Re-Visioning 30s culture: New Directions in Scholarship* (Urbana: University of Illinois Press, forthcoming).

ful anti-racist novel of the boxing profession, *Walk Hard – Talk Loud*. The book cover reads, "A Negro prizefighter in a *SAVAGE* white world!" This was published in 1940. When Zinberg returned from military service, it was produced as the play *Walk Hard* for the American Negro Theater Company in Harlem in 1944. The script was by the African-American playwright Abram Hill, a veteran of the Federal Theater Project of the Thirties.

Four novels appeared before Zinberg became Lacy. One of these, *Hold With the Hares*, was specifically about Thirties radicalism and the struggle to reconcile political ideals with economic survival. Although published in 1948, the work was regarded as so much a part of Thirties culture that the *New York Times* reviewer protested:

> Mr Zinberg's book is well-observed and well-recorded. It is interesting and intelligent. But there is a curiously archaic quality about its idealism. Even the most enthusiastic reader may feel that he would like to take this author by the arm at times and say, "Look, by all means, you may be absolutely right. But it is much, much later than you think."[4]

The reviewer spoke more truthfully than he knew; for Len Zinberg, who was and who tried to remain a Communist, the time *was* much later than he thought. Although Zinberg's views never changed, dramatic alterations in the political climate in the United States forced him to mask that early identity forever; and he was hardly the only one to do so.

In the 1940s, Zinberg had been a public activist in the Writers' and Publishers' Division of the ASP (the Committee of the Arts, Sciences and Professions, organized to support Henry Wallace's Progressive Party campaign). Throughout the Cold War era, as Lacy, he remained part of a private Marxist discussion circle meeting monthly at the home of blacklisted high school principal Dr Annette T. Rubinstein.[5] Rubinstein's salons were attended largely by the circle around *Masses & Mainstream*. This small publication was the vestige of what was once the powerful Communist intellectual magazine of the 1930s, the *New Masses*. According to Rubinstein, Zinberg was obsessed with keeping the truth about his identity as Ed Lacy a secret, even from his literary agents, and related to the discussion group in an increasingly clandestine manner. Zinberg's wife was an African-American writer who was for a period employed as a secretary for the Yiddish Communist newspaper, *Freiheit*. In addition to the danger of literary blacklisting, the Zinbergs were seeking to adopt a child. This was hard enough in those years for an interracial couple, let alone one with allegedly subversive political associations.

To raise the issue of the cultural significance of Lacy/Zinberg is to raise the specter of an "other" Thirties – of components of that era and its legacy that we are just now beginning to discover. We confront two names, two careers, two literary genres, and two political periods (pre-and post-McCarthy). These dual-isms have a unique relevance to what I see as the "moment" of scholarship on the 1930s into which we are now entering in the 1990s. This aspect is especially pronounced in relation to the central strand of Thirties culture on which I have been conducting research for the past two decades – the fiction, poetry, and literary criticism expressive of the radical critique and utopian vision of the left-wing social movements of the time, to which I think the democratizing social and cultural movements of our own day are very much indebted.

Moreover, it is telling that I can feel comfortable raising the name and career of Ed Lacy/Len Zinberg. Why not start with the names of John Dos Passos and John Steinbeck, which would have been *de rigeur* before the 1960s? Or the names of Henry Roth, Richard Wright, and Mike Gold, who were so widely discussed in the 1970s? Or the names of Josephine Herbst and Meridel Le Sueur, who were significantly reinscribed into the 1930s tradition in the 1980s? The choice of Zinberg shows the great distance that I myself have come, with the help of so many others, in rethinking the decade.

After all, my project as a graduate student from 1969 to 1974 was much closer to canonical Thirties concerns, even though the intervention was con-ceived as building a bridge back from New Left to Old. The object was to reclaim the 1930s and 1940s legacy of James T. Farrell as expressing a coherent and usable independent Marxist tradition within US literary radicalism. In the 1970s and early 1980s this expanded to an attempted rescue of US Marxist modernism as a hidden tradition within the cultural Left. The latter half of *The New York Intellectuals* (1987) seeks to document, among other things, the bank-ruptcy of politico-cultural anti-Stalinism divorced from anti-capitalist premises and socialist values. The framework, then, seen in retrospect, was of aug-menting, correcting, and developing the contours of a field for which the main lines had by and large been established.

In the 1990s, many scholars no longer feel that way. The more we have dug, the less we know for certain. We are far less confident than ever about what con-stitutes a decade, a period, a movement; about the parameters of cultural prac-tice; about the evaluation of literary quality; and about the interconnections between literature and politics.

If I hadn't invoked Len Zinberg/Ed Lacy as an entreé to this topic, it would have been just as easy to substitute John Sanford, Frank Marshall Davis, Martha Dodd, Ben Appel, Grace Lumpkin, or H. T. Tsiang. These and many other craft-conscious, as well as class-conscious, writers linked to the 1930s are still awaiting rehabilitation. And there could hardly be a more auspicious time for doing so, now that our own "Berlin Wall" of the US literary canon is in the process of crumbling under the blows of yearnings for cultural democracy.

The invocation of an "other" Thirties, however, is in no sense an effort to *cast out* Dos Passos, Gold, and Herbst, as if we were engaged in a one-on-one competition for "America's Greatest Hits of the 1930s." Rather, what we are seeking to do is to complicate and contextualize all dimensions, the known and the unknown, of that stunning, mystifying, and semi-mythical decade in US cultural life. Our goal is not to displace, according to the hierarchical model of literary scholarship. Nor is it to totally counterpose new discoveries to caricatures of older research, in the sordid tradition of academic one-upmanship.

Factoring in the "other" Thirties means, at first, to add to the growing list of traditional questions and to promote new angles of approach. Later, when the "qualitative leap" to a whole different notion of the 1930s actually occurs, such a new synthesis will be the the result of a collective process. It will be the product, first of all, of the *many* scholars and cultural workers who have tilled the vineyards of the tradition over the decades. But behind them lie the social movements of women, people of color, workers, and students who have created space in academe and US cultural life for such new perspectives through their material struggles, often in the streets, for a better world. And this is a continuation in a later stage of the same efforts promoted by our Thirties ancestors.

For example, a consideration of Zinberg/Lacy prompts us to ask: Is the literature of the 1930s limited to texts that saw publication only between 1930 and 1939? After all, many of the works of the early 1930s were actually written during the late 1920s, pre-Crash, and refer back to previous times. *Jews Without Money* and *The Disinherited*, to take two canonical Left novels of the decade, were largely published in literary journals during the 1920s, and they focus on the pre-and-post World War I years. *Daughter of Earth* was printed in 1929. The famous Gastonia strike novels were based on an event that the novelists either witnessed or read about before the Thirties. At least three of the authors – Fielding Burke, Grace Lumpkin, and Myra Page – were drawn to Communism in the 1920s, not the Thirties.

Likewise, many important texts of later decades could not have been conceived without the Thirties experience behind them. A sophisticated, "Lukácsian," historical novel of the labor movement such as K. B. Gilden's *Between the Hills and the Sea* (1971) is inconceivable without the Thirties in the background, although the events occur between the post-World War II strike wave and the 1956 Khrushchev revelations. John Sanford's extraordinary *A Very Good Land to Fall With* (1987) is in large part a brilliant rumination on reproduced documents and remembered moments of the Depression.

From another angle, the question raised by Ed Lacy's interpolation of African-American characters, culture, and street life into his popular fiction in a central way is actually, in a Thirties context, no surprise at all. White radical writers of that generation, especially Jewish writers, made a *convention* of the idea of creating a figure of cultural resistance around a Black rebel.

Zinberg named his detective Toussaint Marcus Moore – suggesting Toussaint L'Ouverture, the Haitian revolutionary; Marcus Garvey, the most successful Black nationalist of the African Diaspora; and Richard B. Moore, the West Indian Communist who lived in New York. That he should choose this name during the repressive, McCarthyite witch-hunt era was, as we Marxists never tire of saying, "No accident." Zinberg had been preceded by Guy Endore's *Babouk* (named after Haiti's legendary Boukman), John Sanford's "America Smith" (in *The People from Heaven*), Aaron Kramer's *Denmark Vesey*, and many others.

Moreover, Lacy's decision to combine this convention of Red Jewish authors cross-dressing as rebellious Black protagonists in fiction and poetry with the detective mystery genre was also "no accident." When the Thirties Left experience is resurrected in all its fullness, such a move may be recognized as *typical* of Zinberg's generation.

Dashiell Hammett, of course, had been a major figure in the Left of the Thirties and after. But there were other Left Thirties writers out of the *Black Mask* school of hard-boiled detectives, such as William Rollins, Jr. In 1934 Rollins published *The Shadow Before*, one of the most widely discussed of the early Thirties proletarian novels. But earlier he wrote *Midnight Treasure* (1929) and *Murder at Cypress Hall* (1933). Afterwards he alternated between the Spanish Civil War novel *The Wall of Men* (1938) and the thriller *The Ring and the Lamp* (1947). Another example is Mike Quin, a prolific West Coast Communist, whose Thirties poetry and sketches were collected in *Dangerous Thoughts* (1940) and *More Dangerous Thoughts* (1941). He also wrote *The Big Strike* (1947), about the 1934 San Francisco General Strike. Quin, whose real name was Paul William Ryan, had a second, pseudonymous career as a mass market pulp writer under the name "Robert Finnegan." As Finnegan he published *The Bandaged Nude* (1946), *The Lying Ladies* (1946), and *Many a Monster* (1948), before his premature death by cancer.

From my own research, it is clear that the majority of writers produced by the Thirties radical upheaval did *not* follow the trajectory of a Steinbeck or Dos Passos, in literary *or* political career. They entered the arena of what we now choose to call "mass culture." Here, they produced literature along the full spectrum of possibility – from landmarks to formula-work – in science fiction, children's literature, romance, horror, detective, pulp, popular science, adventure, and so on.

Of course, many followed the trajectory of Zinberg; or, to take another example, master pulp writer Jim Thompson, who was of 1930s Red origins as well. First they tried their hand at writing that was closer to canonical Thirties radical fiction. Then, economic survival, political witch-hunts, and personal factors propelled them more directly into the production of mass culture. Chester Himes's evolution was similar. So was that of Frank Yerby.

To declare that the time is right in the 1990s to turn our attention to these kinds of issues, and the host of problems they raise, is not to drive out of Thirties scholarship mainstream Thirties figures such as Dos Passos or Steinbeck. Nor is it to disparage those more conventionally promoted on the Marxist Left, such as Gold, Le Seuer, and Hicks (all of whom also had second careers writing children's literature). Indeed, many of these canonical Thirties writers are very much present in contemporary scholarship.

But we must refuse to cut short the 1930s at 1939, and to limit our generic focus only to the kinds of texts traditionally seen as the site of literary value, or as the kind usually generating radical and resistance cultural practice. If we do *not* refuse, then we will be recycling the very elitism that is anathema to what was most exciting in the 1930s cultural upheaval. Moreover, that refusal will take something very large, complex, and various, with extraordinary implications for enlightening our view of US culture, and reduce it to something relatively small – perhaps something that is not completely without merit, but something close to an "episode" that may have been well-intentioned but is ultimately judged to be an "artistic mediocrity."

However, now that the terrain has been marked out where I think we stand in the 1990s, let us step back a minute to review how one might map the way we got to where we are. Understanding of the evolution of a critical approach in relation to the general social trends is an important part of the self-consciousness necessary for developing scholarship in fresh ways that genuinely assimilate the strengths and rectify the limitations of predecessor efforts.

Rise and Decline of the Liberal Paradigm

There are many signs that we are on the verge of a qualitatively new departure from all previous efforts to theorize and analyze the Thirties Great Depression culture. Reconsideration of US literature of the Thirties, particularly its relation to the Left, is proceeding in the 1990s at a faster pace than at any point since the tail end of the McCarthyite anti-radical witch-hunt of the 1950s. At that time, Walter Rideout's *The Radical Novel in the United States, 1900–1954* (1956) and Daniel Aaron's *Writers on the Left: Episodes in American Literary Communism* (1961) broke with Red-baiting conspiracy theories of left-wing cultural influence to establish a "liberal paradigm" for the study of Great Depression literary radicalism. The two professors' view of literary radicalism, as a well-meaning but modest tradition within US literature that is mainly time-bound to the Thirties, more or less set the parameters of the field for studies in the next two decades.

In brief, Rideout and Aaron's books fostered a twofold paradigm: First, the most important genre for left-wing writing was established as the novel (more by default than by rigorous comparison), which in the Thirties was strongly influenced by documentary techniques. Second, the most dynamic political force on the cultural Left was acknowledged to be the Communist Party, although critics simultaneously suggested that the closer a writer was to the Party, the less authentic the literary achievement was likely to be as a consequence of the internal compulsions to subordinate craft to political ideology.

Thus, within this paradigm, it was possible for students and scholars to agree with Rideout that there were some exceptional achievements among radical writers of the Thirties. His top ten were Nelson Algren's *Somebody in Boots* (1935), Thomas Bell's *All Brides Are Beautiful* (1936), Robert Cantwell's *The Land of Plenty* (1934), James T. Farrell's Studs Lonigan Trilogy (1935), Josephine Herbst's Texler Trilogy (1933–39), and Henry Roth's *Call It Sleep* (1934) – all books by enthusiastic pro-Communists at various points in the Thirties.

At the same time, the paradigm did not challenge the overriding opinion summarized by Aaron that "the strongest writers of the thirties" were John Dos Passos, Ernest Hemingway, Sinclair Lewis, Theodore Dreiser, John Steinbeck, and Thomas Wolfe.[6] All of *these* writers were more erratic in their Thirties relations to Communism. Moreover, if we look closely, the Thirties writings of Hemingway, Dreiser, and Lewis are fairly undistinguished, suggesting that *prior* reputation often played a decisive part in one's stature as major Thirties writer.

For the next decades, apart from new biographies and memoirs of veterans, the most influential of the fresh studies of Thirties radical literary culture mainly augmented the work of Rideout and Aaron. James B. Gilbert in *Writers and Partisans: A History of Literary Radicalism in America* (1968), William Stott in *Documentary Expression and Thirties America* (1973), and Richard Pells in *Radical Visions and American Dreams: Culture and Social Thought in the Depression Years* (1973), filled in details about the anti-Stalinist Left, the documentary form, and the broader shifts in cultural climate during the Depression beyond the Marxist literary Left.[7]

Surprisingly, most of the dissertations written then and through the 1970s – including a plethora about the "proletarian novel," and a number about individuals such as Mike Gold, John Howard Lawson, and Joseph Freeman – were never published. It is difficult to determine whether this was solely due to knee-jerk political prejudice, which certainly existed, or also to weaknesses in quality of the scholarship itself. Starting in the 1980s, however, we began to witness the appearance of an impressive number of new kinds of reprints of Thirties novels, poetry, and anthologies from the Feminist Press, Monthly Review, West End Press, and various university publishing houses.

The original staple of Thirties texts included John Dos Passos, James T. Farrell, Mike Gold, Granville Hicks, and John Steinbeck, all of whom were in print in the 1960s. The new publications since the 1980s include Carlos Bulosan's *If You Want to Know What We Are* (1983), Fielding Burke's *Call Home the Heart* (1983), Meridel Le Sueur's *I Hear Men Talking* (1984), Mary Heaton Vorse's *The Rebel Pen* (1985), Josephine Johnson's *Now in November* (1985), Joseph Kalar's *Poet of Protest* (1985), William Attaway's *Blood on the Forge* (1987), Joseph Vogel's *Man's Courage* (1989), Clara Weatherwax's *Marching! Marching!* (1991), Albert Halper's *Union Square* (1991), Guy Endore's *Babouk* (1991), Mary Heaton Vorse's *Strike* (1992), and Ruth McKenney's *Industrial Valley* (1992). There also appeared rich new anthologies such as Jack Salzman and Leo Zanderer's *Social Poetry of the Thirties* (1978; resurrecting Sol Funaroff, Edwin Rolfe, Joy Davidman, Kenneth Fearing and others) and Charlotte Nekola and Paula Rabinowitz's *Writing Red: An Anthology of Women Writers, 1930–1940* (1987).

In retrospect, I think we can see that the qualitatively new and improved study of the epoch began in earnest with the consolidation of feminism in the academy in the 1980s. Today it seems clear that Deborah Rosenfelt's 1981 essay, "From the Thirties: Tillie Olsen and the Radical Tradition" was a landmark publication.[8]

After this came the now famous "canon debates," raising challenges to the way in which the regnant literary models came to hold sway. At first, the explicit tradition of the Thirties literary Left played no part in these controversies. They concerned mainly the reinscription of neglected texts by women and writers of color, many from the nineteenth century, as well as reinterpretations of classic works and moments in light of their darker and female "others."

However, a major study toward the end of the decade, Vincent B. Leitch's *American Literary Criticism from the 30s to the 80s* (1988), took note of certain patterns of continuity in cultural debate between the Depression and 1980s Left critical trends. In the three years since, it has become clear that the Thirties cultural Left is returning as part of the canon debate in ways far outdistancing the understanding of the tradition's original proponents in the 1960s and 1970s. And here, it may be worth observing that the major reconsideration of the Thirties Left that began in the late 1980s evolved largely independent of, and occurs mainly by coincidence with, the recent crisis of the former Soviet Union and Eastern Bloc countries. Much more decisive for the views and values of the new "revisionist" scholars of the Thirties literary Left has been the multifaceted impact of the decade of the 1960s, which is almost as far from us now as the Thirties was from the era of the New Left at its inception.

Now, in the past three years, these fresh and hitherto neglected primary sources of reprinted fiction and poetry have been joined by a genuine renaissance of critical studies of the Thirties that apply the new methodologies that grew out of the Sixties, especially feminist literary theory and a more sophisticated Marxism. Among the most exciting of such works are Cary Nelson's *Repression and Recovery: Modern American Poetry and the Politics of Cultural Memory, 1910–1945* (1989), Paula Rabinowitz's *Labor and Desire: Women's Revolutionary Fiction in Depression America* (1991), and James Bloom's *Left Letters: The Culture Wars of Mike Gold and Joseph Freeman* (1992).

Such a dramatic appearance of recent radical, Marxist-influenced methodology, along with texts by writers who were previously neglected, suggests to me that, in fact, the late date of this renaissance may be understood partly as a consequence of a necessary time-lag. Most of the new crop of vanguard scholars mentioned above are in their forties and have been following cultural debates for several decades.

One must recall that the boom in Marxist literary theory of the 1960s was mostly European-oriented, due to inspirers such as Lukács, Gramsci, and the Frankfurt School. Decades later, those trends have blended with British "Birmingham School" Cultural Studies, Third World "post-colonial" theory, and feminism to perhaps produce for the first time sufficiently rigorous and comprehensive methods and perspectives to carry out the complex task of replacing the liberal paradigm of the Thirties with one that will more fully allow the return of the repressed tradition.

The recent books by Nelson, Rabinowitz, and Bloom are more aggressively sympathetic than their prominent predecessors to issues of "race," ethnicity, and gender, and to popular literature. They also offer less elitist perspectives on modernism. Moreover, these scholars are ready to reopen the question of literary "value" (quality) in relation to the radical Thirties achievement.

However, it is worth noting that there are some lines of continuity between the liberal paradigm and more radical (methodologically, as well as politically) considerations of the cultural Left. Both, for example, operate on the assumption that the Communist Party legacy is mixed in fairly precise ways, a liberating as well as delimiting force. In the early Thirties, Communists produced organizations and publications that gave voice to a broad range of writers, often from classes, races, and a gender that encountered considerable constraints in the institutions of the dominant culture.

On the other hand, the functionaries in the Communist Party, especially Alexander Trachtenberg and V. J. Jerome, believed Party cadres and institutions could lead and provide direction to such efforts. Moreover, not only such leaders but also most Left writers shared an understandable respect for the state-sponsored literary policies of the Soviet Union. This was a country where they (mistakenly) believed a healthy and enduring socialism was in progress. Although the idea of "leading" a literary movement has shown itself perennially and widely attractive, in the case of the literary Left it resulted in "functionalist" pressures in literary evaluation. What too frequently prevailed among *New Masses* and *Daily Worker* critics was the view that, since all literature obviously has political dimensions and implications, cultural practice should be ultimately evaluated in relation to the more immediate concerns of the vanguard of the working class – that is, the Communist Party and the Soviet Union.

Hence, the difference in emphasis among the scholars of the Thirties literary Left, from the construction of the liberal paradigm to the present, has not been about whether such problematic constraints existed. Rather, their inquiry has concerned the degree of balance between positive and negative aspects. What is often in dispute is the tensive area of art and formal ideology. On the one hand, there is the issue of the autonomy of the writer as agent, complicated particularly if that writer is female or of color. On the other hand, there is the real weight of the impact of political guidance as manifest through reviews and the fate of publications usually under the direction of full-time Party literary-critical functionaries who had the confidence of the top political leaders.

Aaron and Rideout, due to the breadth of empirical research, were actually less mechanical than others in correlating Party policy to literary practice. The most notorious of the simplifiers of the relation between Communist political and literary practice was Philip Rahv in his 1939 essay "Proletarian Literature: A Political Autopsy." There he declared that "It is clear that proletarian literature is the literature of a party disguised as the literature of a class."[9] This is a view that contradicts not only any informed understanding of the complexities of the creative process, but also much of Rahv's own excellent criticism of previous years. Regrettably, this sentiment and perspective was embraced and endorsed much too uncritically by outstanding literary figures such as Alfred Kazin and Irving Howe.[10]

Fortunately, in recent years, we have seen the development of a "New History of American Communism," expressed perhaps in its most admirable form by Robin Kelley's *Hammer and Hoe: Alabama Communists During the Great Depression* (1990). Kelley not only establishes greater agency among activists, but also asserts the ability of such activists to appropriate and transform Party institutions to give voice in many instances to local expression. What is theorized by Kelley for non-literary, and, indeed, in some cases non-literate, militants seems equally apt for cultural workers who conducted most of their writing in isolation and often came to the Left with much prior training in other literary traditions, ideas and ideologies.

What is to be Done?

These new perspectives do not mean that the elements of truth in the traditional critiques of the Old Left politico-cultural experiences are to be jettisoned, or forgotten. This would only result in the critique having to be relearned, probably the hard way – by repeating the mistakes. Rather, the kind of arguments recounted above, along with others for which I lack either time or expertise to consider, need to be reconciled with the traditional scholarship on Thirties culture.

As we know, much of this has centered on the demonstration of correlations between political orientations of the Left movements and changes in styles, themes, and organizational forms of cultural workers. The most famous correlation has concerned the differentiation between the pre- and post-Popular Front era in the Thirties. In the first half of the decade (actually, starting in 1928), the emphasis was on working-class literature, revolutionary ideology, and creating venues to give voice to unknown cultural workers from the plebeian classes. In the second half of the decade, the emphasis was on the creation of a people's democratic literature, anti-fascist ideology, and the development of organizations and conferences with well-known and successful writers. Another familiar division is between the Communist Party-led cultural movement and non-Party tendencies, which were allegedly less directly "political" and more open to modernism.

A new method is required to engage and transcend the binary features of such analyses, based partly on fresh primary research – interviews with veterans of the cultural Left; examination of new archival deposits; and the reading of neglected texts and journals. This effort must be in tandem with a deepening of contemporary theoretical work in the areas of gender, "race," ethnicity, mass culture, utopias (including unacknowledged and acknowledged religious impulses), and national identities.

One feature of the new method will be to contextualize the Thirties experiences within the following decades of the 1940s, 1950s, and 1960s, when many of these same cultural workers continue to produce under new conditions, and, also, interact with younger writers. Studies of the response of US radical writers to issues such as World War II, the McCarthyite witch-hunt, the blacklist, the Korean War, the advent of television, and the rise of the New Left will help us gain a more complex view of the traditions of cultural resistance largely beginning in the Thirties.

A second feature will be to invoke the categories of gender, race, sexuality, and ethnicity in order to produce new areas of knowledge. Whatever the political paradigms promoted by left-wing organizations, and whatever the general features of the national cultural atmosphere, women writers, writers of color, and gay/lesbian/bisexual writers deal with unique issues in their lives and literature. These do not lend themselves to the too immediate political correlations of much earlier scholarship – a scholarship that is, in fact, based mostly on studies of the lives and writings of white males, very often from a few select regions.

In addition to works of radical women and writers in most areas of mass culture, among the most neglected texts have been writings by left-wing Latinos educated in the Thirties tradition (José Yglesias, Angel Flores, Alvaro Cardona-Hine, Bernardo Vega, Jesus Colon); Asian-Pacific Americans (H. T. Tsiang, Carlos Bulosan); writings depicting Native American Indian struggles (by Mari Sandoz, Robert Gessner, Howard Fast); and radical writings within certain ethnic traditions (such as Italian-Americans Carl Marzani, Pietro Di Donato, John Fante, Frances Winwar, and Vincent Ferrini).

In regard to this last category, so-called "white ethnics," it's worth observing how central the radical, Thirties, working-class tradition is to the authentic literary history of most of these groups, especially Italian-American, Jewish-American, and Irish-American. Yet many of us have unpleasant recollections of the upsurge of interest in white ethnicity that occurred in the 1970s, because this incarnation had some features of a racist backlash against gains that had been made by people of color during the 1960s. Perhaps now is the time for a rethinking of these ethnic cultures. After all, it seems to me that if Euro-American ethnic culture were reintroduced in a way that centers the class-con-

THE 1930S LEFT IN US LITERATURE RECONSIDERED

scious, anti-chauvinist, anti-particularist, and anti-racist traditions of Farrell, Di Donato, and Mike Gold, such a cultural revival might have a salutary and uni-fying, rather than retrograde and divisive, impact on the general drive toward cultural democracy that we are witnessing in scholarship today.

Of course, African-American radical writers *have* received considerable atten-tion. But many crucial figures linked to the Thirties tradition have fallen into neglect – such as Gwendolyn Bennett, Arna Bontemps, John O. Killens, Julian Mayfield, Alice Childress, Shirley Graham Du Bois, Owen Dodson, Lloyd Brown, William Attaway, Willard Motley, Frank Marshall Davis, and Lance Jeffers.

Gay, lesbian and bisexual writers of the Thirties – such as Newton Arvin, Harold Norse, Gale Wilhelm, Richard Meeker, T. C. Wilson, Langston Hughes, William Rollins, F. O. Matthiessen, Chester Kallman, and many others – are another group that has yet to receive serious attention. And other unique sub-categories might be theorized as well – for example, the many British, Canadian, and Australian sojourners in the US literary Left. This would include novelists Cedric Belfrage, Christina Stead, Harry Carlisle, and James Aldridge, along with the better-known European literary-political exiles.

A third methodological move (in addition to contextualization and new cat-egories) will be to abandon traditional hierarchies and oppositions between realism and modernism (usually based on select formal features), highbrow and lowbrow culture, and avant-garde and mass culture. Even conventional left-wing categories such as "working class" and "revolutionary literature" must be re-theorized in light of their expansion and complication by writers of color, women, gay/lesbian/bisexual authors, and writers in different regions and workplaces.

Moreover, many writers on the Left moved freely among poetry, drama, reportage, fiction, screenwriting, and other literary forms. The literary achieve-ment of Alfred Hayes is not that unusual in its combing and crossing of genres. He wrote the song "Joe Hill," three volumes of poetry, *The Girl on the Via Flaminia* (1949) and six other volumes of prose fiction, as well as plays, screenplays, and television shows. This is not to say that distinctions of genre, period, and quality can't be made, but only to interrogate from a dialogical perspective the ways in which traditional categories silence and repress many areas of cultural practice, and to see what new generic and evaluative terms may be more effective.

Still, in the end, for all the exciting innovations of our own time, we must not succumb to arrogance. We must be conscious in *our* work of something of which those who have previously constructed versions of the Thirties were perhaps insufficiently aware in *their* work.

Rethinking, re-theorizing and re-visioning the Thirties in the 1990s is a task that cannot escape the influence of debates of the moment that drive and animate intellectual, cultural, and political life at the present time. We know that the liberal paradigm of the Thirties was based on selections of authors and issues that were intimately bound up in the "moment" at which such scholar-ship appeared. Thus it is obligatory that *we* not forget that our own selections of authors and issues are linked to the contradictory and complex location of intellectual and cultural workers at the present moment in national and inter-national history.

Clearly many of the issues that I and others are seeing in relation to the Thirties are partly of fascination for what they might tell us about cultural prac-tice today. I know this is the case in regard to "identity politics"; the cynical attack on alleged "political correctness" in US culture; the defense of multi-cul-turalism; development of feminism; the need to combat homophobia; the sick-ening advance of the "New Racism"; and other issues confronting contemporary cultural workers. There is no harm in this relationship. To the contrary, such feelings of continuity and kinship between issues in our time and those of the Thirties are necessary for the deepening of our critical under-standing of its significance as a living legacy.

What is crucial is to remain fully conscious of this aspect of our work. At the same time, we must realize that each reinvention of the Thirties is not equal to the other. There *can* be progress. If we see the evolution of Thirties scholarship whole, treat it with circumspection (by which I mean critically, but not by cari-caturing our predecessors), the present generation of scholars can recreate that decade more richly and meaningfully than any previous one. Such an advance is the greatest tribute we contemporary scholars and cultural workers devoted to the Thirties can pay to those who lived that decade, as writers and activists; who fought its great battles against racism and fascism, and for the rights of working people; and who suffered the brutal backlash of McCarthyism's attempt to destroy their achievements. What is vital and humane in so much of our work today is possible because of what they lived, wrote, and endured, including the painful recognition of their own mistakes.

In a memorable phrase, Leon Trotsky, who knew more than a few things about literature and social revolution, once recalled: "In my eyes, authors, journalists and artists always stood for a world that was more attractive than any other."[11] Many radical cultural workers of the Thirties didn't read, and didn't think they had any use for, the ideas of Trotsky and other heretical leftists of various persuasions. Of course, the contemporary world situation suggests that they were mistaken in this narrowness in ways that we must never emulate.

Still, regardless of formal ideological "position," the Thirties literary leftists lived out Trotsky's words far better than they knew. Their unfinished project of humanizing and democratizing US culture is among the most attractive moments of our intellectual heritage. Placing ourselves in solidarity with, and critically advancing, that honorable legacy of cultural commitment is precisely what contemporary scholarship on the Thirties is all about.

Notes

1. Cited in Obituary, "Leonard Zinberg, Wrote as Ed Lacy," *New York Times*, Jan. 8, 1968, p. 35.

2. John M. Reilly, *Twentieth-Century Crime and Mystery Writers* (New York: St Martin's Press, 1980), p. 547.

3. "The Right Thing," in Nick Aaron Ford and H. L. Faggett, *Best Short Stories by Afro-American Writers, 1925–50* (Boston: Meader Publishing Co, 1950), pp. 184–8.

4. M. B., "Conscience – or Ambition?", *New York Times*, Oct. 3, 1948, p. 22.

5. Author's interview with Annette Rubinstein, NYC, March 1990.

6. Walter Rideout, *The Radical Novel in the United States, 1900–1954: Some Interrelations of Literature and Society* (Cambridge, Mass.: Harvard University Press, 1956), p. 287; Daniel Aaron, *Writers on the Left: Episodes in American Literary Communism* (New York: Harcourt, Brace and World, 1961), p. 392.

7. To see other ways in which studies that followed Aaron and Rideout expanded the terrain a bit, one might examine two anthologies, *Proletarian Writers of the Thirties* (Carbondale: Southern Illinois University Press 1968), edited by David Madden, and *Literature at the Barricades: The American Writer in the 1930s* (University, Alabama: University of Alabama Press 1982), edited by Ralph Bogardus and Fred Hobson. These collections present a range of essays that make the case for more recognition to be given to previously neglected regions (the South, Mid-West, North West), genres (poetry, documentary), and political traditions (Trotskyism, anarchism).

8. *Feminist Studies* 7 (Fall 1981): 370–406.

9. The essay is reprinted in Philip Rahv, *Essays on Literature and Politics, 1932–1972* (Boston: Houghton Mifflin, 1978), pp. 293–304.

10. For a sharp dissent from Kazin's treatment of the 1930s in his otherwise admirable *On Native Grounds* (New York: Harcourt, Brace and Co., 1942), see my essay, "In Retrospect: *On Native Grounds*," *Reviews in American History* 20 (1992): 276–88. See Chapter 2, pp. 28–39 above.

11. Quoted by Irving Howe in *Steady Work* (New York: Harcourt, Brace and World, 1966), p. 118.

8

From Old Left to New in US

Literary Radicalism

In 1958, the McCarthyite witch-hunt against the Old Left was fading, and the first stirrings of a New Left were were materializing. At that time, Alvaro Cardona-Hine, a thirty-year-old Latino poet, made his debut in the Communist Party-sponsored literary magazine, *Mainstream*. His poem, called "Bulosan Now," was a remarkable statement of refusal to accept the demise of the revolutionary, pro-Communist Filipino-American writer and labor organizer Carlos Bulosan. This author of the searing autobiography *America is in the Heart*, had died in Seattle just two years before. Of him, Cardona-Hine declared:

> . . . no moment knows you dead Bulosan
> or gone or vacant or destroyed . . . .
>
> I can raise the thankful inkwells of my voice
> to place you squarely and concretely among this brutal instant of life
> in irreplacable fashion
> as one who knew how to forever subsist later upon *now*.[1]

Four and a half years afterwards, Cardona-Hine appeared in the *National Guardian*, the left-wing newspaper edited by a group of independent journalists sometimes referred to as "non-Party Bolsheviks" by their Communist Party friends. This time, he offered a trio of poems hailing the Cuban Revolution. These elicited a personal letter of praise from Celia Sanchez, comrade and private sectretary of Fidel Castro, although the first poem, "Passacaglia [a Spanish dance tune] for the bearded truth," depicts the tough revolutionaries of the Sierra Maestra as pacific flower-children:

This chapter is based on talks delivered at the "Interdisciplinary Conference on the History of the 1960s" in April 1993 at Madison, Wisconsin, and at the American Studies Association national convention in November 1993 in Boston, Massachusetts.

the razor lost its edge
its guillotine succumbed at dawn
and the men who had lifted their gaze to the sunlight
were covered with a flowing mantle of curls
which became as sacred as the foam upon their beaches
and as free[2]

Six years later was May 1970 – the moment many regard as the culmination of the student movement of the 1960s, when undergraduates and graduates took over and shut down scores of campuses across the country in protest at Nixon's invasion of Cambodia. At California State College at Hayward, this same Cardona-Hine stood before a crowd of striking students. He read a long tribute to them called "Awake," concluding:

kill them with your beautiful lives in love!
kill them by remaining hollow to their screaming!
kill them by not touching their guns . . . .
love until they beat their plowshares into kisses
until they die in what they are and they too awake
and discover that you were always right
because you are not clutching a dream from yesterday
because your life has become
that great honest muddle of laughter and thieving angel
that gently gently each and every morning
licks your darkness conquers your self[3]

This politico-cultural trajectory of Alvaro Cardona-Hine, between 1958 and 1970, requires at least several comments.

First, it is a trajectory deeply rooted in the traditions of the US Left. This is not only due to Cardona-Hine's literary mentors, who include the obscure proletarian poet Stanley Kurnick and the more flamboyant Communist writer Thomas McGrath. Such roots are also evident in the announcement of his literary presence through the invocation of a dead martyr from the 1930s, Carlos Bulosan. Bulosan was militantly pro-Communist, and wholly devoted to class struggle organizing, mainly cannery and field-workers. Moreover, Bulosan was Filipino-born as Cardona-Hine was Costa Rican-born – and both "anti-coloniaism" and "anti-racism" were among the traditional "Great Themes" of US literary Communism.

Second, Cardona-Hine never limited himself to what are popularly thought to be characteristic "Communist sloganeering" modes of literary expression. This is true even though he was closely connected with the Communist movement, starting as a student at LA City College in the late 1940s. (In fact, Cardona-Hine fled to Mexico for several years in the 1950s after being visited by the FBI.) Attraction to the magical, the mystical, and, frankly, the religious were always there in Cardona-Hine's work, as they are in the works of Neruda and Vallejo, who were, in fact, Cardona-Hine's revolutionary models.

115

Third, the evolution to unambiguous New Left themes and modes of sensibility are clearly evidenced in Cardona-Hine's flower-child vision of the Cuban revolutionaries; later, his outright capitulation to those cultural tropes and styles of expression are overwhelming in the "Allen-Ginsbergian" conclusion to his plea to the striking students at Cal State Hayward.

In February 1993 I visited Cardona-Hine, then seventy years old, who lives high in the mountains north of Sante Fé. There he runs a small art gallery, composes music, and publishes mostly haiku. Zen Buddhism has displaced Marxism as the center of his outlook. Cardona-Hine's story is part of the missing, hitherto unwritten history, of the complex web of links and interactions between the so-called "Old Left" (mostly Communist Party-inspired) and the 1960s New Left in the history of US literary radicalism.

It is well known, of course, that independent literary leftists such as Norman Mailer were productive in the 1950s and formed a kind of cultural bridge to the 1960s. On the one hand, Mailer had been touched by various Old Left currents of Marxism – *Barbary Shore* (1951) shows the impact of an idiosyncratic version of Jean Malaquais's quasi-Trotskyist state capitalism, and *The Deer Park* (1955) refers to Hollywood blacklisting. On the other hand, Mailer wrote the prophetic *White Negro* (1957) and championed sexual revolution.

Moreover, the prominent radical playwrights Lillian Hellman and Arthur Miller, who had backgrounds of association with the Communist Left, were both stars of the New York theater in the 1950s. There they sustained a radical cultural resistance to the Cold War that was later embraced by sectors of the New Left – Hellman with her sensational revival of *The Children's Hour* (originally 1934), and Miller with his oddly similar *The Crucible* (1953).

And then there is the relatively unexplored phenomenon of the migration of a legion of leftist writers from the *New Masses* to the mass market, producing scores of detective, pulp, romance, science fiction, children's fiction, young adult fiction, and historical fiction. A few, like Howard Fast, were public Communists. Most, like the Jewish Communist Len Zinberg, who sold over 28 million copies of his two-fisted tough-guy novels as "Ed Lacy," published under pseudonyms or with their political identity suppressed.

But the clearest way to trace Old Left pro-Communist cultural activity in the Cold War years, as it fed into the 1960s, is through its publications. The major ones of the World War II years were the *New Masses, Directions, Jewish Life, Negro Quarterly*, the cultural pages of *Daily Worker* and *People's World*, and the *Hollywood Quarterly*. In early 1947, a literary quarterly called *Mainstream* was launched by the Communist Party. By 1948, however, a depletion of resources forced the weekly *New Masses* and quarterly *Mainstream* to blend into a monthly *Masses & Mainstream*.

Meanwhile, the West Coast Communist cultural movement, which has its own radical culture history that includes a variety of literary magazines and conferences, launched a "coalition" journal in the autumn of 1951, *California Quarterly*. This lasted until 1955, at which time it was subsumed by *Coastlines*, a new poetry journal. *Writers' Workshop* was another radical periodical; it came out of the San Francisco Workers' School and edited by the novelist Alexander Saxton.

The African-American publications *Freedom* and *New Freedom*, as well as the aforementioned *Jewish Life*, are indispensable for learning about the radical cultural resistance and strands of continuity from the Cold War to the 1960s. In addition, radical writers on the East Coast in the 1950s participated in the National Council of the Arts, Sciences and Professions. They published *Contemporary Reader*, and, later, some of the same individuals brought out *Promethean Review*.

Nevertheless, although writers associated with both Old and New Lefts appear in these publications, the unbroken flow of the cultural traditions and practices of organized Old Left tendencies (here, mainly the Communist Party) into the allegedly fresh and innocent waters of the 1960s New Left is denied (for various reasons) in all extant literary histories. For example, in the historiography of US literary culture, the phrases "US literary Left," "writers on the Left," and "the radical novel" all have applications to periods *distinctly prior* to the era of the 1960s. This is uniform in all major studies of the subject, although recently two dissertations ("Anonymous Toil" by Alan Block, and one in progress by Tim Libretti) have broken that mold.

True, it will be admitted, there *were* radical novels written during the 1960s, but this New Left "literary radicalism" was of a markedly different form; can we really say that the realist narrative of Mike Gold's *Jews Without Money* (1930) is in the same genre as Ken Kesey's fantastic *One Flew Over the Cuckoo's Nest* (1962)?

True, there was also a major upsurge in radical poetry in the 1960s, spearheaded by the Black Arts movement; yet Langston Hughes's "One More 'S' in the U.S.A.," written for the Eighth Convention of the Communist Party, seems worlds apart from Leroi Jones's "Black Dada Nihilismus."

This is Hughes in 1934:

> Put one more *S* in the U.S.A.
> To make it Soviet.
> One more *S* in the U.S.A.
> Oh, we'll live to see it yet.
> When the land belongs to the farmers
> And the factories to the working men –
> The U.S.A. when we take control
> Will be the U.S.S.A. then...

This is from Jones in 1964:

> Poems are bullshit unless they are teeth . . . .
> Fuck poems
> and they are useful . . . .
> We want live
> words of the hip world, live flesh &

117

coursing blood. Hearts and Brains
Souls splintering fire. We want poems
like fists beating niggers out of Jocks
or dagger poems in the slimy bellies
of the owner-jews . . .

However, what is often missed in the kind of sharp juxtapositions I've presented is that Langston Hughes lived to write his tribute to the Black Panther Party and other verse of the 1960s that is remarkably responsive to the new "Black Arts" cultural trend, minus the obscenities. His final book, the vastly underrated *The Panther and the Lash* (1967), prints, side by side, selected poems from the 1930s and 1960s, and they all seem to be of a piece.

Moreover, Hughes is hardly the only one to *carry on the message* from the generation of the 1930s to the 1960s, just as Cardona-Hine is not the only one to express a *fusion or compression* of the two trends.

In place of Hughes one might substitute Walter Lowenfels, who lived three lives as: an expatriate modernist poet of the 1920s and early 1930s; a Communist activist and *Daily Worker* journalist from the mid 1930s until his Smith Act trial in the early 1950s; and a Beat poet, Jazz poet, and hippie flower-child poet, in the 1960s and until his death in 1976. In this last phase, he still remained a Communist Party member while International Publishers issued a book of aphorisms by Lowenfels called *The Revolution is to Be Human* (1973).

This "non-canonical Communist" identity, by the way, caused Lowenfels considerable anguish. As early as 1961 he complained in a letter to his wife about the consequences of his unusual popularity in left-wing circles that were otherwise hostile to the Party: "The peculiar thing about my Marxism is that nobody takes it seriously – either in or out of the Party. 'Oh Walter,' says Harold Rosenberg the [art] critic, 'He belongs to a party all his own.'"[4]

Still, Lowenfels's protest poetry anthologies of the 1960s and early 1970s, usually published by mainstream publishing houses such as Doubleday, Vintage, and Beacon, are, through their contributors, major testimony to the linkage of Old Left/New Left radical poets.[5]

Moreover, for the kind of role Cardona-Hine played as a fusion of both generations, one might substitute any number of Old Left writers of color of the 1950s who helped forge cultural conditions for a New Left sensibility – for example, Julian Mayfield, Ann Petry, José Yglesias, Jesus Colon, Shirley Graham, and Lance Jeffers, most of whom have received far less credit than they deserve for laying the foundations for the multicultural movements of the present.

Or one might turn to the literary careers of several left-wing women, such as Eve Merriam, known among feminists as author of *The Double Bed From the Feminine Side* (1958), *After Nora Slammed the Door* (1964), and *Growing Up Female in*

America (1971), and among the general public for *The Inner City Mother Goose* (1969).

Merriam is an intriguing case because, after the 1960s, when she finally became established, she deliberately obscured her political roots in the Communist cultural movement. Merriam even insisted that she had hid her "feminism" in the 1940s and 1950s, when, in fact, a kind of "premature social-ist feminism" was quite evident in her writing, as in the case of other left-wing women writing in the 1950s such as Meridel Le Sueur and Tillie Olsen. One sees such views clearly in her long poem "Spring Cleaning," featured in a 1952 spread in an issue of *Masses & Mainstream* honoring International Women's Day.[6] Such sentiments are also expressed quite militantly in *Singing of Women*, a dramatic review co-authored with Gerda Lerner and published by the New York Council of the Arts, Sciences and Professions around 1950.[7]

Of course, to talk of such writers as part of the Old Left, mostly Communist, cultural tradition has its dangers; it can be difficult to grasp the *specificity* of the work of individuals who can relate to the ideology and organizations connected with the Communist Party along a continuum of possibilities, as in the case of the mystic/Communist poetry of Alvaro Cardona-Hine. The simplistic cate-gories we've inherited of "card-carrying member" or "fellow-traveler" fail to accommodate the nuances and hybrids one can find among a range of possible responses.

To take another example, the African-American pro-Communist novelist John O. Killens has been pilloried by Harold Cruse and others for adhering to a Party-line socialist-realist aesthetic in the 1950s, which is certainly suggested by Killens' reaction to Ralph Ellison's fiction at the time.[8] Yet to assess Killens primarily through that framework would cause us to misperceive his neglected masterpiece *Youngblood* (1954), a stunning dramatization of the complex interac-tions among class, gender, and race worthy of the 1960s, and even the 1990s. It is a work expressing a rich, Fanonian view of nationalism as a stage to interna-tionalism, climaxing in a powerful deconstruction of the myth of biological "race." The latter is dramatized in a manner accessible to a popular audience through the penultimate scene of a blood transfusion from white worker to Black, which was featured on the cover of the original mass-market paperback edition.

Moreover, conventional labeling hardly accounts for the multiple identities that might be held by an individual such as Lorraine Hansberry, an African-American lesbian/bisexual woman who adhered to Communist Party politics for the decade prior to her entrance into the theatrical mainstream with *A Raisin in the Sun* (1959). To talk of gay/lesbian, bisexual Communist cultural activities in the pre-New Left period is tricky, too, in light of both anticommunist and homophobic censorship; yet such identities were there, for not only did Hansberry contribute to the lesbian journal *The Ladder*, but former Party members such as Harry Hay created the Mattachine Society, and a one-time

Communist poet from Brooklyn College pioneered Beat gay poetry in the 1950s under the adopted name Harold Norse.

Through a glance at the final phase in the life and work of Kenneth Fearing we can perhaps concretize the argument that what came to be seen as New Left cultural trends were in fact quite present in the work of Old Left literary radicals in the period just prior to the rise of the New Left. Whatever may have been Fearing's precise organizational commitment and the heterodoxy of his personal politics, he was treated by other radicals and the popular press in the Depression decade as *the* revolutionary poet of his 1930s generation.

Of course, as with many writers, Fearing's politics evolved away from Leninism by the 1950s when he wrote two novels technically classified as "thrillers," *The Generous Heart* (1954) and *The Crozart Story* (1960), and one more that combined "thriller" features with science fiction motifs, *The Loneliest Girl in the World* (1951), plus the entire anti-witch-hunt "Family Album" poetry sequence of the mid 1950s published in his *Selected Poems* (1956).

The explicit pastoralism and anti-technology bias of Fearing in the 1950s has made him seem like a left-over Luddite in the context of the Old Left; but these also mark him out as a kind of precursor of Mario Savio of New Left fame – the "Berkeley Free Speech movement" leader who said: "you've got to put your bodies upon the gears and upon the wheels [of the machine], upon the levers, upon all the apparatus and you've got to make it stop."[9]

The evanscence of the organized working class as agency in Fearing's worldview also links him forward to the New Left. A similar point can be made about Fearing's view of the centrality of alienation as not just middle-class malaise but a "subjective" factor with harsh "objective" consequences.

Finally, Fearing's complex view of the "culture industry" also anticipates contemporary debate. Mass culture is at once the site of oppression and manipulation, while also the place where resistance occurs as Fearing uses mass culture forms to expose the industry. Although his introduction to his 1956 *New and Selected Poems* was brutally panned by certain reviewers, that brilliant text, "Reading, Writing and the Rackets," is a cultural document more characteristic of the New Left than the Old. Among other things, Fearing's "Twelve Theses" on printed and electronic forms of communication address the transformation in technology that Ernest Mandel theorizes as the basis for a "third industrial revolution" in his book *Late Capitalism* (1975), and that Fredric Jameson uses as a key moment of periodization in his work on postmodernism.

In sum, what I've presented in this essay is not just a comment on the origins of 1960s literary radicalism. Actually, I've been adding my voice to those others who have been arguing for a new periodization of twentieth-century left-wing activity as a whole.

- In past scholarship, the history of the Old Left has been too closely identified with the 1930s, and the late 1930s has been inaccurately depicted as its zenith.
- The standard perception is of the Great Depression as the "heyday" of the Old Left and the 1950s as the time of its rout.
- The 1960s is treated too one-sidedly as inaugurating a new kind of radical literary politics and corresponding "cultural revolution."

What is missed is that the Left cultural practice of the decades of the 1940s, 1950s, the 1960s, and even beyond in a few instances, is all linked to the same tradition. There is a continuity of personnel and themes, along with the additions, developments, and transformations. This is a perspective significantly different from, although not necessarily contradictory to, the Morris Dickstein argument in *Gates of Eden* (1977) that 1950s culture set the stage for the 1960s culture; or the Maurice Isserman argument in *If I Had a Hammer* (1987) that, in the sphere of radical organization, the political rethinking of non-Communist and former Communist 1950s radicals fed into the 1960s.

My own fresh study of the literary record suggests that the 1930s was actually the time when the foundations of the entire mid-late twentieth-century literary Left were laid, and that the New Cultural Left in the 1960s inaugurated not the death of the Old Literary Left but its further development and complication. That's why so many of us intellectually and morally inspired by the New Left have found ourselves continuing to be so deeply immersed in the study of the Old.

Thus the Next Left, to which many of us engaged in the study of literary radicalism are pledged to nurture back to vitality, is not likely to be the negation of predecessor movements, either. Rather, the Next Left will at the least require the incorporation of those predecessor traditions. Moreover, if Trotsky's old law of "uneven and combined development" has application here, this Next Left may even witness an advance to a higher and more successful plane of cultural and political struggle than hitherto anticipated or imagined – a struggle that will bring us closer than ever to the overthrow and abolition of our own "really existing" capitalism, imperialism, racism, sexism, homophobia, and ecocide.

Notes

1. *Mainstream* 11, no. 7 (July 1958): 53–5.
2. *National Guardian*, Dec. 13, 1952, p. 4.
3. "Awake," manuscript of unpublished poem in possession of A.W.
4. Lowenfels to Lillian, Jan. 27, 1961, Beinecke.
5. See *Where is Vietnam?* (New York: Doubleday, 1967), *In a Time of Revolution* (New York: Random House, 1969), *The Writing on the Wall* (New York: Doubleday, 1969), *Poets of Today* (New York: International, 1974), *For Neruda, For Chile* (Boston: Beacon Press, 1975),
6. 5, no. 3 (March 1952): 17–19.

7. Gerda Lerner and Eve Merriam, *Singing of Women: A Dramatic Review* (n.d.: New York Council of the Arts, Sciences and Professions), mimeographed copy in the John Howard Lawson papers, Morris Library.

8. See Harold Cruse, *The Crisis of the Negro Intellectual: From Its Origins to the Present* (New York: William Morrow and Co., 1967), p. 235.

9. Cited in Todd Gitlin, *The Sixties* (New York: Bantam, 1987), p. 291.

PART III

Cultural Theory

9

Leon Trotsky's Contributions to
Marxist Cultural Theory and
Literary Criticism

Professional Critics and Professional
Revolutionaries

The contributions of Leon Trotsky to twentieth-century literary and cultural theory are unique among what is generally regarded as "literary criticism" in the advanced capitalist nations of the West today. By and large literary criticism in countries such as the United States and those of Western Europe is the product of scholars affiliated with colleges and universities, or, in some cases, of journalists writing in mass media publications.[1] The seeming preponderance of "Marxist" critics outside the former Soviet bloc and existing post-capitalist societies (in which Marxism is still the official state ideology) is of the "Western Marxist"[2] variety; that is, often written from an armchair and accordingly divorced from organizational commitment.[3]

Thus, whatever the personal political views of the majority of the university- and business-employed cultural critics, and whatever their social and political commitments might be, the bulk of the literary criticism they produce is filtered through a system of powerful institutional constraints.[4]

It is also noteworthy that critical practice never occurs in a vacuum but is significantly conditioned by the everyday life experience of the critic. Again, in the United States and Western Europe, the critic is most often a teacher who is obliged for an income to have his or her work judged acceptable by a private or state educational institution, or else by a privately owned publication where there is always the threat that he or she might be dismissed or denied future assignments. Moreover, he or she usually inhabits an environment of economic peers with similar cultural, social, and even "racial" features.[5]

In contrast to these "professional critics," Leon Trotsky was a professional revolutionary. Even on those occasions when he received payment for writing,

This chapter originally appeared in *Journal of Trotsky Studies*, 2 (Summer 1994).

he did not regard literary activity as a specialized area of intellectual labor articulated through the network of institutions upon which his livelihood depended.
Rather, writing cultural criticism was one aspect of his efforts to build a political movement based on his understanding of the main trends of contemporary
history. Therefore, any evaluation of his contributions in the area of literary and
cultural criticism must be rooted in an understanding of his central preoccupations and political objectives at various moments in his career.

These moments can be grouped roughly within three broad periods. The first is
the pre-revolutionary period, dating from his initial literary essays around the turn
of the century to the Bolshevik seizure of power in 1917. Writings of these years
include youthful journalistic appraisals of Tolstoy, Ibsen, and Gogol. A distinctive
feature of his early method is readily apparent through his frequent assertion that
every author has a crystallized psychology resulting from social conditions.

A second phase comes in the first five years following the Russian Revolution,
prior to the onset of Trotsky's struggle against Stalin in 1923–24. These years witnessed the greatest fecundity of Trotsky's cultural work, punctuated by the publication of his famous *Literature and Revolution* (1923) as well as *Problems of Everday Life*
(1924). In these writings he vigorously and boldly sought to theorize a relationship
between the cultural legacy of bourgeois society and the politico-cultural tasks of
the epoch of the transition to socialism. Trotsky also promoted in these works a
critical method based on the assertion of social judgments independent of artistic
forms. This produced some brilliant results in practice, but the method is problematic on a theoretical plane due to its separation of content from technique.[6]

The third phase of Trotsky's writing begins with his exile from the Soviet Union
in 1927 and lasts until his assassination in August 1940. In these years, he carried
out the unpleasant but necessary task of documenting and analyzing the effects
of Stalinism on Soviet culture. Episodically, he also assessed a number of recent
novels – the genre he preferred above all – and recorded diary notations of other
readings. After 1933, Trotsky was increasingly active in seeking to draw writers
and artists to the new revolutionary movement that became the Fourth
International in 1938.[7] As such, his perspective underwent several important
changes. Most significantly, he promoted for the first time a frankly "libertarian"
cultural view calling for an "anarchy" of literary production.[8] This is a decided
improvement over the ambiguities of his 1924 formulation for the relation of the
state to various artistic groups and tendencies: "while holding over them all the
categorical criterion, *for* the revolution or *against* the revolution, to give them complete freedom in the sphere of artistic self-determination."[9]

The Evolution of an Aesthetic

As in the case of Lenin, Franz Mehring, and Rosa Luxemburg – not to mention
Marx and Engels themselves – the early literary criticism produced by Trotsky

was animated more by a "Marxist sensibility" than a systematic set of propositions. Moreover, this sensibility was derived from a profound assimilation of the
first principles of historical materialism. Unlike the written texts of later debates
that came to characterize literary discussions among Marxists of the Third
International during the Stalin era, there are in Trotsky no long quotations from
the famous writings of the "founding fathers." For one thing, the anthologies of
Marx and Engels's excerpts and aphorisms on literature and art that are today
familiar to all students of the subject were simply not available at that time.
However, the major biographical sources agree that Trotsky, from the time he set
his mind to it, had a special aptitude for Marx and Engels's method of historical,
social, philosophic, and economic analysis.[10] Moreover, as George Novack
observes, "Trotsky never claimed originality for his theoretical and political positions"; rather, he sought to apply classical Marxism with breadth and subtlety.[11]

Trotsky's two essays on Tolstoy (1908 and 1910) exemplify this approach. His
method, like that of his mentors, tends to privilege realist literature and to seek
the social basis of imagery and characterization. It was also a method that
adamantly resisted the conflation of "political" and "artistic" judgments even
as a social evaluation was provided. His first study, "Tolstoy: Poet and Rebel,"
commences in characteristic fashion by refracting the social origins of the novelist through his personality. Trotsky concludes that, while Tolstoy intellectually
would not defend feudal relations in practice, he was nevertheless "emotionally
bonded" to that system where "everything hinges on cycles of nature" and "one
lives by hearing and obeying."[12] Sharing the judgment of bourgeois critics,
Trotsky declares *War and Peace* to be "best and unsurpassed." His three evaluative criteria are worth noting, for they are premised on an unabashed
Hellenocentrism that may strike us as naively dated today.

First, the novel incarnates the "anonymousness of life and its sacred irre-
sponsibility" in the character of Karatayev. Second, Tolstoy radiates a "Homeric
calm and Homeric love of children." Third, Tolstoy achieves characterization
through a unity of "inner necessity" and "harmony" resulting in an "aesthetic
pantheism." The end result is incisively characterized by Trotsky as the creation
of an "agricultural aesthetic" bonded "back to the *Pentateuch* and *Illiad*." Thus
Trotsky, like Marx and Engels before him, uncritically accepts inherited notions
of aesthetics from the nineteenth-century version of the Western tradition.[13] What
is new and distinctive is Trotsky's ability to infuse these with the perspective and
sensibility of historical materialism, which he brilliantly blends with a detailed
knowledge of the Russian social formation.[14]

The second study, "On Tolstoy's Death," written by Trotsky in Vienna
shortly after the event, establishes a contradiction between Tolstoy's "organic"
ties to an unacceptable ruling class culture and his "moral affinity" to socialist
thought.[15] In his impressively researched book, *The Social and Political Thought of
Leon Trotsky* (1978), Baruch Knei-Paz aptly summarizes the literary values established by Trotsky in this essay: "a liberal attitude in principle to all literature, an

openness to the artistic merits of creative work without regard for the author's political views," but one that is also always asking "the utilitarian question: what does it matter from the perspective of socialism?"[16] Another enduring feature Trotsky establishes in his early work is a non-intrusive, dialectical mode of argumentation. Characteristically, he will first state the viewpoint of an opponent, and then reformulate the issue on a different basis – usually with some impressive twist. At its most effective, the method moves the reader from one view to another. However, it is crucial to realize that within the new view is embedded a dynamic tension stemming from the residue of the earlier proposition reinterpreted in the fresh context.

Art and Society

The second phase of literary criticism, occurring in the years immediately following the Russian Revolution, was indubitably Trotsky's most productive. But its achievement was significantly flawed by Trotsky's failure to foresee the main trend in Soviet society – the appearance of a bureaucratic tyranny led by Stalin that would subvert and negate Trotsky's entire literary projections for the future of the USSR. It was not until 1937 that he would be able to fully come to grips with this phenomenom in his chapter on "Culture and the Soviet Bureaucracy" in *The Revolution Betrayed: What is the Soviet Union and Where is It Going ?*

Trotsky's writings of the early 1920s, especially *Literature and Revolution* (originally a series of articles in *Pravda* that he wrote over two summers),[17] were produced under the impact of the immediate post-revolutionary events of social transformation and civil war. His overriding concern is to rework the complex tension between a view of art as an independent category of aesthetic experience, and the recognition of all culture as essentially ideological (that is, implicitly or explicitly bearing a political message).[18]

Perhaps surprisingly, from a contemporary Marxist perspective, Trotsky argues that the claims of the artist are entirely irrelevant to the multiple functions of the work of art itself. On the one hand, regardless of what the reader or viewer might think about a work of art, it must exist within history and bear a relationship to history. He uses deliberately provocative terms to characterize the socially dependent nature of art, such as "social servant" and "utilitarian."[19]

On the other hand, the techniques attributed by Trotsky as ones intrinsic to art are in no way reducible to politics. He maintains that art is characterized by at least six traits: it finds the necessary rhythm of words for "dark and vague moods"; brings thought and feeling "closer or contrasts them, one with the other"; enriches the "spiritual experience" of the individual and the community; refines feeling, rendering it more "flexible" and "responsive"; enlarges the volume of thought "in advance and not through the personal method of accumulated experience"; and educates "the individual, the social group, the class and the nation."[20]

In sum, Trotsky's view is clearly that art is not "pure." Yet, to deny the "purity" of art from a Marxist view is not to deny its autonomy, praxis, or expansive dimension, rendering it a mere instrument of message. If anything, Trotsky seems to conceive of art as "technique" – devoid of a particular content. Simply put, Trotsky regards art as a technique of articulating moods, formulating diverse relations between thought and feeling, expanding and enriching emotions, and educating us prior to empiric experience in some sort of preparatory way. Upon this foundation, Trotsky sought to elaborate the tasks of Marxism in regard to art as he saw them in the post-Revolution era.

In this local application of his theory, Trotsky demands a kind of "scientific" investigation into the "social roots of the 'pure' as well as the tendentious art."[21] That is, rather than "'incriminate' a poet with the thoughts and feelings which he expresses," Trotsky aims to focus on questions such as the following: To which order of feelings does "a given artistic work correspond in all its peculiarities"? What are the "social conditions of these thoughts and feelings"? What is their location in the "historic development of a society and of a class"? What literary heritage has "entered into the elaboration of the new form"? Under the influence of "what historic impulse have the new complexes of feelings and thoughts broken through the shell that divides them from the sphere of poetic consciousness?"[22]

When Trotsky explores these issues in assessing writers such as Kliuev, Yessenin, Pilnyak, Blok, and Mayakovsky, the result can be characterized as something of a balancing act. He never fails to offer complicated, detailed, and individualized investigations full of verve and wit; yet these are directly set against his insistence on "the subsidiary role which art plays in the social process."[23]

One must conclude that, if Trotsky holds art to be a realm of "techniques" involving emotions, feelings, thoughts, and perceptions, Marxism must be apprehended as a method appropriate to the understanding of the social roots that nourish the various techniques. In particular, it follows that the Marxist critic should be equipped to tell us what produces the content and the form exhibited in art. Such a charge is particularly complex and demanding when it comes to suggesting to what social order the content and form correspond, and what drives new human emotions into the realm of poetic expression.

By mid-career Trotsky had established the fundamental terrain of his cultural theory. From a Marxist view, art is subsidiary to social process. Yet art is simultaneously a category dealing with specialized techniques, and is therefore semi-autonomous and not immediately reducible to political coding.

The Masterwork

The brilliance and relevance of *Literature and Revolution* and related essays of the early 1920s stem from much more than Trotsky's mere articulation of a classical Marxist stance on art and society. Indeed, it is hard to think of another book in world history with an equivalent agenda of complex and burning issues. Among the questions he addresses are the following:

- How does a social revolution affect literature? Does it help literature, hinder it, advance it, retard it, or derail it?
- How do writers relate to the revolutionary process? Can a revolution be accurately grasped and communicated in literature? Are special literary forms necessary to express the revolutionary process?
- How should leaders of a revolutionary government evaluate the literature that grows out of a revolution? Should revolutionaries try to influence literature by encouraging certain schools?
- How should censorship be used in order to defend a revolution? Where should the line be drawn?
- How should one formulate one's expectations for the kind of literature one should expect to appear in the short run as well as the long run, following a successful revolution and the inauguration of a transitional period?

Trotsky uses pre- and post-revolutionary Russia as the laboratory in which to explore these and similar issues. He proceeds from a study of the literature existing in the period before the unsuccessful 1905 Revolution, and concludes with a utopian vision of the literature that he hopes will eventually emerge from the Communist leadership of the 1917 Revolution, along the way covering just about every conceivable stopping point.

For example, his initial chapter, "Pre-Revolutionary Art," encompasses developments in four main areas. He starts with a survey of the literature emerging before 1905, the first great upheaval in modern Russia, which consists in the main of the writing of nobles and peasants. He then turns to the bourgeois literature appearing in what he calls the "intra-revolutionary period," between 1905 and the 1917 Revolution. The next period is marked by the literature of the counter-revolutionaries who fled Russia because of the Revolution (the émigrés); and the last theme taken up is the literature of the counter-revolutionaries who remained inside Russia.

His second chapter, "The Literary Fellow-Travelers of the Revolution," analyzes the work produced by writers obviously more sympathetic to the Revolution than the counter-revolutionaries. The word "fellow-traveler" has acquired a variety of meanings over the years. It was also discussed by Trotsky in "Class and Art," a 1924 speech to the Press Department of the Central Committee of the Communist Party of the USSR.[24] Trotsky applies the term to writers who approve of the abstract goals of the Russian Revolution but are not ready to go all the way with the revolutionaries to achieve them.

In his third chapter, Trotsky moves even closer to the Revolution through a consideration of Alexander Blok, a writer he regarded as partly forming a bridge between the fellow-travelers and the October Revolution. The fourth and fifth chapters discuss two movements – Futurism and Formalism – that try to interact with the Revolution. The sixth chapter analyzes the school of proletarian culture and art, one of the literary schools that is actually a conscious part of the Revolution. The seventh chapter presents Trotsky's recommendations for Communist policy regarding literature. The eighth and concluding chapter contains Trotsky's projections and predictions as to the kind of art he believes the Revolution will ultimately produce upon completion – when all classes have been abolished, and when communism has been established in the USSR.

From the outset, Trotsky applies his dialectical "Marxist sensibility" to the topic. For example, he affirms the priority of the material and social over the cultural by emphasizing that, if Communists had not fought against the counter-revolution and carried out a reorganization of society, there could not even have been a debate over the various cultural policies of the USSR. Moreover, he adds that there will be no opportunity for the debate to continue if the severe economic problems besetting the USSR in the wake of the Civil War are not resolved.

Then, in a characteristic inversion of perspective, Trotsky is equally emphatic that merely establishing a new state and organizing an egalitarian economy is no guarantor of the achievement of socialist goals. According to Marxist theory, he argues, each new revolution in class relations ultimately produces unique changes in the form and content of art and culture. Therefore, until the USSR has developed a new socialist science, culture, and art, one cannot say that a socialist society has been achieved. This is the essence of his aphorism, "the development of art is the highest test of the vitality and significance of each epoch."[25]

Trotsky then deepens this claim by being equally adamant that one cannot achieve a new socialist art or culture through declaring it by fiat or by conducting laboratory experiments. It is first necessary to create a successful society as a whole: "Only a movement of scientific thought on a national scale and the development of a new art would signify that the historic seed has not only grown into a plant, but has even flowered."[26]

Viewed with the hindsight of seventy years, one of the more striking features of *Literature and Revolution* is the degree to which it anticipates Gramsci's familiar adage, "Optimism of the will, pessimism of the intellect."[27] This could hardly be clearer than in Trotsky's scathing critique of the state of Soviet literature at the time. It is especially important to note his view that no particular school or group has as yet proposed a viable or appropriate literary response to the Revolution: "If a line were extended from the present art to the Socialist art of the future, one would say that we have hardly now passed through the stage of even preparing for its preparation."[28]

Although scores of issues are explored in *Literature and Revolution* in a fresh and exciting way, seven are especially enduring.

1. *Trotsky's challenge to the simplistic identification of Futurism with the proletarian revolution.* Trotsky expresses considerable vexation at the fact that the Futurist group in Italy was subsumed into the fascist rather than the Communist movement, as it had been in the USSR. He speculates that the explanation lies in the origins of Futurism, an upsurge of artistic rebels with no definite political leanings. Moreover, in his view, it was not at all inconceivable that the Futurists might at some point have followed most other literary movements in accommodating the establishment and achieving respectability, had they not been drawn into the whirlwind of violent political upheavals before they had time to evolve. What is most noteworthy is that, when social crises occurred in the respective environments of the Futurists in Russia and Italy, this obstreperous artistic tendency tended to dress up its literary rebellion in the political colors of whatever movement was most strongly in ascendancy, regardless of whether it was Left or Right. Trotsky, however, does not deny that the Russian Futurists were genuinely attracted to the dynamic force of the Revolution. He insists, rather, that they erred in thinking that their bohemian (non-conventional) rebellion against bourgeois culture was the genuine artistic counterpart of the social revolution.

2. *Trotsky's theorization of literary tradition.* Although Trotsky advocates the birth of a new culture corresponding to the new social order of the Revolution, he is at one with Marx and Lenin in valorizing tradition. Responding to the Futurist attitude, he states that:

> The working class does not have to, and cannot break with literary tradition, because the working class is not in the grip of such tradition. The working class does not know the old literature, it still has to commune with it, it still has to master Pushkin, to absorb him, and so overcome him.[29]

Instead of positing that each new cultural phase smashes and annihilates the culture that preceded it, Trotsky proposes a dialectical continuity in cultural history. Literary tradition proceeds by a series of reactions, each of which is united to the tradition from which it is seeking to break. Moreover, these developments occur not all at once, but under the stimuli of new artistic needs as the result of changes in the psychology of social classes attendant upon changes in the economic structure.

3. *Trotsky's critique of Russian Formalist criticism.* Trotsky's analysis in this area constitutes a landmark defense of the need for a "totalizing" literary method. His devastating critique of the limits of Formalism has a general relevance to problematic features of certain trends in literary criticism that have periodically come to prominence, as in the case of the "New Criticism" in the United States and the structuralists, post-structuralists, and deconstructionists in Western Europe.

The Formalists were members of a critical school that declared form to be

the essence of poetry, the determinant of poetry's content. These critics concentrated on a close analysis of the sound and meaning of words in poetry. In
interrogating such claims, Trotsky dialectically acknowledges the kernel of truth
in the argument of the Formalists, while excoriating their empty pretensions in
sealing off literature as an autonomous realm:

> Having declared form to be the essence of poetry, this school reduces its task to an
> analysis (essentially descriptive and semi-statistical) of the etymology and syntax of
> poems, to the recounting of repetitive vowels and consonants, of syllables and epi-
> thets. This analysis which Formalists regard as the essence of poetry, or poetics, is
> undoubtedly necessary and useful, but one must understand its partial, scrappy, sub-
> sidiary and preparatory character.[30]

4. *Trotsky's opposition to the fomenting of a "proletarian culture" in the immediate post-
revolutionary USSR.*   The argument he advances here is one of the most well-
known and controversial of his entire life. It forms not only the central part of
the book, but informs the work as a whole. Perhaps the most succinct summary
of Trotsky's views is presented in the Preface to *Literature and Revolution*:

> It is fundamentally incorrect to contrast bourgeois culture and bourgeois art with
> proletarian culture and proletarian art. The latter will never exist, because the pro-
> letarian regime is temporary and transient. The historic significance and the moral
> grandeur of the proletarian revolution consist in the fact that it is laying the founda-
> tion of a culture which is above classes and which will be the first culture that is truly
> human.[31]

Trotsky's argument derives from the underlying thesis that it is erroneous to
make a historical analogy between the bourgeoisie's creation of its own culture
and the proletariat's similar endeavor. The comparison is false for two reasons.
First, the purpose of the proletarian revolution is, in fact, the creation of a *classless* society and correspondingly a *classless* culture. Second, and perhaps more
important, in Trotsky's view a basic difference exists in the historic destinies of
the bourgeois and proletarian classes.

The bourgeois way of life developed organically over the course of several
centuries, whereas the proletarian dictatorship, in Trotsky's estimation, would
last years or decades but not longer – certainly not centuries. Moreover, the life-
span of the proletarian dictatorship, the transitional phase between a dictatorship of the capitalist class and a communist society devoid of classes, would be
filled with savage class struggles allowing little or no room for the organic
growth of new cultures. The fledging USSR was only one country and economically a backward one at that, with all the major capitalist nations dedicated to
its extermination.

According to Trotsky, the reason that the bourgeoisie can create its own
culture more easily is because, even under feudalism and absolutism, before it

had gained political domination, this class possessed significant wealth, social power, and education. Moreover, there were bourgeois forces operating in almost every field of activity. In contrast, the most that the working class is able to gain under capitalism is the social ability to overthrow capitalism. The proletariat, he claims, differs from the bourgeoisie markedly in that it is a propertyless, exploited, and uneducated class. It emerges from bourgeois rule in a condition of cultural pauperism, thus finding itself severely handicapped in any attempt to originate a new and significant phase in the development of the human mind.

Trotsky assessed the situation of the USSR in the 1920s as one where the working class was not even at the point of *trying* to give birth to a new special culture; rather, the reality was that only a small group of intellectuals was trying to do this through their journals and proclamations. As Trotsky wittily points out, one can't create a class culture behind the back of a class. It is true, he acknowledges, that a few gifted worker poets have emerged; but the artistic achievement they have attained is largely due to their apprenticeship with bourgeois or even pre-bourgeois poets. Trotsky declares it demagogic to treat such efforts, valuable as they might be, as more than they are – as new and "epoch-making" art.[32]

5. *Trotsky's proposals for Communist policy toward art.* Trotsky is responding to the charge that, if he denies the possibility of a distinct proletarian art under the dictatorship of the proletariat, he therefore must be an advocate of complete eclecticism – an anything-goes attitude toward culture and cultural policy. His response is well worth quoting at length; if these words had been heeded in the Third International, the Communist movement throughout the world might have avoided many cultural policies that discredited it even in the eyes of those sympathetic to its political aims:

> The Marxian method affords an opportunity to estimate the development of the new art, to trace all its sources, to help the most progressive tendencies by a critical illumination of the road, but it does not do more than that. Art must make its own way and by its own means. The Marxian methods are not the same as the artistic. The Party leads the proletariat but not the historic processes of history. There are domains in which the Party leads, directly and imperatively. There are domains in which it only co-operates. There are, finally, domains in which it only orientates itself. The domain of art is not one in which the Party is called upon to command. It can and must protect and help it, but it can only lead it indirectly. It can and must give the additional credit of its confidence to various art groups, which are striving sincerely to approach the Revolution and so help an artistic formulation of the Revolution. And at any rate, the Party cannot and will not take the position of a literary circle which is struggling and merely competing with other literary circles.[33]

Much of the rest of the chapter in which this argument is set forth further elaborates the authentic communist-humanist values held by those who led the Bolshevik party in the pre-Stalin era. Trotsky warns that, even though Marxism puts society first, exaggerated attacks against "individualism" are dangerous. This is because of the dual role individualism has played. Historically, individualism has as many progressive and revolutionary effects as reactionary ones. In fact, the working class under capitalism, Trotsky maintains, suffers not from an excess of individualism but from an atrophy of individualism. Even now, in the transitional years of the Revolution, the personality of the Soviet workers is not yet sufficiently formed and differentiated. Trotsky holds that to form and develop an individual personality is of equal importance to training an individual in industrial skills. He is also annoyed that some Communist thinkers apparently believe that the reading of traditional bourgeois literature might sap the workers' sense of class solidarity. He retorts: "What the worker will take from Shakespeare, Goethe, Pushkin, or Dostoyevsky will be a more complex idea of human personality, of its passions and feelings, a deeper and profounder understanding of its psychic forces and the role of the subconscious, etc. In the final analysis, the worker will become richer."[34]

6. *Trotsky's discussion of "certainties and hypotheses" about prospects for the future.* By "certainties" he is referring only to the "art of the revolution," based on the experience of the Revolution and the dictatorship of the proletariat. In contrast, the "hypotheses" are what he offers in regard to "socialist art," that can only come to life in a classless society, and about which it is therefore possible only to speculate.

He holds that the genuine art of the Revolution, which throbs with all the class conflicts and political passions of the time, belongs to the dictatorship of the proletariat, a transitional phase between capitalism and socialism. This he calls the realm of necessity (where one does what one must to survive) as opposed to the realm of freedom (where one does what is possible). From this perspective, the possibilities of the transitional period of the proletarian dictatorship are highly limited. Only in the classless society will human solidarity be able to come to full fruition:

> the powerful force of competition, which, in bourgeois society, has the character of market competition, will not disappear in a Socialist society, but, to use the language of psychoanalysis, will be sublimated, that is, will assume a higher and more fertile form. There will be the struggle for one's opinion, for one's project, for one's taste. In the measure in which political struggles will be eliminated – and in a society where there will be no classes, there will be no such struggles – the liberated passions will be channelized into technique, into construction which also includes art. Art will then become more general, will mature, will become tempered, and will become the most perfect method of the progressive building of life in every field. It will not be merely "pretty" without relation to anything else.[35]

As for the literature of the Revolution itself – even that has not yet emerged; it is still groping for expression.

Nevertheless, while acknowledging that other Communist intellectuals had come to similar perspectives, Trotsky is distressed about the currency of the view that literature of the Revolution must become more "realistic" in order to fully develop. His response is to agree that, yes, in the broad philosophic sense, the art of the revolutionary epoch cannot achieve greatness unless it is deeply sensitive to social reality. But he also thinks that it is preposterous to try to foster "realism" in the narrow sense, as a distinct literary school of which the subject is the "common" experience of "common" people.

Here Trotsky declares the falsity of the view that such a school of literary realism would necessarily have to be inherently progressive; by itself, realism was neither revolutionary nor reactionary. To the contrary, in Russia, due to the peculiarities of historical development, there had been a "Golden Age of Realism" during the era when the aristocracy had been most entrenched. This is why the radical Populist writers who rose against the aristocracy had used a tendentious style, which eventually turned into pessimistic symbolism, against which the Futurists had rebelled.

Trotsky is unambiguous in arguing that it is deleterious to cultural production to promote one style as politically superior to another; among other reasons, because the mutation of style occurs against a definite social background reflecting changes in the political climate. In a formulation that is central to any Marxist theory of forms, he asserts that new styles grow out of old styles, as their dialectical negation. They revive and develop some elements of the old while abandoning others:

> Evidently there are sentiments and thoughts which feel crowded within the framework of the old methods. But at the same time, the new moods find in the already old and fossilized art some elements which when further developed can give them adequate expression. The banner of revolt is raised against the "old" as a whole, in the name of the elements which can be developed. Each literary school is contained potentially in the past and each one develops by pulling away hostilely from the past.[36]

Trotsky also holds that the culture of the future will not cast aside totally earlier literary genres and forms. He expresses dismay that some Communist critics apparently had argued that tragedy will disappear because such antiquated pre-socialist notions as religion, fate, sin, and penance are at the center of the tragic motif. In response, he points out that the essence of tragedy lies in the larger conflict between humanity's awakened mind and its constricting environment; that this is a conflict inseparable from human existence which will manifest itself in different forms in all stages of history. Religion, Trotsky maintains, did not create tragedy but only served to express it. Moreover, the Greeks, Shakespeare, and Goethe each expressed tragedy in different ways.

Even though Trotsky affirms that all anticipations of art under socialism are by definition hypothetical, he nevertheless strives to discern elements that might point toward socialist art amidst the confused, occasionally meaningless innovations which abounded in Soviet culture during these early post-Revolution years. Taking an example from architecture, he notes that the "constructivist" school of Tatlin (emphasizing industrial materials) rejects oramental forms, advocates "functionalism," and draws up ambitious blueprints for garden cities and public buildings that are worthy of a socialist society. Unfortunately, these plans, Trotsky points out, take little account of what is materially possible in the USSR at the moment, although it is significant that they still contain what he thinks are fruitful rational elements and valuable intuitive premonitions of the socialist future.

7. *Trotsky's comprehensive defense of the socialist vision and the socialist future.* The very last pages of *Literature and Revolution* offer a compelling response to the Nietzschean view that humanity under socialism would be passive and herd-like, with all competitive and combative instincts extinguished. Trotsky counters with a "utopian" vision, more accurately a "practical utopia," that is largely derived from a plausible if optimistic view of the possibilities for humanity once the distortions of class exploitation have been eliminated.

He argues that socialism, far from suppressing human instincts for activity and growth, will fully unleash those instincts by encouraging them toward higher purposes. In a society free from class antagonisms there will be no competition for profits and no struggles for political power, hence humanity's vast energies and passions will be devoted to creative activity in the fields of tech-nology, science, and art. New political parties will spring into being, dramat-ically unlike old parties. They will contest with one another over ideas, social planning, trends in education, styles in the theater, in music, and in sport; and over schemes for new transporation networks, the fertilization of barren deserts, the regulation of climate, advances in chemistry, and the like. Moreover, these vital contests, which Trotsky speculates will be exciting, dramatic, and passion-ate, will embrace society as a whole, not merely intellectual elites.

To be sure, says Trotsky, these are all remote prospects. Immediately ahead will be an epoch of fierce class struggle and war against the old ruling classes on an international scale from which humankind might well emerge impoverished and destitute, requiring that decades must then be spent in the conquest of poverty and backwardness. Moreover, during these difficult times the nascent socialist society will be gripped by the need for industrial expansion and the attainment of material comfort. But when this transient phase passes, a vista will be opened for humanity which our imaginations of the present are incapable of grasping.

The Exile Period

Of interest in Trotsky's criticism in the 1920s and the 1930s is his attitude toward the experimental literature now known as modernism. An important

aspect of his assessment of this genre is his longstanding opposition to the dom-
inance of any particular literary school, regardless of the political claims of its
adherents. The danger of supporting a particular literary trend is further under-
scored by his belief that the culture of the revolutionary movement of his day
was at a very primitive stage. Thus Trotsky's basic sympathy for tradition, and
for the realist genre of fiction, was balanced on principle by an openness to all
art forms, and a demand for tolerance for the greatest degree of experimentation: "Poets, painters, sculptors and musicians will themselves find their own
approach and methods, if the struggle for freedom of oppressed classes and
peoples scatters the clouds of skepticism and of pessimism which cover the
horizon of mankind."[37]

Nevertheless, despite all that has been made of Trotsky's late 1930s
collaboration with André Breton, and some passing references to psychoanalysis in his own criticism, there is little evidence that Trotsky read many surrealist or other avant-garde works. His comments on modernist works, such as
Journey to the End of Night (1933), reveal his traditional preoccupations, such as
the refraction of national culture through language: "Céline's style is subordinated to his receptivity of the objective world. In his seemingly careless,
ungrammatical, passionately condensed language there lives, beats, and
vibrates the genuine wealth of French culture, the entire emotional and mental
experience of a great nation, in its living content, in its keenest tints."[38] On the
other hand, in his exile, Trotsky appears to be more insistent than ever in identifying potential links implicitly existing between the more rebellious forms of
art and rebel politics:

> Living creativeness cannot march ahead without repulsion away from official tradi-
> tion, canonized ideas and feelings, images and expressions covered by the lacquer of
> use and wont. Each new tendency seeks for the most direct and honest contact
> between words and emotions. The struggle against pretense in art always grows to a
> lesser or greater measure into the struggle against the injustice of human relations.
> The connection is self-evident: art which loses the sense of the social lie inevitably
> defeats itself by affectation, turning into mannerism.[39]

Does this alter in any significant way his stance on the relation of political
commitment to artistic practice? His original view was that, within limits, it is
permissible to urge certain values and perspectives on the artist. The danger is
in attempting to provide precise leadership for the arts and in transgressing
boundaries of areas not appropriately the terrain of Marxism. As I quoted
earlier:

> The Marxian method affords an opportunity to estimate the development of the new
> art, to trace all its sources, to help the most progressive tendencies by critical illumina-
> tion of the road, but it does not do more than that. Art must make its own way and
> by its own means. The Marxian methods are not the same as the artistic.[40]

This meant in practice that while a political party might protect and assist artistic movements, it should in no way endorse a literary circle in competition with other literary circles.

However, what was new by the mid 1930s was that Trotsky began to put a special premium on the current within modernism drawn to the Left – most notably the French surrealists and dissident Communists gravitating toward *Partisan Review* magazine in the United States.[41] In his famous "Manifesto: Towards a Free Revolutionary Art," written in collaboration with Breton, Trotsky appears to regard left-wing modernism as the highest form of art, which he refers to simply as "true" art: "True art, which is not content to play variations on ready-made models but rather insists on expressing the inner needs of man and mankind in its time – true art is unable not to be revolutionary, not to aspire to a complete and radical reconstruction of society."[42]

In this context, Trotsky speaks of a category of "independent revolutionary art." Politically, the category meant militantly anti-capitalist, anti-fascist, and anti-Stalinist – but specifically excluding the view that equated Stalinism with fascism. In other words, a political trend compatible with Trotskyism but much broader, reaching out to anarchists, left social democrats, independent communists, and others drawn to the Left whose ideas were not so well formed. In 1938 Trotsky sought to unite such forces in the International Federation of Independent Revolutionary Art, and it seems probable that his writings at that time were modulated to appear more attractive to the existing radical modernist milieu, although he was clearly enthuiastic about Diego Rivera's art. In any event, the beginning of World War II in September 1939 truncated Trotsky's efforts to unite revolutionary artists.

Conclusion and Caveat

In summary, Trotsky's contributions to literary and cultural theory, of which *Literature and Revolution* comprises the central moment, must be grasped as an evolutionary project with some incomplete parts, gaps, and (sometimes implicit) self-corrections. His youthful writings constitute an impressive application of basic Marxist principles to mainly Russian texts and events. In mid-life, under the impact of new circumstances created by the Russian Revolution, there occurs a creative leap to original and enduring contributions. Finally, with the writings of the last decade of his life Trotsky enters a period of adjustment and reworking of earlier propositions in light of the unanticipated triumph of Stalinism and the exigencies of building a new international revolutionary movement under the difficult conditions of the 1930s.

Trotsky's extraordinarily rich body of writing on culture must be regarded as a component of the foundation for contemporary Marxist criticism, especially as it relates to two urgent concerns. The first is that the evolution of Trotsky's writings up through *The Revolution Betrayed* (1938) helps explain what occurred in the cultural realm under the name of "Marxism" in the USSR. While the record is clear that a potentially liberatory doctrine became the rationale for political domination and control of the arts, Trotsky's work demonstrates both the authentic character of the potential that was crushed and the heroic legacy of an effort to defend artistic integrity on Marxist principles.

The second area of special value is that Trotsky's views provide possible solutions to theoretical and practical problems faced by left-wing cultural workers in the West, the Third World, and in the crumbling post-Stalinist states – all areas where authentic Marxism may still be recouped as the theoretical and practical instrument of liberation. Trotsky's appraisals of tradition, experimentation, literary value, diverse critical schools, and the relation between culture and class, along with the examples of his analyses of texts, remain superb starting points for critical exegesis and cultural policy.

However, in both efforts, we must make every effort to critically scrutinize and update Trotsky's legacy. For example, in 1994, while admiring Trotsky's lifelong devotion to human self-liberation and his intransigent opposition to intellectual mystification and despair, there is reason to conclude that his acceptance of the Enlightenment tradition was too complete. His "faith" in the Enlightenment's reified categories of science, reason, and progress was far too one-sided, as well as Eurocentric.[43] This means that there are good reasons to rethink the basis of his assessment of cultural advance and retardation of the early USSR as compared to the West.

Contemporary Marxist critics might not discern the working class and peasantry of the early USSR as being as barren of cultural achievement as Trotsky suggests in *Literature and Revolution*. While Trotsky was hardly an "elitist," his examination of the cultural activity of these two classes may in some measure be judged to be vitiated by what contemporary Marxists now regard as a patriarchal, Eurocentric literary tradition – a rendering of judgments according to models of high cultural attainment based too one-sidedly upon Dante, Shakespeare, and Goethe. Marxists presently studying the cultures of less industrialized countries are far more alert than Trotsky to the genuine complexity of the daily life, activities, and art of women and the subaltern classes – especially of those hitherto regarded as "primitive," "uncultured," and "uncivilized."[44]

Perhaps the most significant caveat in assessing Trotsky's achievement concerns his theory of the transitional era, which was the basis of much of his thinking on cultural policy and possibility. To what extent has history verified his understanding of the post-Revolution USSR – either as he saw it in 1922 as simply the dictatorship of the proletariat; or as he saw it after the consolidation of power by Stalin – as fundamentally progressive in its economy yet qualitatively compromised by bureaucratic degeneration? Unless one succumbs to the characterization of such societies as being in some sense authentically "socialist," which I certainly am absolutely unwilling to do, then one must call into question Trotsky's belief that the Russian Revolution inaugurated a transitional stage that would rapidly, over several decades, evolve into socialism and then communism. Was the post-1917 stage of the Russian Revolution something other than a transient transition? Will societal transitions occur in far more complex and prolonged ways than Trotsky imagined? Was 1917 an aberration caused by historical peculiarities?

Finally, the utopian vision that closes *Literature and Revolution* requires augmentation by what one has been learning over the past few decades about "cultural difference" from feminists, people of color in the external and domestic colonies of imperialism, other subjugated minorities, the environmental movement, and recent radical religious trends such as Liberation Theology. Trotsky, like Marx before him, drew too exclusively and uncritically on what he saw as best in the Western tradition and the Enlightenment. The human ideals – Aristotle, Goethe, Marx – that Trotsky admired came from a tiny portion of humanity; they were by no means as "universal" in their outlook and achievement as Trotsky portrayed them.

These and other problematic features of Trotsky's cultural contributions could be the worthy subject of lengthy future expositions. Whether or not such inquiries will come to pass may well be bound up in the fate of the world socialist movement as it enters the twenty-first century. The collapse of the Soviet regime in 1989 has unexpectedly opened the door wide to the possibility of a new socialist revival in which a reconsideration of Trotsky's cultural as well as his political writings might well be a significant component. At this point, though, it remains unclear as to just who and how many will pass through that door. However, considering the horrors inflicted by today's global capitalism – hi-tech wars, unrelenting racism, murderous inter-ethnic hatred, mass starvation – it is urgent that alternative courses for humanity receive the utmost consideration by this as well as the next generation of scholars and activists.

Notes

1. In a relatively few cases, a self-employed individual, a full- or part-time industrial or agricultural worker, or a salaried left-wing political activist may contribute substantial cultural criticism to a paper, journal, or political organ that is independent of universities or business corporations.

2. See Perry Anderson, *Considerations on Western Marxism* (London: New Left Books, 1976).

3. In Western Europe, the number of academic literary critics with a Marxist party affiliation is miniscule; it would be surprising to find as many as a dozen in the United States.

4. In the United States and Western Europe, these constraints are in the form of academic journals, university and commercial publishing houses, professional organizations, networks of "readers" who evaluate their colleagues on behalf of various administrative bodies, and, often in the truly decisive positions, bureaucrats worried about the budgets of universities and periodicals – and who are frequently ignorant of the subtleties of the discipline. Useful insights into the complicated situation of literary criticism in the academy can be found in Richard Ohmann, *Politics of Letters* (Middletown, Conn.: Wesleyan University Press, 1987).

5. For example, although the population of people of color in the United States is approximately

20 percent, literature teachers prior to the recent decade were 99 percent white.

6. Such a schism has fallen in disfavor among more rigorous Marxist critics since the publication of Fredric Jameson's *Marxism and Form* (Princeton, NJ: Princeton University Press,1974).

7. See the excellent studies in the following issues of *Cahiers Leon Trotsky*: "Trotsky et les intellectuels des États Unis," 19 (Sept. 1984); "Trotsky et les écrivains français," 25 (March 1986); and "Trotsky, la littérature et les écrivains," 47 (Jan. 1992).

8. The exact quotation is: "If, for the better development of the forces of material production, the revolution must build a *socialist* regime with centralized control, to develop intellectual creation an *anarchist* regime of individual liberty should from the first be established. No authority, no dictation, not the least trace of orders from above" (emphases in original). See "Manifesto: Toward a Free Revolutionary Art," in Paul N. Siegel, ed., *Leon Trotsky on Literature and Art* (New York: Pathfinder, 1970), p. 117. The manifesto was signed by André Breton and Diego Rivera, but Trotsky wrote most of it.

9. Leon Trotsky, *Literature and Revolution* (Ann Arbor: University of Michigan, 1960), p. 14.

10. See, for example, the sections on Trotsky's youth in Baruch Knei-Paz, *The Social and Political Thought of Leon Trotsky* (Oxford: Oxford University Press, 1978).; Isaac Deutscher, *The Prophet Armed* (New York: Vintage, 1963); and Edmund Wilson, *To the Finland Station* (New York: Doubleday, 1940).

11. George Novack, "Introduction" to Leon Trotsky, *Problems of Everyday Life and Other Writings on Culture and Science* (New York: Monad, 1973), p. 11.

12. All quotations from this essay can be found in Leon Trotsky, "Tolstoy: Poet and Rebel," in Siegel, ed., pp. 127–41.

13. That version is now in the process of unraveling through the impact of works such as Martin Bernall, *Black Athena* (New Brunswick, NJ: Rutgers University Press, 1989).

14. It would be hard to surpass Norman Geras's remarkable discussion of the young Trotsky's writings in "Literature of Revolution," in his collection, *Literature of Revolution: Essays on Marxism* (London: Verso, 1986), pp. 217–67.

15. Quotations from this essay can be found in Siegel, ed., pp. 143–7.

16. Knei-Paz, p. 462.

17. The second part of *Literature and Revolution* consists of Trotsky's essays penned between 1908 and 1914, yet to be translated into English. In this present essay, the first part is treated as a book in itself.

18. A fine study of Trotsky's views on the relation between art and ideology can be found in Cliff Slaughter, *Marxism, Ideology and Literature* (London: Macmillan, 1980), pp. 86–113.

19. Siegel, ed., pp. 30–31.

20. Ibid., p. 30.

21. Ibid.

22. Ibid., pp. 30–31.

23. Ibid., p. 31.

24. It appears in Siegel, ed., pp. 63–82.

25. Trotsky, *Literature and Revolution*, p. 9.

26. Ibid.

27. For the detailed discussion of Gramsci's concepts of optimism and pessimism, see Antonio Gramsci, *Selections from the Prison Notebooks* (New York: International, 1971), pp. 173–8.

28. Trotsky, *Literature and Revolution*, p. 12.

29. Siegel, ed., p. 130.

30. Trotsky, *Literature and Revolution*, p. 164.

31. Ibid., p. 14.

32. Ibid., p. 197.

33. Ibid., p. 218.

34. Ibid., p. 225.

35. Ibid., p. 230.

36. Ibid., p. 323

37. Siegel, ed., p. 114.

38. Ibid., p. 193.

39. Ibid., p. 201.

40. Ibid., pp. 55–6.

41. For studies of Trotsky's relations with surrealists, see Marguerite Bonnet, "Trotsky et Breton"

and Gérard Roche, "La rencontre de l'aigle et du lion," in *Cahiers Leon Trotsky* 25 (March 1986): 5–18 and 23–46. An analysis of Trotsky's associations with the *Partisan Review* group is central to Alan M. Wald, *The New York Intellectuals* (Chapel Hill: University of North Carolina Press, 1987).

42. Siegel, ed., p. 117.

43. A stimulating comparison of Trotsky to Walter Benjamin, from a slightly different perspective, can be found in Enzo Traverso, "Walter Benjamin et Léon Trotsky," *Quatrième Internationale* 37–8 (August-October 1990): 97–104.

44. For an influential work bridging literary theory and anthropology along these lines, see James Clifford, *The Predicament of Culture: Twentieth-Century Ethnography, Literature, and Art* (Cambridge, Mass.: Harvard University Press, 1988). Of course, one should not exaggerate Trotsky's tendency toward an emphasis on high culture to the point of ignoring his important writings contained in *Problems of Life* (1924), with chapters on vodka, the church, cinema, etc.

10

Literary "Leftism"

Reconsidered

I

A reconsideration of US left-wing literature of the 1930s, particularly its relation to the Communist Party, is now proceeding at a faster pace than at any
point since the tail end of the McCarthyite anti-radical witch-hunt of the 1950s.
At that time, Walter Rideout's *The Radical Novel in the United States, 1900–1954*
(1956) and Daniel Aaron's *Writers on the Left: Episodes in American Literary
Communism* (1961) broke with Red-baiting conspiracy theories of "Communist
infiltration of the arts"[1] to inaugurate a liberal paradigm for the study of the
literary radicalism that reached its apex in the 1930s.

Through the use of extensive primary sources (interviews, letters, unpublished manuscripts, and a wide reading in left-wing publications), the two scholars forged an influential view of the Left literary tradition of the 1930s and after
as a sincere but misguided effort boasting a few genuine but modest achievements. In the 1960s and 1970s, a flood of subsequent studies offered variant
interpretations – some more hostile to Red writers, but the majority more sympathetic – without displacing this dominant paradigm.

A qualitatively new and improved study of the epoch began in earnest with
the consolidation of feminism in the academy in the 1980s, which cast a fresh
eye on hitherto neglected pro-Communist writers such as Tillie Olsen, Meridel
Le Sueur, and Josephine Herbst. Next arose the now-famous "canon debates,"
challenging the way in which the regnant models of "literary excellence" came
to hold sway. At the present moment there are hopeful signs that a fresh
examination of left-wing writers of color may be under way.

In these same years of intense rethinking, an impressive number of new kinds
of reprints of 1930s novels, short fiction, reportage, and poetry were published
by the Feminist Press, Monthly Review, West End Press, and various university

---

This chapter originally appeared in *Science and Society*, 57, no. 2 (Summer 1993).

presses. The original staple of 1930s radical texts were by John Dos Passos, James T. Farrell, Mike Gold, Richard Wright, Granville Hicks, and John Steinbeck. The books appearing in the 1980s and early 1990s include Carlos Bulosan's *If You Want to Know What We Are* (1983), Fielding Burke's *Call Home the Heart* (1983), Josephine Johnson's *Now in November* (1985), Joseph Kalar's *Poet of Protest* (1985), Meridel Le Sueur's *I Hear Men Talking* (1984), Joseph Vogel's *Man's Courage* (1989), Mary Heaton Vorse's *The Rebel Pen* (1985), Clara Weatherwax's *Marching! Marching!* (1991), Albert Halper's *Union Square* (1991), Guy Endore's *Babouk* (1991), Mary Heaton Vorse's *Strike* (1992), and Ruth McKenney's *Industrial Valley* (1992). Well-selected anthologies such as Jack Salzman and Leo Zanderer's *Social Poetry of the Thirties* (1978) and Charlotte Nekola and Paula Rabinowitz's *Writing Red: An Anthology of American Women Writers, 1930–1940* (1987) have also expanded the availability of 1930s texts.

In the past three years, the new editions have been joined by a genuine renaissance of fresh critical studies applying the new methodologies that grew out of the 1960s, especially feminist literary theory and a more sophisticated Marxism. Among the most provocative of such works are Cary Nelson's *Repression and Recovery: Modern American Poetry and the Politics of Cultural Memory, 1910–1945* (1989), Paula Rabinowitz's *Labor and Desire: Women's Revolutionary Fiction in Depression America* (1991), and James Bloom's *Left Letters: The Culture Wars of Mike Gold and Joseph Freeman* (1992).

Now appears James F. Murphy's *The Proletarian Moment: The Controversy Over Leftism in Literature*, carrying a brief but unequivocal endorsement by Cary Nelson in a preface.[2] Its aim is to correct "one of the most glaring misinterpretations in the writing of recent American literary history" (p. 195). Surprisingly, the post-1960s concerns of gender, race, mass culture, and literary theory have no role in Murphy's correction. Instead, he focuses exclusively on the question of who actually led the campaign against and dealt the final blow to literary "leftism" within the cultural movement led by the US Communist Party (CP-USA). Was the struggle against vulgar, sectarian, and dogmatic versions of Marxist cultural theory and practice waged mainly by the writers around *Partisan Review* magazine, with the death blow coming as a result of the Popular Front turn in 1935? Or was the "leftism" trend repudiated by the cultural leadership of the CP-USA itself, prior to and independent of the new outlook ratified by the Seventh World Congress of the Comintern?

As Murphy documents, "leftism" was a significant phenomenon in Communist cultural circles in the USSR and Germany as well as the United States in the 1920s and early 1930s. While its exact meaning is uncertain, and the term was never embraced by those accused of practicing it, Murphy uses "leftism" to refer to critical views hostile to the entire bourgeois literary heritage, including modernism (that is, the self-conscious formal experiments of T. S. Eliot, James Joyce, et al.); more concerned with sociological labeling than with literary-specific "aesthetics"; and favoring immediate political impact over the subtleties of literary technique.

145

Murphy is in accord with most previous scholars such as Rideout and Aaron in his belief that such attitudes constituted a genuine source of contention in the cultural movement led by the CP-USA. What is unique is his argument that leftism was repudiated and defeated by party cultural officialdom in the United States *prior* to and independent of the shift to the Popular Front, which he claims was also the case with the defeat of "leftism" in the USSR and Germany.

Of course, the record shows that, in 1935, many of the organizations, publications, and literary assumptions of the early 1930s were replaced by a call for a democratic, anti-fascist literature, and a desire to mobilize the best-known writers toward this end. This switch has long stood as a watershed in theorizing the course of left-wing politics during the Depression decade in many arenas beyond mere cultural policy. But Murphy insists that the repudiation of leftism occurred earlier; it was a result of the CP-USA cultural leadership's embracing anti-"leftism" on its own as "the culmination of a long process that began with the Proletcult controversy in the Soviet Union in the early twenties" (p. 191).

In other words, Murphy holds that this struggle was between more sophisticated and less informed versions of Marxism, with the sophisticated version winning out as time went on, new experiences accrued, and additional texts by Marx and Engels came to light. Significantly, this was an internal evolution separate from the polemical efforts of the editors of *Partisan Review* magazine, which has been long regarded to be the chief antagonist of leftism in that era.[3] Even more surprising, Murphy insists that the official Communist Party orientation was not antagonistic to but actually in *support* of literary modernism: "In the *Daily Worker* and *New Masses* a favorable attitude toward modernism persisted to the end of the decade" (p. 147).

If Murphy is accurate, the idea that *Partisan Review* led a unique struggle in support of modernism and against leftism is a fabrication initiated by the *Partisan* editors themselves. He believes his view is a crucial corrective: "In numerous books and articles the criticism of leftism is described as a dissident position that first emerged in the original *Partisan Review*, and was directed against views that dominated the proletarian literature movement and were propagated by the *New Masses*. The first formulations of this interpretation can be found in articles written by members of the original *Partisan Review* staff" (p. 2). Murphy insists that the arguments of *Partisan Review* were then taken over wholesale and uncritically by all subsequent scholars for various "political" reasons.[4]

The most problematic feature of Murphy's book is that he has close to no evidence for the more sensational of his claims – that the CP-USA cultural leadership was open to modernism, and that all scholars prior to Murphy uncritically repeat *Partisan*'s self-aggrandizing history of the events. What the record more accurately shows is that some writers who employed modernist techniques were treated sympathetically by the CP-USA cultural leadership if they politically supported the USSR and the CP-USA's orientation. It would also be more accurate to say that many scholars (including myself) have seen the most effective critiques of "leftism" coming from the pages of the early *Partisan Review* – although it certainly does not follow that all have therefore viewed that journal as the first or sole voice against "leftism."

On the other hand, several of Murphy's underlying premises strike me as the indispensable foundation for all future work on the period; for example, Murphy is on solid ground when he remarks of debates about the specific nature and function of creative literature, and the relation between art and politics, literature and propaganda, and fiction and journalism, that "The arguments and positions formulated on these questions in the *New Masses* and other organs of the proletarian literature movement were by no means as simple and crude as has often been suggested, and deserve review for their own sake " (p. 3).

II

The difficulty for the reader of Murphy's book is to throw out the bath water while saving the baby. Unfortunately, in aiming his blast against those who have shown sympathy for *Partisan Review*'s version of the 1934–36 controversy, Murphy creates a simplistic amalgam of a wide range of scholars who couldn't possibly have similar motives, political or literary, and who disagree on substantive aspects of the "leftism" debate. This secret team of scholars and memoirists includes mutually antagonistic veterans of the decade such as Malcolm Cowley and Max Eastman; post-World War II liberals such as Aaron, Rideout, and Murray Kempton; 1960s radicals of different types such as James Gilbert, myself, and Lawrence Schwartz; and miscellaneous individuals who happened to have written an essay with a reference to the topic, such as Alvin Star and Jack Salzman. His villain in the field of scholarly studies of radical drama is Ira Levine, the author of a little-known dissertation, "Left-wing Dramatic Theory in the American Theatre" (1985), while the major books, such as Morgan Himmelstein's *Drama Was a Weapon* (1963) and Malcolm Goldstein's *The Political Stage* (1974), are never mentioned.

With such a wide range of names and texts at his disposal, Murphy is situated to combine decontextualized quotations to prove just about anything he wants. He shifts among names and manipulates sentence fragments to fabricate a consensus, a homogeneous "other," of incompetent and/or unscrupulous people who swallowed and then promoted the *Partisan* line. Regrettably, Murphy never summarizes on its own terms the work of a single one of these alleged apologists for *Partisan Review*, which could be accomplished in a page or two. Instead, each work, whether book-length, multi-volume, or a brief essay, is represented by a sentence, or sentence fragment, inserted in a highly constructed sequence of contexts. This makes for a tedious kind of formulaic reading. Every few pages Murphy informs us that, contrary to this or that scholar (the appropriate name can be chosen from his hit list), the opposite is allegedly the case. The problem for the targets of Murphy's assault is that it would be an incredible bore to recon-struct what each of these diverse figures was trying to do, and to then show how these efforts differ from the simplistic views that Murphy attributes to them. In other words, Murphy makes his case in such a way that, to try to set the record straight, one would have to go to such lengths of documentation that it would fill most of this journal and put even the most sympathetic readers to sleep!

Since Murphy allows no distinctiveness or subtlety to the views of those jammed together in a pro-*Partisan Review* gang, the arguments of many are never addressed, let alone refuted. All I can offer here is the generalization that most of these scholars made different kinds of claims, and the degree of merit varies. A review of their work according to the standards of scholarly "fair play" – which usually requires that one try to make a plausible case for an opponent's view prior to demolishing it – would result in a richer and more subtle grasp of past literary scholarship in this area.

My own view is that such careful critique would produce conclusions similar to what many younger scholars in the field of US radical history (such as Maurice Isserman, Mark Naison, Robin Kelley, and Paul Buhle) have argued in the 1980s and 1990s: US Communism was not free of political dependency on the Soviet Union, or of the normal institutional constraints that flow from hierarchy and bureaucracy; but Communist Party members and sympathizers chose this dependency out of certain convictions, and they appropriated the leadership's directives and orientations in ways demonstrating rank-and-file agency as well as a responsiveness to local conditions.

It is also my opinion that the phenomenon called "leftism" has sources in two areas. One source is over-simplified, mechanical Marxist thinking that appeared (and still appears) naturally in all radical movements, sometimes promoted by anti-intellectual, workerist elements but just as often by purist, college-educated zealots. The other source is the tendency of some officials in Party institutions to judge culture expediently, or functionally, in terms of wanting to treat politically sympathetic authors well, and help promote art that might assist current policy. As a result, resistance to "leftism" within the movement might be generated in various ways: possibly promoted by Communists of broader cultural sensibility, but also instigated by changes in policy that produce more or less flexibility in judging what kinds of culture assist the current political orientation.

The above analysis suggests that what we call "leftism" never really dis-appears from a radical movement; moreover, it plays various roles under differ-ent political circumstances. In fact, a study of CP-USA cultural policy covering more years than does Murphy's would reveal many similar conflicts between a desire for greater autonomy by writers and a demand to write more simply on the part of some Party functionaries and zealous rank-and-filers. A variant of "leftism" was clearly present in the attack on Albert Maltz in the post-Browder era, and cultural "leftism" was discussed again in the wake of the 1956 Khrushchev revelations. If one examines lesser-known debates in party cultural organs, one can see many familiar traits in disagreements around such matters as the treatment of Arthur Miller's *Death of a Salesman*, the reluctance by some Communist editors to publish Tom McGrath's poetry, and the assessment of anti-racism in post-World War II Hollywood films. Thus it is not surprising that Murphy can find patterns similar to the US controversy in debates in the USSR, Germany, and elsewhere.

However, Murphy confuses the matter unnecessarily by the way in which he too readily conflates the issue of specific pro-modernist sympathies into the other features of "leftism." If Murphy is correct – and I think he is – that most previous scholars failed to demonstrate the degree to which writers other than those linked to *Partisan Review* took up the cudgels against "leftism," it does not follow that actual sympathy for modernism as a school existed among the CP-USA cultural leadership. Opposing "leftism" and supporting modernism are hardly identical.

For example, Murphy presents as an instance of "leftism" a 1925 article in the *Daily Worker* by one Robin Dunbar dismissing all literature that is not explicitly Marxist-Leninist and that is not written by workers for workers (p. 58). He then shows how Joseph Freeman, in contrast, made an effort to "go beyond sociological analysis in literary criticism" (p. 62). Murphy also notes that Mike Gold, despite many vulgar statements against "bourgeois" literature and formalism, praised "the language of the intoxicated Emerson," the "clean, rugged Thoreau," and the "vast Whitman" (p. 68). This is fair evidence that the more extreme forms of "leftism" were rejected by leading writers for Party publications.

However, all his examples proving that the CP-USA cultural leadership held sympathy for modernism are much weaker. We are told that party journalist A. B. Magil in a *New Masses* article endorsed Anatole Lunacharsky's view that "even in the period of its decline the art of a dying class is still capable of making significant contributions in the field of form" (p. 80). Magil is also quoted as reporting that the 1931 Kharkov Conference "recognized the positive value of some of the experimental movements" (p. 80). We are also told that Granville Hicks praised John Dos Passos's *The Forty-Second Parallel* and *1919* for "creating new forms for the just representation of both the forces of life and the forces of death in our war-torn society" (p. 138).

But these and Murphy's other examples offer nothing comparable to the serious engagement with T. S. Eliot on the part of *Partisan Review* editor William Phillips, nor the evolving view of Philip Rahv and Phillips that the modernist revolution in literary sensibility was a counterpart of the Marxist-Leninist revolution in political sensibility.

Arguments that literature should be vivid, forged with craft, and so on are testimony to genuine literary concerns on the part of Party intellectuals. This degree of authentic literary sensibility should be acknowledged. At the same time, it should not be confused with a defense of modernism. If Murphy wants to make a convincing case that the CP cultural leadership was sympathetic to

literary modernism, as this is conventionally understood, he should have identified authoritative Communist Party cultural figures and reviewed their records
in detail. The most important of these would be V. J. Jerome (Isaac Jerome
Romaine, 1896–1965), who was placed in charge of cultural work in the 1930s.
But Jerome's name never even appears in the book.[5]

III

Dismay at Murphy's polemical overkill , and disagreement with his handling of the
modernist aspect of the "leftism" controversy, should not obscure the admirable
features of his study. Foremost is his view that one must base one's argument on the
documented record, not on *post facto* memoirs; the latter are primarily rationalizations of the "victors," who, in this society, I might add, have become victors more
through supporting than defying the ruling social order and its dominant culture.
Specifically, in the case of the battle over literary modernism, Murphy accurately
observes that the story of the victors has been that of the leading *Partisan Review*
editors, who have repeatedly referred back to struggles over leftism and modernism as justification for their tortured and unsavory political trajectory since World
War II.[6] All such claims about the past record should not be taken at face value but
treated with a healthy skepticism – a skepticism which is usually aimed 100 percent
only at the other side, the CP-USA's cultural leadership.

A second noteworthy feature of Murphy's method is his use of a comparative
dimension in studies of the literary Left. Despite national differences,
Communist literary movements existed in numerous countries, in many
instances producing debates that were roughly analogous. Thus Murphy
includes enlightening material on controversies about leftism in both the USSR
and Germany.[7] He also pays special attention to the possible influence on US
writers of authoritative statements from abroad, and the appearance of influential writings (for example, letters by Marx and Engels on literary questions)
in *International Literature*, a significant journal published in English in Moscow.

A third attractive feature of Murphy's method is his broadening out of the
frame of reference for considering the politics of literary disputes in a few new
areas. For example, when discussing reviews of controversial books he turns to
the literary page of the *Daily Worker* in addition to the more regularly consulted
New Masses and *Partisan Review*. He also augments discussions of problems in
poetry and fiction with a consideration of similar issues in drama, the genre that
was in many ways the dynamic center of Left culture in the 1930s.

The problem of an organized political movement's relation to culture has
come up repeatedly in the theory and practice of US radicalism – not only in
socialist movements, but in the women's movement, labor movement, and movements of people of color. If "leftism," as I see it, grows from a combination of
overzealous individuals and the exigencies of institutions trying to "lead" cultural

activities, then we can expect the reappearance of individuals and functionaries who insist that art must be aimed at reaching "the masses" (or, at least, their estimate of the consciousness of these allegedly homogeneous masses); who judge the quality of artistic creations primarily by the backgrounds (class, gender, race, ethnicity) of the artist; who disparage difficulty in form or subject matter as "elitist"; and who resort to knee-jerk political coding of artistic forms and subject.

Hence, the debate over leftism and modernism presents many lessons for cultural workers today. After reading Murphy's indictment of previous scholarship and his interpretation of the "leftism" controversy, my opinion remains that the revolutionary Marxist essays in *Partisan Review* between 1934 and 1938 (that is, specifically prior to Philip Rahv's 1939 "Proletarian Literature: A Political Autopsy," an outrageous caricature published in *Southern Review*) present some of the most powerful and thoughtful critiques of vulgar Marxist thinking in the arts. But Murphy, despite his regrettable polemical overkill, has demonstrated that there remains much more to be gleaned by reading widely, deeply, and carefully, and without conventional anticommunist preconceptions, into the literary legacy of our Red ancestors.

Notes

1 See Eugene Lyons's *The Red Decade* (New York: Bobbs-Merrill, 1941) for one of the most popular versions of this approach.

2 James F. Murphy, *The Proletarian Moment: The Controversy Over Leftism in Literature* (Urbana: University of Illinois Press, 1991).

3 *Partisan Review* was a US Marxist journal established in 1934 by Communists but which grew increasingly independent before relaunching itself in 1937 as a champion of both modernist sensibility and quasi-Trotskyist politics.

4 Some of these reasons he specifies precisely; for example, Murray Kempton (in *Part of Our Time*, 1955) and Walter Rideout allegedly wanted to aid the Cold War, while Malcolm Cowley (*Dream of the Golden Mountains*, 1964) wanted to "disown" his "radical past" (p. 2). Other scholars, for reasons that are never explained by Murphy, simply repeat "the *Partisan Review*'s version of the discussion over leftism" (p. 3). I don't believe that Murphy produces sufficient documentation to justify *any* of these charges about motivation.

5 This is hardly the only significant blunder. Key literary texts of the time such as E. A. Schachner's "Revolutionary Literature in the United States Today" (*Windsor Quarterly*, Spring 1934) are never mentioned; the political trajectory of Marxist critic Alan Calmer is misrepresented; and other political and literary episodes are ineptly described. These would be forgivable if Murphy, and Nelson in his foreword, were not so adamant in insisting that only Murphy has done his homework in the reading of left-wing publications.

6 After a fling with Trotskyism in the late 1930s, Phillips and Rahv progressively moved to a stance conciliatory to Cold War anticommunist liberalism in the late 1940s and 1950s. Then, in the 1960s, Rahv stunned his associates by returning to a kind of elitist Leninism before his death in 1973. Today, Phillips's views are hardly distinguishable from neo-conservatism.

7 However, Murphy states that the material summarized is not original: "This section [on Germany], as well as the one on the Soviet Union, is intended as background to the discussion in the United States, and does not claim to add anything new to research already done by others" (p. 17).

11

Cultural Cross-Dressing:

Radical Writers Represent

African-Americans and Latinos

in the McCarthy Era

I

In his 1945 sonnet, "The Negro's Tragedy," Claude McKay argues that

> Only a thorn-crowned Negro and no white
> Can penetrate into the Negro's ken,
> Or feel the thickness of the shroud of night
> which hides and buries him from other men . . . .
> There is no white man who could write my book,
> Though many think their story should be told
> Of what the Negro people ought to brook.[1]

Nevertheless, long before the post-World War II era, Euro-American left-wing writers regularly produced books on aspects of African Diaspora life. A veritable tradition of white radicals creating African-American protagonists to dramatize their views and concerns started in the early Depression with Scott Nearing's *Free Born* (1932), John Spivak's *Georgia Nigger* (1932), and Guy Endore's *Babouk* (1934). Similarly, V. J. Jerome and Sol Funaroff wrote poems in what they imagined was "Black dialect."[2]

In addition, leftists of those years unabashedly published empathetic novels about Native American Indians, including Robert Gessner's *Broken Arrow* (1933), and Howard Fast's *The Last Frontier* (1941). Gessner's work was dedicated "to the many white friends of the Indian who have fought to protect him from their own civilization."[3]

Most of these writers were Jewish-American and male, and usually pro-Communist at the time they published such works. One exception is Dorothy Myra Page, who was a Communist novelist but who was not Jewish; she fea-

---

This chapter was originally presented at the April 1992 national convention of the Society for Multiethnic Literature in the US at UCLA in Los Angeles, California.

tured several African-American characters centrally in *Gathering Storm: A Story of the Black Belt* (1932). Another is the best-selling mystery-romance writer Laura Caspary. Although she was Jewish, Caspary's novel of "passing," *The White Girl*, appeared in 1929, before the period of Communist Party membership that she describes in her autobiography, *The Secrets of Grown-Ups* (1979) and fictionalizes in her novel *The Rosecrest Cell* (1967).

Just before that, in 1925, Maxwell Bodenheim, also Jewish (he was born Bodenheimer) and also a Communist Party member in the 1930s, published *Ninth Avenue*.[4] This novel depicts a white woman's affair with Eric Starling, an African-American poet who "passes" and who considers himself an enemy of the Negritude movement of the 1920s. The blurb on the paperback reads: "He loved her too much to marry her – without telling her of his Negro blood."[5]

In the early 1940s, novels by white radicals featuring African-American characters tend to become less bound to conventional, 1930s radical plots of strikes, lynchings, and collective rebellions, such as those characterizing the works of Page, Endore, Spivak, and Nearing. John Sanford's *The People from Heaven* (1943), Bucklin Moon's *The Darker Brother* (1943), Benjamin Appel's *The Dark Stain* (1943), Howard Fast's *Freedom Road* (1944), and Henrietta Buckmaster's *Deep River* (1944) are typical of the trend.

However, the novel by Sanford, born Julian Shapiro, a Party member at the time, is aggresively militant. He depicts a Black woman, America Smith, raped by a white thug in upstate New York; she executes the man after the rest of the white community fails to bring him to justice. The title, *The People from Heaven*, is a bitterly ironic reference to whites, based on a letter where Christopher Columbus describes the way in which he and his fellow Europeans were first perceived by the indigenous peoples they would soon assault: "And the others went running from house to house and to the neighboring villages, with loud cries of 'Come! come to see the people from Heaven!'"[6]

Sanford's novel is among the high points of a trend that lasted well into the Cold War years, where it appears that radicals increasingly experimented with forms and styles, combined with varying degrees of stridency, to advance what may be regarded as a tradition of Euro-American left-wing writers culturally "cross-dressing." That is, while looking to people of color as symbols of resistance, radical whites created non-white characters as the major spokespersons to explain and dramatize the themes of counter-hegemonic culture. Aiming to reach as broad an audience as possible, many of these writers chose for the most part to produce realist-naturalist novels, and poetry that was decidedly non-modernist.

An example of the latter is Aaron Kramer's admirably lucid pamphlet-poem *Denmark Vesey* (1952), partly inspired by his reading of Herbert Aptheker's *American Negro Slave Revolts* (1943). According to a sympathetic reviewer in a left-wing publication, "You can read read it without a dictionary, rush through it as you would a thriller"[7] Jewish radical poets Martha Millet and Eve Merriam also contributed immediately comprehensible verse on the African-American struggle to Communist publications in the Cold War years.

A novel of love in the same anti-racist tradition is *The Well of Compassion* (1948) by David Alman, who would soon become secretary of the Committee to Secure Justice for Morton Sobell, co-defendant in the Rosenberg case. Previously Alman had written a sensational book, *The Hourglass* (1947), about a Southern Black woman raped by the leading white citizens of her town. *The Well of Compassion* is an anti-racist tale of an African-American male artist who marries a white woman. At the beginning of the book, Alman felt it necessary to insert: "I am a white man married to a white woman. I would have married this woman if she was the color of night."[8]

Perhaps the most prolific figure in this tradition of Jewish Reds creating rebellious Blacks as their spokespersons is Earl Conrad (born Earl Cohen), who shuttled between novelized biographies and biographical novels of African-Americans. In 1942 he published *Harriet Tubman: Negro Soldier and Abolitionist* under the imprint of the Communist Party publishing house, International Publishers, and in 1943 a full-length biography of Tubman.[9] In 1947 he published *Jim Crow America*, a "report on the real life of the Negro American."[10] This had its Southern counterpart in *Southern Exposure* (1946), by Stetson Kennedy, who was also white and Red. (Kennedy fled from Florida to Eastern Europe during the Cold War, although he returned disillusioned with Soviet Communism.)

In 1950, Conrad co-authored *Scottsboro Boy* with Haywood Patterson (one of the frame-up victims in the notorious case). This was followed by two novels of African-American life, *Rock Bottom* (1952), about Leeha Whitfield's journey from Mississippi to Harlem, and *Gulf Stream North* (1954), about African-American fishermen.

Among the most original contributions to this tradition was *The Big Boxcar* (1956), by the Southern independent radical Alfred Maund. Here the format of the *Canterbury Tales* is refunctioned into stories of racial oppression told by a group of African-Americans who have sneaked into a boxcar traveling across the South.

However, the most striking development in cultural cross-dressing by radicals during the Cold War era may have been the production of texts about Latino struggles. The most famous is the script of *Salt of the Earth* (1954), produced by blacklisted Hollywood radicals Michael Wilson, Herbert Biberman, and Paul Jarrico (all three Red, the last two Jewish). Two other blacklistees, however, made equally unusual contributions.

Philip Stevenson – a novelist in the 1920s, playwright in the 1930s, and screenwriter in the 1940s – wrote a four-volume series of novels about mid-1930s Chicano/Mexicano miners struggles in the Southwest. Due to Stevenson's blacklisting after refusing to name names in 1951, all four were published under the pseudonym "Lars Lawrence": *Morning, Noon and Night* (1954), *Out of the Dust* (1956), *Old Father Antic* (1961), and *The Hoax* (1961). Collectively he called these "The Seed"; Stevenson was on the verge of completing yet another volume when he died on a trip to the Soviet Union. Stevenson's books were mostly ignored by the popular press, but their merits were debated in the Communist literary publication, *Masses & Mainstream*.

In the same period Gordon Kahn, a blacklisted Hollywood screenwriter who evaded his subpoena by fleeing to Mexico, drafted the manuscript of a novel he called "A Long Way from Home" about a Chicano draft resister during the Korean War. Kahn was Jewish and Red; although he had written screenplays for famous films such as *All Quiet on the Western Front* and *The African Queen*, he was forced to earn money during the Cold War by selling articles to *Holiday*, *Playboy*, and elsewhere under the name "Hugh C. Gloster." *A Long Way from Home* was published posthumously by Bilingual Press in 1989, a leading Chicano publishing house, which issued it in its series of "Chicano Classics."

It is also noteworthy that, in the Cold War years, left-wing Latino writing by Latinos was advanced by the publication of sections of Jesus Colon's *A Puerto Rican in New York* (1961) in the *Daily Worker*. Moreover, *The Memoirs of Bernardo Vega*, about the Puerto Rican Community in New York, was written in the 1940s (although not published in Spanish until 1977 and in English until 1984), and in the late 1950s former *Daily Worker* film critic José Yglesias was preparing *A Wake in Ybor City* for its 1963 publication. Another Latino, the poet Alvaro Cardona-Hine, contributed poetry to *Masses & Mainstream* during the 1950s.

II

Contemporary argumentation about speaking for the "other," often suggesting the virtual impossibility of ever doing so, was expressed in a memorable manner a few years ago by Gayatri Chakravorty Spivak's "Can the Subaltern Speak?"[11] More recently, the question of whether whites should "retreat" from such efforts has been considered in a rigorous and provocative way by Linda Alcoff's essay, "The Problem of Speaking for Others,"[12] in a recent issue of *Cultural Critique*.

Of course, the decision of many white radical writers in the Cold War era to create a resistance culture by depicting the struggles of people of color is an established fact; there is no way now, forty years later, that they can in any meaningful way "retreat," although a few may wish they had done so if they were around to hear some of the contemporary debates. On the other hand, present day cultural critics may not be the first ever to try to come to grips with the problem of representing subaltern groups and "speaking for"; perhaps a closer look at the practice of the 1950s will reveal some partial anticipations of contemporary attitudes, not to mention a few insights we have yet to consider in our own day.

The cultural cross-dressing of radical writers I have so far examined raises issues also seen in some of the theoretical work in studies of gender cross-dressing. In gender cross-dressing, it has been argued by Marjorie Garber's *Vested*

Interests: Cross-Dressing and Cultural Anxiety (1992) and elsewhere, a person biolog-
ically of one sex appears in public in the guise of another. In this creation of a
"third" category lies the potential of breaking the deadlock of binarism, of indi-
cating the constructed nature of gender categories, and of generally calling into
question simplistic identities based on myths of gender. Beyond this, the cross-
dresser has the potential of assuming new kinds of power, as in the case of a
woman who dresses like a man and thereby attains access to male space.

From this vantage point, the experience of white radicals representing people
of color under Cold War pressure reveals a varying range of strategies and
degrees of consciousness. Surprisingly, there are cases where the category of
"authenticity," so central in recent debates about representation and theories of
alternative canon-formation, is conceptualized in ways dramatically different
than that of directly recreating the concrete experience of subaltern subjectiv-
ities and their environments.

For example, poet Aaron Kramer's primary concern after reading the story of
Denmark Vesey's revolt in Herbert Aptheker's study was a desire for a literary
form – one with which he felt comfortable – to communicate his feelings to a
broad audience of receptive progressives. Thus he created "an ambitious narrative work, a dramatic ballad." When I asked Kramer what impelled him to
choose Vesey as his subject during the Cold War, he responded that it was his
long-standing identification with the African-American political struggle, which
could be traced in almost every one of his books from *The Alarm Clock* (1938) on,
and even further back in a poem on the Scottsboro case in 1933, written when
Kramer was barely twelve. That identification peaked with his intensive involvement in the short-lived journal *Harlem Quarterly* around the outset of the
McCarthy repression. In those years he was an active member of the Harlem
Writers' Group, working almost as much in Harlem as at home for a year or two.

In addition, Kramer felt impelled to focus on the Vesey rebellion as his theme
because of the post-war climate and the anti-radical witch-hunt. He observed
that the *National Guardian*'s decision to feature sections of *Vesey* at that time makes
it "clear that the editors and their readers understood what I was really talking
about when I used an episode from history." Waldemar Hille, a radical composer, leaped at the chance to set the poem as an oratorio, and he started
working on it as soon as the book was "unveiled" at a huge series of LA celebra-
tions during Kramer's 1952 visit. According to Kramer, "[Hille's] choruses and
audiences also understood utterly that my poem was as much about 1952 as
about 1822. The response was immense." The sections of the poem that
aroused such audiences the most included "Vesey Speaks to the Congregation,"
"A Meeting at Vesey's," and "The Sentence is Announced." The last-men-
tioned was performed at West Coast meetings for Ethel and Julius Rosenberg,
who were appealing their death sentences for alleged espionage. "Every word
in the entire book, and the private printing of the book itself, was an act of defiance," Kramer recalls. "That year I was on fire."

When asked about "authenticity" in regard to his depiction of African-American rebels, Kramer responded that he "never for a moment considered the use of dialect. Neither photographic nor audio realism was among my aims, nor did I try for detailed historical accuracy."

Vesey and his rebellion were for Kramer "symbols of a heroism in the face of repression and annihilation, symbols too of a resistance tyranny could not crush." He recalled that he would not have considered "localizing into dialect and other details a grandeur huge and universal, which I had long been training myself to present with my own music, imagination, and language." Kramer additionally pointed out that in his many public readings of Black poets, with Langston Hughes and others, "I have always avoided choosing poems in dialect; trying to 'act Black' on a stage or on radio simply goes against my grain. . . . It just strikes me as unseemly."[13]

A recording of the 1954 performance of Kramer's *Vesey* in Los Angeles at the First Unitarian church, following the Rosenberg execution, is available.[14] Listening to it in the 1990s, one might conjecture as to whether Kramer's Vesey creates a "third." The majority of his audience would certainly have known Kramer as Jewish-American, and they would learn Vesey's identity as African-American quickly from the way the poem commences with the slave trade. But local detail of language and personality are subordinated to forging a bond of common interests between resisters of 1950s McCarthyism and rebels against the nineteenth-century slavocracy. The European oratorio form (that is, chorus, orchestra, and soloists, and a libretto of sacred character without stage action), which composer Hille episodically blends with African rhythms and spirituals, reinforces the theme of an idealized multicultural blending of art forms in the service of universal human emancipation. If Kramer in some way creates a "third," his Vesey is not a deconstruction or destabilization of "racial" types in the post-structuralist sense, but rather the extraction of a common element of resistance behavior to be potentially shared by all, regardless of the superficial trappings of "race."

The strategy, in fact, is tantamount to a partial "retreat." In other words, through form and style, Kramer makes it clear that he has no desire to "speak for" Vesey or African-Americans; rather, events of Vesey's life and struggle have inspired him, Kramer, to a solemn and respectful recreation in the forms that Kramer himself knows best and that he felt could be used to affect his audience.[15]

III

A radically different approach is suggested by the work of Gordon Kahn, who seems to be primarily drawn to the ironies and idiocies (although they are dangerous idiocies) of racial discourse in his truly extraordinary novel *A Long*

Way from Home. The text, written in Mexico but intended for a commercial publication in the United States that never came, is 455–pages long in very small print and admits no easy summary. To my knowledge, a more relentless interrogation of racial ideology by a Euro-American has never appeared. It would be hard for even the most contemporary text to outdo Kahn's scenes on the border between Mexico and Texas, where the Chicano protagonist Gilberto Reyes engages in a battle of wits with one Fred Bishop, the white man who allegedly knows more about Mexicans and Chicanos than they know about themselves.

Bishop went to Mexico City College; he's married to a Mexican; and he carefully states that any generalizations to be offered are not about "all" but just about "certain Mexicans." Yet, despite his good will and desire to be Gilberto's buddy, he inevitably makes statements that drive Gilberto into a rage. It seems likely that Kahn introduced Bishop partly as a stand-in for himself – to self-reflexively remind the reader that the auctorial hand that appears so confidently to unravel the enigma of Chicano identity is not itself infallible. In a memorable sequence, Bishop constructs for Gilberto a vision of the way Mexicans allegedly relate to machines. Then Gilberto boards a bus and watches the actions of the bus driver whose behavior proceeds to contradict Bishop's image, not by violating every prediction but by showing that the situation is far more complex than Bishop's short-hand stereotypes.

Kahn's Gilberto is sufficiently realized and autonomous to make this convincingly the story of "one white Mexican who turned brown and was giving them all the finger."[16] Like *Salt of the Earth* and Stevenson's "The Seed," Kahn's work is bilingual and multicultural. Like the Puerto Rican Piri Thomas's *Down These Mean Streets* (1967), Kahn presents Latino identity as a shifting category, to be reformed through critical consciousness combined with praxis. Kahn seems to be fostering as well a kind of Fanonian view of nationalism that must be autonomously reclaimed as a prerequisite to participation in an internationalist context.

In a contribution to the *Dictionary of Literary Biography* on "Literature Chicanesca,"[17] Antonio Marquez uses that term for literary works about Chicanos written by non-Chicanos. Marquez endorses the view that all such literature, including John Nichols's much-admired *The Milagro Beanfield War* (1974), is limited by a perspective "from the outside looking in."

In a response to Marquez, Juan Bruce-Novoa suggests that, in fact, Nichols's work might alternately go into a a separate category of "almost-almosts" (Bruce-Novoa is being sarcastic here) "for those authors who cannot pass the blood test, but whose writings are culturally and ethnically Chicano."[18] *A Long Way from Home*, as well, might be considered as a text similar to that of Nichols. Clearly this is suggested by its publication by Bilingual Press as a "Chicano Classic," and the arguments of the Introduction to the edition by Santiago Daydi-Tolson.

IV

It may be true that the position of being "outside" a culture can never be transcended. However, all outside positions are not the same. As Linda Alcoff observes in "The Problem of Speaking for Others," positions might be seen as "multiple with varying degrees of mobility." Kramer and Kahn seem to me to provide two variants of a self-awareness of one's outside position.

Kramer refuses from the outset to declare himself "Black" or to make any gesture toward the illusory pose of self-abnegaton for which Spivak, in "Can the Subaltern Speak?", criticizes Foucault and Deleuze. Kramer makes a partial retreat from "speaking for" by eschewing "dialect" (local speech) and by introducing the oratorio approach. The "third" that is created – Kramer's slave-rebel Vesey – is publicly acknowledged to be neither the authentic African-American nor a mere persona for the radical Jewish poet. Vesey is a kind of hybrid creation, a utopic image of a blended racial/cultural unity in the sphere of political solidarity.

Of course, the predominance in Kramer and Hille's work of European cultural tropes and references, and the imaginative depiction of African-American experience in these terms, renders this effort suspect. This is the case with virually all attempts at universals and cosmopolitanisms, which are so often only masks for Eurocentrism, although it is important to note that Kramer does characterize the New World conquest as an "unholy genesis."[19] Still, even if naive by the standards of the 1990s, Kramer's approach at least has the virtue of refusing a pretense of "black authenticity"; "Denmark Vesey" is an effort, however flawed, to speak "about," rather than "for."[20]

Kahn, in contrast, *does* aim for authenticity in language, running the greater risk of arrogant domination, of unacknowledged cultural imperialism. Yet, he is partly rescued through his dialogic structure: Gilberto is the center of consciousness, but flanked North and South by two older, persecuted Jews, who also suggest elements of Kahn's perspective and thereby further complicate our sense of auctorial intervention. Moreover, Gilberto is problematically engaged by a wide range of Anglo and Mexicano characters. As a result, the reader is given surprisingly concrete analyses of the particular power relations of the characters, and is alert to the limitations of the author's "outsider" status. Perhaps because Kahn first mastered the language and familiarized himself with the culture of Mexico, his strategy seems closer to "listening to" or "speaking with," rather than "speaking for," even if the last cannot be totally avoided.

In sum, Kramer and Kahn in different ways engage strategies designed to, hopefully, minimize the misrepresentation of the racial other; they seem aware of the discursive dangers of "outside" positions they cannot escape. Thus, following Alcoff's distinctions, while their outside locations "bear" on the meanings of the texts, the locations do not mechanically "determine" the meanings.

If these judgments are fair, then what may partly account for the accomplishments of Kramer and Kahn is the peculiar "moment" of the witch-hunt era in which leftists who did not bail out through naming names and bathetic confessions found their ability to pursue their literary careers as widely as possible, even as whites, blocked – blocked by a stigma. This stigma, vastly intensified from what it was in the 1930s and 1940s, was their being targeted for demonization and for unofficial as well as official blacklisting through the ideology of "anticommunism," which in the form characteristic of the McCarthy era has marked similarities to racism, anti-Semitism, and homophobia.

While no artist can ever be free of the possibility of "using" the racial other for neurotic gratification, the basis may have been here in 1950s resistance literature for cross-cultural relationships founded more on common feelings about the reigning US social order than ever before. Kramer, as a Jewish Red,[21] felt the impending doom of the Rosenbergs in ways that impelled him to invoke the story of Denmark Vesey with its "informer theme." Similarly, Kahn's escape to Mexico to evade a subpoena to "name names" may have struck him as analogous to the situation of a Chicano fleeing across the border to escape a summons to extend US hegemony in Korea.

Anti-racist white cultural and political rebels of the 1990s may lack perfect models in the Euro-American Old Left. But in the 1950s tradition of anti-McCarthyite cultural resistance, we may have some honorable ancestors.

Notes

1. Claude McKay, "The Negro's Tragedy," *Selected Poems of Claude McKay* (New York: Harcourt, Brace and World, 1953), p. 50.

2. See V. J. Jerome, "A Negro Mother to Her Child," *Daily Worker,* Nov. 15 1930, p. 4; Sol Funaroff, "Negro Songs," *Exile from a Future Time* (New York: Dynamo, 1943), pp. 1–23.

3. Dedication, Robert Gessner, *Broken Arrow* (New York: Farrar and Rinehart, 1933).

4. Many more titles could be cited, depending on how widely one cast one's net. For example, in drama, Eugene O'Neill, who had a flirtation with the Left in the World War I period, wrote *The Emperor Jones* (1920) and *All God's Chillun Got Wings* (1924), both starring Paul Robeson.

5. Cover, Maxwell Bodenheim, *Ninth Avenue* (New York: Avon Paperback Reprint, 1951).

6. Quoted on the title page of John Sanford, *The People from Heaven* (New York: Harcourt, Brace and Company, 1943).

7. J. S. W., "Our Hope Has Saucy Wings," *New Frontier* (Toronto), courtesy of Aaron Kramer.

8. Dedication to *The Well of Compassion* (New York: Simon and Schuster, 1948).

9. Earl Conrad, *Harriet Tubman* (Washington, DC: Associated Publishers, 1943).

10. From the jacket of *Jim Crow America* (New York: Duell, Sloan and Pearce, 1947).

11. In Cary Nelson and Lawrence Grossman, eds, *Marxism and the Interpretation of Cultures* (Urbana: University of Illinois, 1988), pp. 271–313.

12. *Cultural Critique* 20 (Winter 1991–92): 5–32.

13. Letter from Kramer to Author, Feb. 20, 1992.

14. Copy in possession of Aaron Kramer.

15. Nevertheless, I don't mean to discount the degree of accuracy in Kramer's poem, nor his efforts to collaborate where possible with African-Americans in its creation and performance. In a letter of Feb. 4, 1994, Kramer told me that he submitted a draft of the poem to the African-American actor Frank Silvera, and published only after receiving Silvera's enthusiastic comments. Moreover, after publication the poem was praised by Langston Hughes and John Lofton for its

representation of history, and Kramer was invited by the editors of *Dictionary of American Negro Biography* to contribute the entry on Vesey.

16. Gordon Kahn, *A Long Way from Home* (Tempe, Ariz.: Bilingual Press, 1989), p. 417.

17. Volume 82.

18. Juan Bruce-Novoa, "Canonical and Non-Canonical Texts," *The Americas Review* 14, nos. 3–4 (Fall-Winter 1986): 127–8.

19. Aaron Kramer, *Denmark Vesey and Other Poems* (New York [no publisher credited]: 1952), p. 5.

20. At that same time, Kramer welcomed African-American collaboration and participation in performances. In a letter to me of Feb. 4, 1994, Kramer recalls that "most of the soloists and half of the choir in each performance were African-Americans . . . . the Charleston audience of African-Americans who sat in Vesey's very church were (according to Roby Cornwall) profoundly moved by the recording of *Vesey*. The work, it might be pointed out, ends with a blues poem. Blues is a form Langston Hughes taught me to love as a child, and I often used it – into the mid-'60's, with 'Blues for Medgar Evers' and 'St Nicholas Avenue Blues' (an elegy for Hughes) – both published in *Freedomways*."

21. "Jewish Red" is my own designation, not Kramer's, meant honorifically, and referring to committed radicals – for example, "Red Emma" Goldman, the anarchist – not just people in the Communist movement. Naturally, in the 1950s "Red" was an epithet hurled at marchers in May Day parades, usually accompanied by hurled projectiles such as bottles and rocks. Kramer would have defined himself as a people's poet and internationalist.

12

The Utopian Imagination

Michael Löwy, ed., *Marxism in Latin America from 1909 to the Present*. Atlantic Highlands, NJ: Humanities Press, 1992. 296 + lxix pp.

Michael Löwy, *On Changing the World: Essays in Political Philosophy, from Karl Marx to Walter Benjamin*. Atlantic Highlands, NJ: Humanities Press, 1993. 189 pp.

Michael Löwy, *Redemption and Utopia: Jewish Libertarian Thought in Central Europe. A Study in Elective Affinity*. Stanford, Calif.: Stanford University Press, 1992. 276 pp.

The appearance in English of three new books by the Brazilian-born Marxist Michael Löwy may at long last consolidate his reputation in the United States as one of the most eloquent, erudite and creative voices of our time on behalf of emancipatory socialism. Until now, the extraordinary breadth of his *œuvre*, combined with its only partial translation into English, has imparted an elusive quality to Löwy's writings as they have become available to US readers, despite his high rate of productivity and the international acclaim accorded to his work on the theory of the "national question" and on the philosophy of the young Georg Lukács.

First known among scholars and activists in the Latin American solidarity movement in the United States for his sophisticated Trotskyist appreciation of *The Marxism of Che Guevara* (New York: Monthly Review Press, 1973), Löwy had earlier completed a doctoral dissertation on the revolutionary theory of the young Karl Marx. This work, still untranslated but published in French as *La théorie de la révolution chez le jeune Marx* (Paris: Maspero, 1970), anticipated in its focus the first two volumes of Hal Draper's *Karl Marx's Theory of Revolution* published by Monthly Review Press in 1977 and 1978.

After establishing himself in philosophical and sociological circles with his monumental book *Georg Lukács: From Romanticism to Bolshevism* (London: New Left Books, 1981), Löwy appeared to shift gears with a compelling defense of

---

This chapter is to appear in *Against the Current*, forthcoming (1994).

Trotsky's Theory of Permanent Revolution, *The Politics of Combined and Uneven Development* (London: Verso, 1981). Meanwhile, he steadily produced essays translated into English on Lenin's philosophy, romantic anti-capitalism, Walter Benjamin, Rosa Luxemburg, Max Weber, Herbert Marcuse, Antonio Gramsci, and religion in a range of international publications, including *New German Critique*, *New Left Review*, *Telos*, *Monthly Review*, *Against the Current*, and *International Marxist Review*.

Those fluent in French may have been aware of his *Festschrift* co-edited with Sami Naïr honoring his teacher, Lucien Goldmann, *Goldmann* (Paris: Éditions Seghers, 1973); his book on the sociology of knowledge, *Paysages de la verité* (Paris: Anthropos 1985); and his recent study of romantic anti-capitalism co-authored with Robert Sayre, *Révolte et mélancholie* (Paris: Payot, 1992). Löwy's favorable assessment of Liberation Theology, an example of which appears in *Marxism and Liberation Theology* (Amsterdam: Notebooks for Study and Research No. 10, 1989), earned him a satiric fictional portrait as Father Rossi in Tariq Ali's novel *Redemption* (Harmondsworth: Penguin, 1990).

Löwy's three latest publications will demonstrate to US readers the cohesion and coherency that actually lie at the core of his achievement.[1] However, it may also be helpful to consider several of the factors accounting for the range and diversity in Löwy's work. First is Löwy's unique origin – born in São Paulo in 1938 of Jewish refugees from Austria who had earlier traveled to the USSR in search of work during the Depression. Radicalized in his high school years in the 1950s and politically influenced by a local follower of Max Shachtman (a founder of US Trotskyism and leader of a dissident current after 1940), Löwy made a pilgrimage from Brazil to Paris to study with Lucien Goldmann, a former student of Lukács and among the foremost Marxists of his generation. Then followed five years of teaching in places such as Israel and England before settling in France with a position at the University of Paris VIII and finally as Research Director in Sociology at the Centre National de la Recherche Scientifique in Paris.

Second is Löwy's unfashionable political stance, which has sustained him for thirty-five years as a militant in various revolutionary socialist organizations. Steeped in the revolutionary traditions of Latin America as well as Europe, Löwy is a much too genuinely unorthodox thinker to join the herd of "unorthodox Marxists" coalescing in the universities since the decline of radicalism in the 1980s. It is true that Löwy's classical Marxist and Leninist stance is somewhat apart from the canonical versions of Bolshevism with which we are familiar in the United States; Löwy prefers the young Lukács to Plekhanov, is skeptical of any parallel between a dialectics of social development and a "dialectics of nature" (although he otherwise admires Engels), participates in international surrealist circles, and treats Liberation Theology with a seriousness that causes him to rethink and challenge what have sometimes passed as Marxist and Leninist pieties about the irreconcilable politics allegedly flowing from philosophical materialism and idealism.

At the same time, Löwy stands apart from the familiar, garden-variety type of "heretical Marxist" in the United States who ritualistically arrives at the "brilliant" discovery that "Leninism leads to Stalinism," insists that party commitment precludes individualism, and conceives of his or her role as primarily excoriating those of us in the activist/organized Left for failing to see all the subtleties and complexities noted from an armchair observation post. In other words, Löwy's unorthodoxy, like Rosa Luxemburg's, is a genuine expression of revolutionary praxis – not just another excuse for sideline criticism or academic careerism.

This may help account for a third reason why a substantial US audience may have had past difficulty in gaining a perspective on Löwy's achievement. Unlike his more familiar leading contemporaries who have likewise produced brilliant contributions to Marxist culture – Fredric Jameson and Perry Anderson, to name two for whom I have the highest regard – Löwy is equally at home whether he is writing philosophical, historical, and sociological analysis for scholarly contemplation, or meticulous programmatic critique and exegesis for immediate, practical implementation. A book such as *The Politics of Combined and Uneven Development*, or, to take another example, his stunning sixty-five page "Introduction" to *Marxism in Latin America*, bears the unmistakable marks of decades of first-hand political experience, in which the theoretical questions *really matter* because the well-being and maybe even the lives of struggling individuals are at stake.

Factors such as these have probably caused Löwy's achievement to "fall between the cracks" of conventional disciplinary and other classificatory categories. Only a few activist-scholars in the United States, such as Manning Marable, even make gestures toward crossing such borders. No doubt many of Löwy's political associates immersed in day-to-day struggles are less cognizant of his philosophical and sociological contributions, while his intellectual admirers fail to respond to the political Löwy. Yet the unique component of his achievement lies precisely in the integration of these two halves; each nourishes the other, and the totality of his work can only be grasped in the intimate interaction of theory and practice, the unity of philosophical subject and political object.

One could hardly hope for a more useful introduction to the evolution of Löwy's intellectual achievement than *On Changing the World*. This third volume in the Humanities Press series "Revolutionary Studies," edited by the Trotskyist historian and activist Paul Le Blanc, will enormously aid students of Marxist theory through its assemblage and reprinting of fourteen of Löwy's most stimulating essays on European and Latin American political culture. An incisive Preface by Löwy situates these texts within the broader debates over the meaning of socialism.

His definition of socialism is, first of all, in the classical vein – "a society where the associated producers are the masters of the process of production" (p. ix). But it is also a definition clearly differentiated from Maoist and Stalinist authoritarianism – "democratic rights – freedom of expression and organization, universal suffrage, political pluralism – are not 'bourgeois institutions' but hard-won conquests of the labor movement" (p. ix). Most significantly, perhaps, for debates of the current moment, Löwy radically differentiates his project from that of the proponents of market socialism. He argues that the failure of Soviet and other post-capitalist societies was not a consequence of unrealistic aims on the part of their leading parties, but, rather, because their "break with the productivist pattern of industrial capitalism and with the foundations of modern bourgeois civilization was not sufficiently radical" (p. xi).

Thus the tradition that Löwy upholds within Marxist thought is in sharp distinction to those theorists from Plekhanov to Althusser who are actually rooted in the eighteenth-century "ideology of progress." In Löwy's view, they erroneously regard the socialist project as simply removing "the relations of production that are an obstacle for the free development of the productive forces" and follow "the bourgeois/positivist model, based on the arbitrary extension to the historical sphere of the epistemological paradigm of the natural sciences, with its 'laws,' its determinism, its purely objective 'prediction,' its linear evolutionism" (p. xi). In contrast, Löwy takes his stand on behalf of "utopia," which implies "a new way of producing and living, with productive forces of a qualitatively different nature" (p. xi). This, he believes, is the main content of a Marxism based upon "the philosophy of praxis and the dialectical/materialist method . . . the analysis of commodity fetishism and of capitalist alienation...the perspective of workers' revolutionary self-emancipation" (p. xii).

The fourteen essays that follow the Preface recapitulate Löwy's journey to his present position, the stages by which he has enlarged upon (*not* recanted or repudiated) the original vision of Marxism held at the time he published his book on Lukács. The most significant component in this process of enrichment is Löwy's reassessment of romanticism, which he defines as "the protest against industrial/bourgeois civilization in the name of precapitalist values" (p. xiii). Dramatically, he rejects his earlier treatment of romanticism as antithetical to Marxism, now embracing romanticism as a "hidden moment" within Marxism that must be regarded in the "forefront" of the contributions of theorists discussed in this essay collection – Marx, Engels, Lenin, Rosa Luxemburg, Lukács, Gramsci, Marcuse, and Benjamin.

His masterful survey, "Marxism and Revolutionary Romanticism," is obviously a key text in this evolution. Here he establishes a far broader understanding of romanticism as a world outlook than the more familiar simplifications of romanticism as merely as nostalgia for feudalism. In an erudite review of scholarship and the ideas of influential romantic thinkers, Löwy further specifies, and personally identifies with, a sub-trend of "revolutionary romanticism"; this means a renaissance of precapitalist elements of social existence "worth conserving" (the phrase is from Martin Buber in reference to the Jewish-

German libertarian socialist Gustav Landauer). In one of Löwy's most creative moves, he maps the terrain of possible evolutions from the romantic matrix to alternative outcomes such as "Past-oriented or Retrograde Romanticism," "Conservative Romanticism," and "Disenchanted Romanticism" (p. 2–3).

It is not possible to fairly summarize and describe even a small portion of the complex and stimulating ways in which this argument is developed throughout the rest of the volume. What is clear is that Löwy's studies of the Utopian Vision, Liberation Theology, Lenin's "April Theses," Luxemburg, Gramsci, and Lukács, the French Revolution, and the four essays mainly about Walter Benjamin are consistent – and persuasive – in their elaboration of the "hidden moment" within Marxism. The argumentation culminates memorably in his link between the prophetic images and allegories of Benjamin, and the emergence of the two late twentieth-century social movements of ecology and anti-nuclear pacifism. Löwy is entirely sympathetic to the view, inspired by Benjamin, that "the revolution is not 'progress,' improving the established order . . . . It is a 'messianic' interruption of the course of history . . . the emergency brake that brings to a stop the headlong rush of the train toward the abyss" (p. 22).

Marxism in Latin America from 1909 to the Present is a signal contribution to the understanding of the lessons to be learned from a century of struggle against US imperialism "in our backyard." Divided into four major sections ("The Introduction of Marxism to Latin America," "The Revolutionary Period," "Stalinist Hegemony," and "The New Revolutionary Period"), the volume embraces close to fifty different contributors (some appear more than once, such as Luis Emilio Recabarren, Julio Antonio Mella, José Carlos Mariátegui, Vincente Lombardo Toledano, Fidel Castro, and Ernesto Che Guevara). Although no single compilation can claim to be comprehensive or definitive, Löwy has achieved a major breakthrough by bringing together a combination of key political documents, influential manifestos and speeches, representative "positions" of a variety of organizations, and trenchant critiques from revolutionary Marxist (especially Trotskyist, Sandinista, and Brazilian Workers' Party) perspectives.

Redemption and Utopia is in large part the culmination and application of many strands of thought found in *On Changing the World*. Here Löwy extends the "elective affinities" he finds between revolutionary utopian politics and heretical forms of religion, originally noted in Liberation Theology but now discovered as well in Jewish-German messianic culture. Nine incisive chapters pursue this theme in the lives and work of over a dozen figures, including many Löwy has not previously explored such as Martin Buber, Franz Rosenzweig, Gershom Scholem, Leo Löwenthal, Franz Kafka, Erich Fromm, and Bernard Lazare.

These three books provide an opportunity for a reassessment of Löwy's scholarship of the period following the publication of his book on Lukács. He is now in an enviable position to step back and map out his direction for the 1990s and beyond. Some weaknesses and limitations of his work so far – problems shared by many others of us – may now be rectified. One is the systematic neglect of feminist issues and a feminist method in these studies. Here, the remedy will not be just a matter of "adding on" a female to his list of case studies. He already did this by including a sole essay on Rosa Luxemburg alongside the thirteen others on men in *On Changing the World*, and he might possibly have done something similar by stretching his definitional borders a bit to include Hannah Arendt, Rachel Varnhagen, or Simone Weil along with those central European Jewish males in whom he has perceived an "elective affinity" in *Redemption and Utopia*.

Instead, the rectification must come through reformulating basic issues around women's concerns. This would be consistent with his remark on page 19 of *On Changing the World*, where he calls for "the integration of feminism as an essential and permanent dimension of the Marxist program." Such an effort would undoubtedly expand the cultural breadth of his politico-intellectual project.

Moreover, while Löwy's work by far transcends the narrow Eurocentrism of most Marxism produced in Western Europe, due in part to his multi-continental origins and participation in the international socialist movement, there remain significant limitations. In particular, the components of his work responsive to the African Diaspora and indigenous people seem unnecessarily small. When he offers examples of underground, anti-bureaucratic currents, they are too frequently limited to the European revolutionary tradition. The figures who qualify for his "elective affinity" in this particular study are, as he freely acknowledges, only those similar to his own family's background; one might almost forget that Löwy has demonstrated in earlier books that he is a thoroughgoing internationalist who also feels a genuine cultural consanguinity with many other like-minded people regardless of regional/ancestral commonalties.[2] Romantic anti-capitalism, Löwy's crucial, and, yet, in my view, oddly underdeveloped category, would become far richer and have greater explanatory force if expanded to include not only some currents within feminism (Margaret Fuller, George Sand, and Christa Wolf are possibilities), but also the Negritude movement, Harlem Renaissance, Latin American *modernismo*, the *corrido* balladeers, and so forth.

In its present form, the centrality he gives to even the most palatable current of "revolutionary romanticism" may be a bit hard for some of us to swallow. This is not because one is a vulgar "positivist" but because one is justifiably suspicious, as was Marx, of attempts to celebrate elements of medieval society by idealizing them (mainly achieved by highlighting some features and ignoring others), and, also, because many of us feel alienated from Marx and Engel's unabashed Hellenocentrism.

Of course, the question of resolving the need for a socialist incorporation of romanticism, like earlier debates over incorporating elements of Existentialism and the current controversy over postmodernism, hinges largely upon one's definition. According to conventional usage, romanticism is virtually the obverse of Marxism in its extreme celebration of individualism and "instincts" (including a dubious notion of "genius"), anti-scientific bias, and philosophical idealism. Conventional studies in romanticism (to which Löwy's work bears some resemblance), tend to have an individualist/biographical focus, and to contain little information about how the retrieved visionary impetus embedded in texts admired by the scholar might be integrated into practical social movements.

Finally, it is worth remarking on the degree to which Löwy's work is fixated on "high culture," something of a contradiction to his strong identification with surrealism, an artistic movement that aspired to burst the barriers between the constructed categories of the "elite" and "mass." I particularly recommend that Löwy explore the connections between his concept of revolutionary utopia and the "critical utopia" that emerged from the feminist, anti-racist and gay/lesbian science fiction of the United States after the 1960s, as in the work of Joanna Russ, Ursula K. LeGuin, Marge Piercy, and Samuel R. Delaney.[3] Nevertheless, by a selective emphasis and interpretation of certain elements within romantic thought, Löwy *does* seem to render the anti-capitalist/revolutionary strain within it quite recuperable. Surely an interrogation and enlargement of the category along the above lines would only make it far more viable.

Notes

I wish to thank Ellen Poteet for comments on an earlier draft of this essay.

1 Actually, an earlier version of *Marxism in Latin America* was published in French in 1980 and *Redemption and Utopia* is a translation of a work appearing in 1988; the essays comprising *On Changing the World* first appeared between the mid 1970s and 1990.

2 Other books by Löwy evidence a close sympathy with Latin American revolutionaries, Liberation Theologists, Gramsci, etc.

3 A superb study of this trend is Tom Moylan's *Demand the Impossible: Science Fiction and the Utopian Imagination* (New York: Methuen, 1986).

PART IV

Anti-Racism

13

The Roots of African-
American Communism

Robin Kelley has produced a brilliantly researched and theorized exposition of the appropriation and transformation of US Communist ideology and institutions by the indigenous African-American community of Alabama.[1] This is a book that has the potential for revolutionizing the study of the African-American and broader Left in the 1990s through its compelling methodology and the nature of the information disclosed. Moreover, Kelley's conclusions may also be a stimulant to creative thinking about socialist and anti-racist activism at the present moment.

Hammer and Hoe is hardly the first in the new "revisionist" trend in the study of US Communism, mainly associated with New Left activists turned professors. These radical academics took a cue from the "history from the bottom up" school, pioneered in scholarly studies by Jesse Lemisch and E. P. Thompson,[2] although aspects of the approach were similarly anticipated by extra-academic left-wing scholarship in preceding decades.[3] In the 1980s, a number of impressive studies of the US Left were produced by Paul Buhle, Maurice Isserman, and others who sought to rethink Communism from a rank-and-file perspective.[4] The most concentrated reinterpretation of the Communist Party's approach to the anti-racist struggle was Mark Naison's *Communists in Harlem During the Depression* (1983).[5] Kelley's work incorporates yet dramatically extends and in some ways challenges the achievement of this group of New Left historians.

Perhaps Kelley's boldest move is to side-step what could easily have turned into a tedious refutation of the mainstream trend in the historiography of the Left, which is liberal anti-Communist. His book stands as an implicit refutation of the shelfload of books by Theodore Draper, Harvey Klehr, and Wilson Record, in which the Communist experience is interpreted mostly through the malignant lens of increasing Soviet manipulation.[6] Kelley seems to understand,

This chapter originally appeared in *Against the Current*, 8, no. 4 (September–October 1993).

intuitively if not explicitly on a theoretical level, that these authors are mainly guilty of the sin of *omission*. Especially as they approach the 1930s and after, they fail fairly to depict positive achievements of the Communist movement or to include substantial episodes that contradict their mostly cynical hypotheses. Moreover, a few of the "horror stories" recounted in earlier histories, such as Harold Cruse's claim that the Communist Party stole money collected by the Committee to Defend the Scottsboro Boys (nine African-American youths framed up on rape charges in Alabama) to buy new printing presses for the *Daily Worker*, rest on unsubstantiated gossip.[7] Still, in the end, there can be no question at this late date that Cruse and others are accurate that the Communist Party was deformed, organizationally and politically, by its unbreakable connection with with the totalitarian regime headed by Joseph Stalin.

What *is* in dispute, and hotly so, is the degree to which the Communist rank-and-file were "malleable objects," to use a notorious phrase by Irving Howe and Lewis Coser, of those responsible for such deformations.[8] Was the sum total of the Communist impact an "enormous waste," to quote Howe and Coser again,[9] or did the progressive effects of Communist-led activity, in the short as well as long run, out-weigh what was discrediting? To what extent do the categories appropriate to "Stalinism" – a term meaning the (evolving) political outlook that rationalized rule by the Soviet elite – usefully explain the bottom-up activities of Party supporters in their unions, communities, and cultural works? Should "Stalinist deformations" be assessed as a manifestation of the logic of Leninism, or explained as the consequence of the displacement of Leninism by an alien (anti-Marxist) politics and practice?

Kelley's research and manner of presentation provide the freshest answers to many of these questions to date, so long as one keeps in mind that he is opening doors to further research and understanding, not closing off debate. Rather than refute his scholarly predecessors point by point – indeed, the names of Klehr, Howe and Coser, Cruse, and Record never even appear in the index![10] – Kelley simply presents some of the fascinating material that such writers have failed to see or acknowledge in their work.

Moreover, this alternative presentation is offered from a Marxist perspective and within a framework that acknowledges what remains valid in the conventional historiography of Communism. An opening "Prologue" provides a socio-economic history of Birmingham, Alabama, the pivotal urban industrial center for the unfolding story. This is followed by five chapters under the rubric "The Underground" which survey the interaction between Communist ideas/institutions and African-Americans in the unemployed movement, the struggle of sharecroppers, the labor movement, and political defense work.

Then comes a stunning exegesis of "The Culture of Opposition" in which resistance is theorized according to concepts adapted from the Italian Communist Antonio Gramsci's ideas about hegemony, and US cultural theorist George Lipsitz's notion of "collective memory." Kelley gives numerous

examples where African-American Communists acted like "trickster characters" in Black folklore to distribute literature and gather weapons. They
reworked familiar spirituals into Marxist hymns, changing the refrain about
Jesus from "Give Me That Old Time Religion" to read, "It was good enough
for Lenin, and it's good enough for me." Vivid memories of the Civil War
encouraged African-American radicals to draw tremendous hope and strength
from the belief that "Russia" was a powerful ally that would aid them in a new
and more complete social transformation.

After this are five chapters under the rubric "Up from Bolshevism." These
study the arenas in which Popular Front policies were employed between 1935
and 1939. The book concludes with a brief but incisive summary of the consequences of these events for Alabama racial politics in subsequent years.

Hammer and Hoe is striking because Kelley – using oral history, private papers,
local newspapers, and other primary materials – shows how African-American
Alabama Communists incorporated the surface features of Communism into a
local radical tradition deeply steeped in in religious symbols and community
resistance. The slogans of the Third Period, calling for self-determination in the
Black Belt (a region of the South which still had a majority African-American
population in many counties), responded effectively to already existing nationalist sentiments. The class-based politics of the International Labor Defense was
the answer to frustration felt because of the inability of the middle-class NAACP
to militantly champion the rights of those on the bottom.

Here it is worth noting that Kelley deviates significantly from others in the
New Left School of American Communism in his more critical approach to the
Popular Front – the policy by which socialist economic transformation was subordinated to the liberal capitalist program of bourgeois democracy for the sake
of unity against the right-wing and fascist threats. Indeed, not only does he score
the contradictions of the Popular Front on empirical grounds, but he concludes
that the Popular Front was really more of concern to whites in the Party than
Blacks. In sum, he insists that, in the South, the "Third Period" (the 1928–34
era of ultra-revolutionary policy) was not merely class-against-class reduction-
ism; on the contrary, the centrality of the "Black nation thesis" meant the promotion of a kind of regional-cultural autonomy through advocacy of the right
of African-Americans to choose to control regions of the South where they constituted a majority of the population. On the other hand, the Popular Front
cannot be uncritically celebrated for its unleashing of multicultural democracy,
due to the heavy element of cross-class opportunism.

The doors opened by Kelley are many, not the least of which is the possibility for the extension of this methodology to other regions, additional racial and
ethnic groups, women, more arenas of political struggle, and radical political
tendencies other than the Communist Party. Moreover, particular episodes,
such as Kelley's discussion of the efficacy of armed self-defense among the
African-American population, might be used to provide a comparative frame-

work for considering the controversial application of this strategy in later situations in the 1960s, such as the armed actions of the NAACP chapter in Monroe County, North Carolina, and the community self-defense policy of the Black Panther Party.

Still other areas of inquiry, raised within the topic of the book itself, remain to be rounded out with more research and thought. Kelley provides surprisingly frank information about the Communist Party membership of many individuals in the South, often accompanied by fascinating mini-portraits of activists who are Black and white, female and male. Yet, for all the general emphasis of the book concerning culture and psychology, he may not always have pursued his subject into the more controversial areas. For example, in Richard Wright's collection *Uncle Tom's Children* (first version, 1938; additional stories, 1940), also based on oral histories of African-American Southern radicals and similarly replete with songs and religious references, the climactic tale, "Bright and Morning Star," presents an interracial love affair between a Black male and white female Party activist. Yet no hint of interracial sex appears in any of the numerous stories recounted by Kelley.

Indeed, the personal lives of the Black Communists are presented as squeaky clean and as idealized as the fictional William Christman, the African-American Abraham Lincoln Brigade Veteran in Alexander Saxton's novel *Grand Crossing* (1943). It is understandable that a public image of upstanding family men and women, adhering to the segregated sex code of the South and 100 percent free of any hint of homosexuality, was promulgated for self-defensive purposes by revolutionaries who were trying to survive among a Southern population indoctrinated with the view that Communists stood for the virtual nationalization of white women (p. 28). Still, anyone with first-hand experience in the reality of the social life of the Left may feel that the version uncritically offered here may well be several steps removed from the "personal truth" of the Alabama radical movement.

Another unfinished strand of Kelley's story may be that of Black–Jewish relations within the Left. Kelley makes a point of ethnically identifying all African-American activists, several of the WASPS, and a select number of Jewish-Americans who were indigenous to the South as well as implanted. Episodes such as the Communist Party's replacement during the Popular Front era of the Northern-born Jewish-American Nat Ross with the Southern-born WASP Rob Hall suggest the possibility that Kelley's data may lead to new insights regarding the controversial topic of the role of Jewish Communists in the African-American struggle. Yet there is no follow-through, and other key Jewish-American radicals are not identified as such – including prominent ones such as playwright John Howard Lawson (the family name was Levy), and, later, in the Epilogue, Herbert Hill of the NAACP. The full potential for generalization on the subject of Black–Jewish relations remains unrealized.

Finally, there is the general theoretical position to consider. Kelley makes a convincing case that the substantial achievements of Alabama African-Americans in the Great Depression were not the result of being "radicalized" by the Communist Party. Rather, the Depression conditions interacted with the local practices of resistance. When Communist organizers appeared on the scene from the North, the local Black population found what it needed to achieve political coherence in the Communist slogans, and in making use of Communist institutions to educate and organize. Moreover, this indigenous radical movement at the "base" persisted with consistent features in spite of political changes in line at the "top." In fact, according to Kelley, the Southern Communist movement, unlike the Northern, experienced a distinct resurgence among African-American militants when it abandoned the Popular Front during the period of the Hitler–Stalin Pact (fall of 1939 to spring of 1941).

However, the foundation of this movement was originally rural agricultural labor through sharecropping; thus the mechanization of such labor and depopulation of the countryside undermined it and eventually caused its decline. Nevertheless, the impact of these years of struggle was so great that the afterglow of the tradition lived on in different forms – often by individuals influenced by the Communist movement but not so identified – until it blended with the Civil Rights movement. Eventually a number of veterans of the experience became well-known and influential figures, usually as organizers, teachers, and even government officials.

Kelley's argument would suggest that revolutionary socialists of the 1990s must start not by seeking to "radicalize" the oppressed with our own Marxist strategies, but by studying the already existing forms of oppositional culture in the new sites of resistance and rebellion – in the present case, the urban ghetto. It then falls upon us to develop a political strategy and organizational forms through which those indigenous means of expression can be realized at the same time as they can creatively interact with those lessons from Marxism that remain valid today.

Unfortunately, history and cultural formation fail to stand still and there are important factors unaccounted for in this model. One is that white and Black radicals were impelled toward extraordinary acts of heroism in the face of KKK vigilantes and gun thugs, many of which are recounted by Kelley, partly due to a belief in an already existing utopia. The USSR, as it figured in the imaginations of these radicals, was a religious and secular Promised Land, proving that their dreams were obtainable and also offering real material aid. Visits to this Promised Land rarely contradicted preconceived fantasies, helping to fortify the cadres in their struggle. Today there is no substitute to fill that void; indeed, the Left is overrun with skepticism about the possibility of a democratic-collectivist alternative to the market system.

In addition, Euro-American and Jewish-American revolutionaries who braved the armed force of the racists were welcomed by African-American militants as brothers and sisters in struggle – including, amazingly, the acceptance by Blacks of even some local whites who had previously been in the Ku Klux Klan (p. 28). Since the late 1960s, however, even the most well-meaning white radicals are not especially welcome in the Black community; often they are urged by African-American militants to "organize your *own* community." Conspiracy theories and anti-Semitic variants of Black nationalism combined with a real history of betrayal and exploitation of African-Americans by whites make racial unity among different non-white groups difficult. In fact, although urban centers are the sites of oppression of Chicanos, Puerto Ricans, Latin American immigrants, Asian-Americans, Arab-Americans, and others, cross-racial unity even among people of color is also rare. Add to this the enormous challenge posed by the gang and drug cultures, and one's effort to create a con-temporary version of a formula by which revolutionary socialism and the indigenous resistance struggles of people of color can unite seems a near-Sisyphean task.

And then there is the notion of resistance culture as theorized by Kelley. Can it be true that, similar to what is claimed by some contemporary theorists of popular culture, African-American radicals simply take what they want and need from Left politics – rejecting what is alien to their situation, and empow-ering themselves with subversive appropriations? Is it all just a spontaneous process, the activation of "collective memory"? Doesn't something need to be done to help insure that such rebels will take only the most effective tools?

Looking back at the 1960s, it seems to me that the results were far from ben-eficial when Third World, as well as disoriented white, radicals simply appropri-ated the guerrilla warfare strategy of the Left in the colonial world and tried to apply it in US, German, and Italian conditions. Moreover, looking more inter-nationally at the Vietnamese and even the Cuban experiences in relation to the USSR, it seems fair to speculate that, when one interacts with a Stalinist move-ment, no matter how autonomously in local practice, there still can be many "bad habits" – organizationally, culturally, politically – appropriated along with the material benefits.

However, it would be preposterous to demand that Kelley's book provide answers to all or even most of these questions. Rather, what he has done is to present us with fresh tools and a stunning case study that ought to enable activist-scholars in contemporary struggles to continue the pursuit of answers to these and other enigmas at a far more advanced level than was previously possible.

Notes

1. Robin Kelley, *Hammer and Hoe: Alabama Communists During the Great Depression* (Chapel Hill: University of North Carolina Press, 1990).

2. See Jesse Lemisch, "Jack Tar in the Streets: Merchant Seamen in the Politics of Revolutionary America," *William and Mary Quarterly* (July 1968); and E. P. Thompson, *The Making of the English Working Class* (1963).

3. See George Novack, *America's Revolutionary Heritage* (1976), C. L. R. James, *The Black Jacobins* (1938), and Herbert Aptheker, *American Negro Slave Revolts* (1943).

4. See my more extensive comments in reviews of Maurice Isserman's *Which Side Were You On?* (1982) and Paul Buhle's *Marxism in the USA* (1987) in *The Responsibility of Intellectuals: Selected Essays on Marxist Traditions in Cultural Commitment* (Atlantic Highlands, NJ: Humanities Press, 1992), pp. 112–16 and 122–5.

5. Reviewed favorably by this author in *Socialist Action*, (Oct. 1984), p. 14.

6. See Draper's outstanding *The Roots of American Communism* (1957) and *American Communism and Soviet Russia* (1960); Klehr's *The Heyday of American Communism* (1984); and Record's *The Negro and the Communist Party* (1951).

7. See Cruse, *The Crisis of the Negro Intellectual: From its Origins to the Present* (New York: William Morrow and Co., 1967), p. 148. Cruse's book is a radical nationalist perspective, however, not liberal anti-Communist.

8. See Irving Howe and Lewis Coser, *The American Communist Party: A Critical History* (New York: Praeger, 1962), p. 506. Although this is a brilliantly written left-wing socialist critique of the Communist Party, its reductive attitude toward "Stalinism" resembles that of the liberal anti-Communists such as Draper and even neo-conservatives such as Klehr.

9. Ibid. p. 499.

10. Draper's name appears only in connection with his May 9, 1985 *New York Review of Books* essay attacking the New Left revisionists of Communist historiography. However, the works of many of the traditional scholars are listed in the excellent bibliography to the volume.

14

The Subaltern Speaks

In a well-known argument, "Can the Subaltern Speak?", Marxist-deconstructionist critic Gayatri Chakravorty Spivak raises complex questions about the ways in which scholars, writers, and historians from the Western elite aspire to give "voice" to the colonial subjects, the Third World subalterns, of their First World societies.[1] Are there techniques by which such authors might allow subaltern subjects to represent themselves with maximum authenticity? Or must even well-meaning Western writers, no matter what their literary strategies, be doomed instead to reproduce simplistic versions of their own culture's "others"? *Babouk*, a 1934 work just republished in Monthly Review's "Voices of Resistance" series, is an early example of an effort to negotiate this tension in the form of an experimental novel.[2] In this case, the Western author and colonial subject are positioned in the text to speak from distinct but complementary perspectives.

At the time of the novel's first edition, Guy Endore was the 34-year-old US author of four previous books and several translations from the French. Originally nudged toward the Left in the 1920s by a fellow Columbia University student named Whittaker Chambers (a Communist writer who became an underground agent and, in the 1940s, a notorious informer), Endore was impelled by the events of the early Depression to declare his revolutionary sympathies. The form he chose was a historically based novel challenging the distortions of the official historiographers of New World slavery and colonialism. The result was *Babouk*, a fast-paced, multiply voiced narrative of a Mandingo storyteller by that name. Through the words of Babouk and many others, including the author himself as an outraged and ironical commentator on the events, Endore telescopes the factors precipitating a slave insurrection in the Caribbean.

Kidnapped from Africa in the mid eighteenth century by the French, Babouk

---

This chapter originally appeared in *Monthly Review*, 43, no. 11 (April 1992).

is brought to San Domingo (now Haiti) where he struggles during two decades to develop a "story" to tell that will unite his fellow captives in revolt against their European masters. According to contemporary reviews of *Babouk,* the historical revelations and author's viewpoint were sensational and unprecedented in literature of its day. Surprisingly, nearly fifty years later, the work still seems fresh and original in many respects. The two Caribbean scholars who co-authored the Afterword to the Monthly Review edition affirm a remarkable degree of accuracy in the facts of slave life and resistance.

Fortuitously, the publication of *Babouk* also gives voice to a very different kind of subaltern stratum in the historiography of US literature and radical culture. This is the long-repressed tradition of "literary communism" that appears in the works of scores of novelists who have been twice neglected: first, by the traditional "canon" of US literature; second, by the Left's own "canon." The former reduces the "Left" literary contribution to figures such as John Steinbeck and John Dos Passos. The latter, until just recently, was fixated mainly on Mike Gold, Granville Hicks, the Hollywood Ten, and the early Richard Wright.[3] Endore is one of hundreds of radical writers in various genres – including many women and writers of color – who fell between the cracks of both classificatory systems.

Such exclusion was by no means the result of a lack of productivity or even success in sales on Endore's part; he published twelve novels, including the frequently reprinted horror classic *Werewolf of Paris* (1933) and the Book of the Month Club international best-seller *King of Paris* (1956). The more probable reason for neglect is that Endore fails to exhibit the canonical features of radical writers as they were established either by university scholars, as in Daniel Aaron's *Writers on the Left* (1961), or by the Left's own representation of its legacy, as in Joseph North's *New Masses: An Anthology of the Rebel Thirties* (1969).

The omission of Endore, however, is far more comprehensible than the regrettable "disappearances" of John Sanford, Martha Dodd, H. T. Tsiang, and so many other novelists of exceptional craft and originality. Even apart from his obscured political identity, the elusive Endore is not what he seems in many respects. The name sounds French, which fits logically with the subject matter of many of his books; in fact, he was Jewish-American and actually born Samuel Goldstein in New York City in 1900.

While receiving a BA (1923) and MA (in European languages, 1925) from Columbia, he impressed classmates with his suave European cultivation, poise and sophistication. Yet his father, Isidor Goldstein, had been a coal miner in Pittsburgh, and his mother, Malka Halpern Goldstein, committed suicide four years after her son's birth, partly in response to the family's dire poverty. Soon after, Endore's father changed the family name to obliterate the past, placing the children in a Methodist orphanage. But then his father sold an invention and dreamed that his dead wife commanded him to use the money to obtain a European education for their children. This inaugurated a bizarre five-year sojourn in Vienna where the Endore children were left alone under the care of a Catholic governess. When the elder Endore vanished and the money ran out, Guy and his siblings were sent back to Pittsburgh to live communally. Later, Guy squeaked his way through Columbia by renting his dorm bed out to a wealthier student and sleeping on the floor.

Endore's Communism, too, must be documented in less "canonical" forms than that of a Mike Gold. Although he reviewed occasionally for *New Masses*, he and his wife, Henrietta Portugal, moved to Hollywood in the mid 1930s after becoming radicalized. There he was more directly associated with West Coast left-wing literary publications such as *Black and White* and *The Clipper* (for which Endore wrote the Introduction to the Greenwood Press reprint in the 1960s); he also taught fiction writing at the Los Angeles People's Educational Center. As part of the Hollywood branch of the Communist Party, Endore was in units organized precisely so that one might deny membership if necessary; thus, like others, it was easy for him to be ambiguous about the details of his Party associations in later years.

Although blacklisted during the 1950s, Endore was never called before a witch-hunting committee, nor did he serve time in jail. In 1956, he was profoundly traumatized by the Khrushchev revelations, and his political mentor, Samuel Ornitz (a novelist, screenwriter, and one of the Hollywood Ten), died soon after. These and other factors led him to abandon the struggle for principled reinstatement in the film industry in 1958, just prior to the reprieve that came to many in the 1960s. Hence he is only peripherally mentioned in studies of the infamous blacklist episode.

However, the most probable explanation for Endore's disappearance from Left cultural history is that, although a committed Marxist for two decades, he never wrote strike novels, proletarian novels, anti-war novels, or novels of intellectuals undergoing political conversions to socialism. Mostly he wrote books that he thought would sell. These are elegant, erudite, and witty fictionalized biographies of Cassanova, Joan of Arc, the Marquis De Sade, and Rousseau; mystery novels on psychoanalytic and linguistic themes; and occasional horror stories which, along with his classic *Werewolf of Paris*, have earned him entries in most reference books on the subject. Before the blacklist, he was in the 1930s a screenwriter for films such as *The Devil Doll* and *The League of Frightened Men*, and, in the 1940s, *Song of Russia* and *The Story of GI Joe*. Late in life, after his bitter disillusionment with Stalinism, Endore threw himself heart and soul into supporting a controversial Southern California experimental commune for reformed drug addicts and alcoholics. He became its chief pamphleteer, intellectual guru, and author of its definitive history, *Synanon* (1968).

As a left-wing political activist, Endore was best known as a pamphleteer for anti-racist causes. He wrote one of the major pieces of material for the Scottsboro Boys, *The Crime at Scottsboro* (1938), as well as two major pamphlets for the "Sleepy Lagoon" case (sometimes referred to as the "Chicano

Scottsboro"), which sold many thousands of copies. He read voluminously in Marxist history – although he was simultaneously interested in mysticism, Yoga, vegetarianism, theosophy, and anti-vivisectionism – and labored throughout his life on an unpublished "History of Human Skill."

A logical starting point for assessing Endore's literary strategy in *Babouk* is to contrast his depiction of a rebel slave on an island with that of Shakespeare's more famous slave-rebel in his last play, *The Tempest* (1623). Whatever the literary merits of *The Tempest*, it is unlikely that Shakespeare created Caliban with the objective of vivifying or activating the colonial subject from the perspective of the subject himself. Rather, most commentators regard the portrait of Caliban as confirming the ideological precepts of the master class and culture of Shakespeare's time.

In contrast, Endore's complex characterization of Babouk, his dramatization of the enslavement process, his elaboration through dialogue of the socio-economic infrastructure of the island of San Domingo, his depiction of the interaction between European masters and slaves of color, and the manner in which he relentlessly details the climactic rebellion on the island all suggest that Endore's literary project is founded on opposite premises. Starting with the title, *Babouk*, named after the slave rebel who is himself designated as story-teller, Endore wishes to center, valorize, and powerfully name the protagonist. Shakespeare, according to most interpretations, named Caliban as a cruel joke that only reflected his own cultural ignorance ("Caliban" comes from "cannibal," itself a botched reference to the Caribbean). Endore, as a kind of acknowledgment of his own inadequacy to speak "for" the subaltern, introduces himself as author in a subordinate position, as a kind of technician who facilitates the narrative. Moreover, he strategically takes advantage of his omniscient status to hurl barbs and brickbats at the European colonizers and their apologists – often by juxtaposing quotations from history books that reveal the Europeans' ignorance and hypocrisy. Shakespeare, however, identified himself mainly with Prospero, the aristocratic magician-storyteller of his isle, who torments Caliban by conjuring up vicious attack-dogs to chase him down.

Politically, Endore wrote *Babouk* on the way to Communism, about which he had been thinking-at-a-distance for some time. To his surprise, the novel was criticized in the *New Masses* (October 23, 1934) by the African-American Communist critic Eugene Gordon (later, a Howard University Professor of Philosophy) as too nationalistic in political orientation. Gordon noted that, even though the Communist slogan "Black and White Unite and Fight" is mentioned in passing toward the end of the book, the climactic episode of the slave rebellion is clearly Black *against* white. Endore defended himself in a letter to Gordon remarking that it was hard to promote a Leninist political line "in an historical novel antedating Lenin," and, also, that Haiti was one of those countries where "there are no whites to unite with," as in India, China, and the Malay States.[4]

Nevertheless, the political implications of the novel were meant to operate on two levels: the racial-nationalist uprising is regarded as a kind of necessary stage of cultural affirmation that must come prior to a successful class-based uprising when conditions are appropriate. There is no doubt that Endore intended *Babouk*'s eighteenth-century uprising as a way of talking about the situation of the early Depression. To his publisher James Henle, owner of Vanguard Press, Endore wrote: "[The struggle] of the Negroes in 1791 is being repeated today in new forms. I feel that a great deal of interest in my book will come from those who are interested or participating in this struggle."[5]

Still, it is fair to query the extent to which the creation of *Babouk* was Endore's means of assuaging his personal guilt, working out his own neuroses, or projecting his individual anger onto a character alleged to be a genuine representative of colonial resistance. After all, there is no doubt that an author's work can never be entirely free of the psychological and cultural influences of his personal life and cultural milieu. As a Jew who was placed in a Christian orphanage in Cleveland, Endore first felt drawn to African-Americans who were also outsiders. Later, in New York City he was personally wounded by anti-Semitism. In the late 1940s, Endore referred to *Babouk* in a letter to Lillian Smith, the Southern author of *Strange Fruit*, who had just published a treatise on racism:

> Inasmuch as I myself once wrote a book about Negroes, a novel, *Babouk*, 1934, unread, almost unprocurable, I feel that I must say a few things about your point of view [on African-Americans], though I daresay I have not one-tenth your experience in the matter. Perhaps being a Jew gives me some rights. Phil Silvers [the comedian] used to say: "A Negro is only a Jew in technicolor," and perhaps having personally been segregated, shoved off sidewalks and called a Jew bastard, who knows, I may be closer to this problem than a Southern white. I know you have felt it, have suffered it, because we're not islands, we're not that much individuals, and yet you slipped, right in your foreword [to *Killers of the Dream*]: "Why has the white man dreamed so fabulous a dream of freedom and human dignity and again and again tried to kill his own dream?". . . In my novel I made the dream of freedom and dignity a dream of a black man, and I pointed out that the planters of Haiti could not believe that this dream had originated in a black skull: it must needs have come from some rabble-rousing French revolutionary. For everything, good or bad, even a dream, must come from a white.[6]

Whatever our independent assessments of Lillian Smith's work, or of Endore's success or failure in giving "voice" to the colonial subaltern, this letter affirms his self-perception as a conscious radical artist opposed to the do-gooder, uplift tradition of the liberal. Even a complex work of art such as *The Tempest* fails to confront head-on the impossibility of the dominating culture giving voice to the dominated; Endore, whatever his failures, at least makes an effort to seek ways of expression to differentiate the world-view of the subaltern.

Of course, the creative process is far more complex and ambiguous than the translation of a theoretical proposition into characters and action. There is evidence of the importance of personal aspects to Endore's identification with Babouk even beyond his sense of Jewish–Black bonds, and his anti-colonialist awareness of some of his culture's racist attitudes toward people of color. For example, Endore was always obsessed by feelings of uprootedness and homelessness. As late as the mid 1950s he wrote in response to a publisher's questionnaire to authors:

> Thus I cannot honestly say that I am anything. Everything sort of cancels itself out in me. I am neither European nor American. Neither Jew nor Christian. Neither of the country nor the city. Neither of this century nor the last. Neither rich nor poor. And in my studies I've been similarly divided: torn between the sciences and the arts. And these contrasts and cleavages have remained with me to this date.[7]

Such an ambivalent sense of self may explain how the final version of *Babouk* seized hold of him in spite of his intention to write a very different kind of novel.[8] According to Endore's personal records, following the success of *The Werewolf of Paris*, he was offered a book contract for another adventurous mystery story. Since he knew French and had studied the French colonial relation to the French Revolution during a post-graduate sojourn in Paris, he conceived of a romantic adventure of the slave trade period and traveled to Haiti to undertake the research. Once there, according to his letters and his Oral History taken at UCLA, he became fascinated with the African stories that he encountered in documents about slave life. Suddenly he found himself writing a totally different kind of novel than he had intended, based around a teller of these stories – a character he fashioned from the figure of an early rebel slave called "Boukman." Endore recalls in his Oral History:

> I began reading the history of the French Revolution, studying the role of slavery and learning the fables of the Africans. I truly admired their ability to devise brilliant stories, so I inserted them in the text. I also wanted to give the Negro people a historical novel that would really be theirs. Other historical novels were about rich and important people, and this bothered me personally. I went to Haiti for this project. Century publishers had requested the book but then refused to publish it. They saw it as too revolutionary. No one would take it until Vanguard Press.

A letter to Endore from the publishing house of Simon and Schuster confirms the response that the manuscript received: "This is a powerful, moving piece of work. It won't sell because it's just too horrible. The reviews would warn people away from it. We would be afraid to handle it."[9]

The reviews more or less bore out the above prediction. Even the Left, with the exception of a long and favorable review in the Trotskyist *New International* (by the poet Florence Becker, January 1935) and an unsuccessful effort at a dramatization by Paul Robeson, failed to respond with much interest or under-standing. Twenty years later, Walter Rideout undoubtedly felt justified in giving only one sentence to *Babouk* (and to Endore, for that matter) in his monumental 340–page book on the radical novel: "Guy Endore's *Babouk* is chiefly interesting as an excursion into economic history, for it details the conditions which, in 1791, at last pushed the slaves of San Domingo into bloody revolt against the white planters."[10]

Yet this is hardly how the book looks in 1991, at least for those of us investi-gating matters such as "cultural difference," construction of the subaltern colo-nized subject, and other preoccupations of the contemporary Cultural Studies movement. The few pages on economic matters dispersed throughout the book are less of a distraction than a concretization of essential information about the international division of labor that the reader needs to know; and, even here, Endore uses the material to raise fundamental questions about the role of slavery and colonialism in the rise and ideological construction of "Western civilization." Moreover, the overriding theme is that of cultural differences among the kid-napped slaves, and Babouk's efforts as political leader, storyteller, and ideologist to rework African stories, and later on Christian myths, to unify them for revolt.

The narrative strategy is extraordinary for its time. From the very first page, where the kidnapped Africans who have been brought to the coast erupt into debate over the significance of the "Nigger Taster" (one of the European slavers was employed to lick the sweat of every captive as a way of supposedly estimat-ing the captive's health), Endore strives to depict the intrusion of the Europeans into Africa from the *diverse* perspectives of the indigenous peoples. The Africans from various tribes argue among themselves as to what is happening to them, responding according to their various cultures.

Endore maintains this perspective as the novel evolves through the "Middle Passage" (a term for the trans-Atlantic voyage of the loaded slave ship) and then to Haiti, where Babouk rises to a political leadership through his storytelling. The book is too rich in issues of cultural difference to lend itself to brief summary, but among the more striking points are:

● Endore's frequent ironic paralleling of European and African cultures, the allegedly "civilized" and the "savage."
● His usually implicit, but sometimes explicit, linkage of the formation of racist ideology in the colonial period to the continuation of racial oppression in the 1930s.
● His ability to identify substantially with the situation of the Africans, while eschewing any effort at idealization; many of the stories Babouk tells to unify and mobilize are blatant lies, and the range of behavior on the part of the Africans is diverse, such as that of the Maroons who return escapees such as Babouk to the French as part of the *modus vivendi* they have worked out to maintain their independent communities.

184

- His effort to show the subversion of European Christian culture by the slaves, as in the scene where a priest insists that Babouk take off his snake charm and wear a cross, and Babouk responds by breaking the same charm in half and wearing the broken snake charm as a cross.
- His effort to transform the conventional European novel genre to create a new form appropriate to his non-European subject, as in his use of the drum-dialogue poem in the closing pages.

Of course, I am not a scholar of the eighteenth-century Caribbean and cannot vouch for the degree of accuracy with which Babouk and the other enslaved Africans are rendered. My guess is that the book, once it receives the attention it deserves, will be regarded as fairly authentic because Endore incorporated so many primary materials of the slave experience into the text. The scholarly Afterword by Gaspar and Trouillot remarks on only two disagreements, concerning the characterization of enslaved women and the number of free Africans depicted, although questions may be raised about other matters such as the references to cannibalistic practices in Africa. Also, the predominant voices are male, although the perspectives of several enslaved African women are occasionally voiced.

The major role played by documentary materials in assembling *Babouk* reflects not only a literary strategy popular in the 1930s, but also one that is characteristic of much writing by people of color themselves – from geographical details of Frederick Douglass's *Narrative* (1845) to newspaper stories incorporated into Richard Wright's *Native Son* (1941). Documentation is necessary when the truth of oppression has been masked so often by the dominant culture. In fact, many of the historical episodes described in the "Middle Passage" of *Babouk* also appear in Robert Hayden's innovative poem of that name (the initial version of which was completed in 1943), based partly on research Hayden conducted on the Federal Writers' Project in the late 1930s. It also appears that Herman Melville may have drawn on some of the same documentary materials as well, for there is a striking resemblance between the fate of the head of his rebel slave Babo in "Benito Cereno" (1856) which was displayed on a pike with a warning sign beneath, and the head of Babouk in Endore's novel:

> And there his head was exhibited upon a pike. And a placard was placed at the foot of it, and it read: "Babouk, chief of the rebels!" And history tells us that "death had brought into relief upon his frozen countenance all the hideous cruelty of his savage nature. His eyes were still open and sparkling and seemed to be encouraging his men on to the massacre." (p.174)

Endore presents this quote, attributed to "History," in a context that exposes "History" as ideology. This produces somewhat the same effect as Melville's inclusion at the end of his story of the outrageously falsified court testimony about Babo's shipboard uprising against Captain Benito Cereno.

How should we assess *Babouk* in 1991? We read, teach, and act in a culture that normally ranks novels as "high" or "low, " "great" or "second rate," "classic" or "entertainment," "art" or "propaganda," etc. Ironically, it is the enshrinement of works such as *The Tempest* – which have cultural influence but which are hardly appropriate models for all significant literary practice – that makes it so difficult for a text such as *Babouk* to obtain a hearing on its own terms.

This is a lost text of 1934 – one that sold 400 copies, then had its plates destroyed, and then remained virtually unmentioned in literary history for the past fifty-seven years until its reprinting in the summer of 1991. *Babouk*, therefore, is a work whose literary value remains largely to be constructed by readers and scholars of the present day. In my view, there is reason for optimism about the audience that this novel of anti-colonial resistance may now find in the 1990s, due to the context of the radical reconstruction of US culture currently under way. This is a text pointing precisely to many areas of literary investigation that are center-stage among the activists and cultural workers seeking to reforge a new, more liberatory Marxism, and a fresh vision of cultural possibility in a world in which colonial subalterns and their Western masters will at long last no longer constitute pre-eminent categories thwarting the potential of all our lives.

Notes

1. See "Can the Subaltern Speak," in Cary Nelson and Lawrence Grossman, eds, *Marxism and the Interpretation of Culture* (Urbana: University of Illinois Press, 1988), pp. 271–313.

2. Guy Endore, *Babouk* (New York: Monthly Review Press, 1991). Foreword by Jamaica Kincaid. Afterword by David Barry Gaspar and Michel-Rolph Trouillot.

3. We are now in the process of a major reconsideration of US Left writers through the recent scholarship of Cary Nelson, Paula Rabinowitz, Douglass Wixson, James Bloom, Constance Coiner, and others.

4. Endore to Eugene Gordon, Oct. 29, 1934, UCLA.

5. Endore to James Henle, July 24, 1934, UCLA.

6. Endore to Lillian Smith, Oct. 18, 1949, UCLA.

7. Undated original at UCLA.

8. It is worth noting that there are significant differences between Endore's novel and his subsequent pamphlets on Scottsboro and Sleepy Lagoon. The latter disclose paternalistic attitudes that I myself don't detect in the novel. Perhaps this difference is testimony to the way in which Endore truly gave himself over to the experience of writing *Babouk*. In a note among his papers, he says that he "became black" when writing the book, as if he had undergone a semi-mystical experience. Of course, Endore's status as a spokesperson for the Western elite is far more ambiguous to begin with than that of Shakespeare and Lillian Smith; as a revolutionary, he felt at odds with the rulers of his country and culture.

9. Clifton Fadiman to Endore, March 31, 1934, UCLA. Fadiman also characterized the politics of the novel as "*Daily Worker.*"

10. Walter Rideout, *The Radical Novel in the United States, 1900–1954: Some Interrelations of Literature and Society* (Cambridge, Mass: Harvard University Press, 1956), p. 194.

15

The Anti-Racist Imagination

Alexander Saxton, *The Rise and Fall of the White Republic: Class Politics and Mass Culture in Nineteenth-Century America*. London: Verso, 1990. 397 pp.

The socialist intellectual who participates in several generations of radical activity has the potential of developing left-wing thought in increasingly rich and complex ways. Such is the case with Alexander Saxton, the proletarian novelist of the 1940s and 1950s turned Marxist historian in the 1960s and after. *The Rise and Fall of the White Republic* is testimony to the sophistication and power of the anti-racist imagination as it has evolved over five decades of cultural and political struggle by partisans of socialism.

Saxton's personal and political trajectories confirm as well as challenge received stereotypes of the US radical intellectual. Born in 1919 in Great Barrington, Massachusetts, the son of Harper and Brothers editor-in-chief Eugene Saxton, he graduated from the elite Phillips Exeter Academy and enrolled at Harvard, a background recalling many twentieth-century progenitors of the intellectual Left starting with John Reed. Saxton, however, rejected Greenwich Village as his cultural mecca. In a combination of literary, political, and cultural rebellion at the end of the 1930s, he moved to Chicago, where he mostly remained until 1943. During those years he graduated from the University of Chicago and briefly attended graduate school in architecture. But mainly he worked in Chicago-area railroading jobs (as a wiper in a roundhouse and a switchman), and wrote his first radical novel, *Grand Crossing*, published in 1943.[1] The book is a semi-autobiographical study of the radicalization of an upper-class college student through his friendship with a Jewish leftist, an African-American Communist, and several Chicano residents of the Peoria and Halstead Street area of Chicago.

This chapter originally appeared in *Monthly Review*, 45, no. 3 (July–August 1993).

Following three years of Merchant Marine service in World War II, Saxton spent two years carefully rewriting *The Great Midland* (1948), the novel that he had sketched out in his spare time at sea. When it was published, he had already moved to Marin County, California, where he worked first for the shortlived Committee for Maritime Unity (headed jointly by Harry Bridges of the West Coast Longshoremen and Joe Curran of the National Maritime Union), and then as regional director of the Henry Wallace Progressive Party campaign. Much of the next decade was spent working as a construction carpenter in the Bay area and serving in various unpaid positions for the Brotherhood of Carpenters as local union president, executive committee member, and delegate to the central labor council and building trades councils. *The Great Midland*, regarded by Saxton and others as his major achievement in fiction, most significantly alternates between the story of David Spaas, a Communist trade union activist and anti-fascist fighter in Spain and World War II, and Pledger McAdams, leader of African-American railroad workers who are repeatedly betrayed by their own union. The most complex character in the novel, however, is Spaas's wife, Stephanie. She is the major site of internalized ideological struggle between middle- and working-class pressures, having previously left Spaas for an aristocratic philosophy scholar.

Bright Web in the Darkness (1958), Saxton's last published novel (he also produced some short fiction while editing *San Francisco Writers' Workshop*, the literary journal of the California Labor School[2]), further escalates the complexity of his approach to the nexus of race and class. This time the story is centered on an African-American woman, Joyce, working as a welder in a shipyard but dreaming of a career as a pianist. Her character and other features of the plot militate against the simpler choices and easier optimism of *The Great Midland*. *Bright Web in the Darkness* is, in fact, a novel anticipating some of the uncertainties about the prospects of radical struggle that would help precipitate a new kind of Left in the next decade.

In the early 1960s Saxton entered another phase in his effort to comprehend and combat racism in US culture. He received an MA (1962) and Ph.D. (1966) in History from Berkeley, and moved to UCLA in 1967, from where he recently retired. In 1971, Saxton published a signal contribution to the debate about the causes of the late nineteenth-century anti-Asian racism on the West Coast. *The Indispensable Enemy: Labor and the Anti-Chinese Movement in California* prefigures his more recent book through its incorporation of traditional economic-determinist explanations (the so-called "cheap labor argument") of the phenomenon into a more sophisticated explanation of racism's ideological functions. He treats primarily the California aspects of state-wide party politics and the organized labor movement, but also considers some trends in national culture.

Now Saxton has come out with *The Rise and Fall of the White Republic*, surely a major achievement marking a dramatic advance and potential turning point in the way we think about the persistence of racist ideology. True to the pattern of

Saxton's earlier writing, this is a work neither repudiating nor imitating his former attitudes and approaches. As before, in both fiction and scholarship, the functions and impact of racism, especially in regard to US working people, is of major concern, although the working class is hardly idealized, appearing mainly as fragmented and indecisive. Moreover, as in the case of *The Indispensable Enemy*, the economy, politics, and culture of the larger part of the nineteenth century is his primary arena of inquiry, with only some concluding remarks addressed to later consequences. Nevertheless, rather than concentrating primarily on a state or region, the new work surveys the major trends of racist ideology all across the continent. Finally, reflecting an astute awareness of contemporary discussions of culture and politics, Saxton's inquiry engages the media, electoral campaigns, popular theater, fiction, mythology (especially the legends of Davy Crockett and Kit Carson), and other aspects of mass culture that "renovated, rehearsed, and fine-tuned" racism (p. 387).

Among the remarkable contributions of *The Rise and Fall of the White Republic* is the introductory theoretical chapter called "Historical Explanations of Racial Inequality," an earlier version of which appeared in *Marxist Perspectives* 2 (Summer 1979). This is an impressive defense of the cogency and superiority of classical Marxist principles as demonstrated in the concrete case of US white supremacism. Such principles are evidenced in Saxton's straightforward explanation that the notion of white racial superiority peculiar to the United States grew out of "rationalizations and justifications of the slave trade, slavery and expropriation of land from non-white populations" (p. 1), with versions of this belief then refunctioned in different contexts by ruling elites to create and sustain various class coalitions.

However, in differentiating the ideological from the economic explanation of racism, but showing how the former incorporates and complicates the latter, Saxton enriches the classical Marxist tradition. He demonstrates how it can become a flexible framework that still towers above all rival schools. This is further shown by Saxton's offering his own modification of the traditional definition of ideology: "It does not insist that ideas, values, and behavior patterns necessarily originate from, or can be manipulated only by, a ruling class. Nevertheless, upper classes enjoy obvious advantages in gaining acceptance of *their* constructs, especially with the proliferation of mass media" (p. 388). Regrettably, however, Saxton does not incorporate systematic gender analysis into his explanatory model, nor does he provide more than glimpses of gender issues (for example, in his provocative discussion of the way in which the novelist Harriet Beecher Stowe analogizes gender and race in *Uncle Tom's Cabin*) in the massive text that follows.

The body of the work itself is an extraordinary architectural structure in which the various components of his hypotheses are tested through the incisive exploration of historic moments, episodes, personalities, and cultural phenomena, demonstrating a mastery of detail that no book review could possibly recapitulate. Its form is triadic, but the conventional Hegelian structure which so frequently appears in Marxist and non-Marxist writings alike is intentionally complicated. Saxton places both his thesis (the character of the class coalition of the National Republicans/Whigs) and antithesis (the Jacksonian Democrats) in Part I, and his synthesis (the Republican Party in the West, and the part racism played in inhibiting challenges to industrial capitalism) at the end. A segment of four chapters called "Transitions" comes in the middle. These explore various means by which racist ideas were popularized through black-face minstrelsy and the evolving construction of Western heroes, and also examine the role of the journalist George Wilkes and various novelists in expanding and solidifying the Republican Party ideology.

The uncompromising anti-racism of this work – regarding not only the assaults on African-Americans, but also Native American nations, Asian-American immigrants, and the Mexican people – shines through the scholarly arguments of every page, putting to shame canonical liberal texts such as Arthur Schlesinger, Jr.'s *The Age of Jackson* (1945). It is significant that Saxton commences with a substantial critique of John Quincy Adams because Adams, being anti-slavery, can be mistakenly taken as anti-racist. Yet Saxton documents that in "soft" (Saxton's term for moderate) ways, Adams was fomenting a political party no less founded on race than that of his rival Democrats.

Saxton is especially adept in this kind exposé because he conceives of the discourse of racism in terms of an entire US political culture, with his use of the complex category of "race" shifting from coalition to coalition, retelling a tale that is modified to fit the needs of the moment. In short, racism continues because it "sustained important interests of ruling classes or class coalitions" and is "generated and regenerated as part of the process of class conflict and compromise" (p. 385). Thus Saxton deals yet another blow toward demolishing the mythological model of good anti-slavery versus bad pro-slavery forces in US history. As he argues on page 148, *all* parties were white supremacist; it is only a matter of "hard" versus "soft" racism, or, as the sociologist Pierre van den Berghe puts it, competitionist and paternalist varieties. The paternalism of Adams represents the soft, and the competitionism of Jackson the hard. Chapter 13, "Class Organization in a Racially Segmented Labor Force," where Saxton's unparalleled knowledge of Western political and labor history comes into play, is just one of the many striking elaborations of this argument.

Saxton raises so many complex issues and casts his net so wide that there are no doubt weaknesses to which specialists in different areas might legitimately object. Perhaps, as was said about his earlier scholarly book,[3] Saxton's discussions of race are too limited to representations by the whites, rarely disclosing to the reader the viewpoint of the targets of racism (people of color) themselves. He may also hold an exaggerated notion of non-interaction between the dominant culture and its "others" (see p. 390). Saxton's analysis, too, might benefit from a global context – what was happening in Japan or Europe. Still, his conclusion that "white racism in the United States during the nineteenth century was continually constructed and reconstructed out of particular historical circumstances" (p. 391) is consistent with the most advanced thinking on US racial theory, which can be found in writings such as Barbara Fields's "Ideology and Race in American History," in Morgan Kousser and James McPherson's *Race, Region and Reconstruction* (1982), Michael Omi and Howard Winant's *Racial Formation in the United States from the 1960s to the 1980s* (1986), David Roediger's *The Wages of Whiteness: Race and the Making of the American Working Class* (1991), and E. San Juan, Jr.'s *Racial Formations/Critical Transformations: Articulations of Power in Ethnic and Racial Studies in the United States* (1992).

By offering a materialist explanation of the refunctioning of racism in the post-Civil War ideology of the nineteenth century, *The Rise and Fall of the White Republic* courageously addresses some of the most complex and problematic issues in the politics and culture of the United States. The method represents an augmentation and correction of classical Marxism in light of a combination of meticulous primary research and a searching dialogue with the most up-to-date trends in the theory of culture, race, and ideology. While Saxton calls his book only "a modest contribution," it actually constitutes a stunningly imaginative historical explanation of a decisive moment in the ongoing differential treatment of non-European people of color in the United States. Such an achievement in creative scholarship is also motivated by a concern with the impact of racism in our own time. Moreover, an important part of its depth, focus, and precision stems from the author's having been tempered in the crucible of experience, during decades of political commitment and first-hand engagement in class and anti-racist struggle.

Notes

1. The most substantial article on Saxton's personal and literary career to date is Frederick Stern, "Saxton's Late-Proletarian Triptych: To Chicago and West," in *Midamerica* 7 (1980): 135–55. Some additional details about Saxton's political activities are in Norman Canright, "Alexander Saxton and *The Great Midland*," *People's World*, Jan. 13, 1949, p. 5.

2. See "Labor Statesman" (Spring 1952): 35–8, and "The Old Man" (Spring 1953): 38–46.

3. See the otherwise mostly favorable review by Wen H. Kuo of *The Indispensable Enemy* in *American Political Science Review* 70, no. 3 (Summer 1976): 984.

16

Belief and Ideology in the
Work of Robert Hayden

To grasp the complexity of the tension between belief and ideology in the work of Robert Hayden, it may be useful to observe that, while Hayden's *œuvre* manifests important continuities, it can also be divided into periods. At the least, there are "Early," "Middle" and "Late" periods, although John Hatcher's *From the Auroral Darkness: The Life and Poetry of Robert Hayden* (1984) employs a more elaborate division and Pontheolla Williams's *Robert Hayden: A Critical Analysis of His Poetry* (1987) proceeds mainly according to titles of Hayden's poetry collections.

For me, a periodization of Hayden's work discloses a telling dialectic of change and permanence. The "change" is that formal political stances become less confrontational in his work after the early 1940s, at the same time that his attitudes toward religious doctrines and poetic tastes undergo development. The "permanence" lies in the tensive relationship between belief and ideology that remains constant, despite the shifts in perspective. I would characterize Hayden's intellectual attitude from first to last as expressive of a tension between a "will to believe" in a political or spiritual doctrine, and a heretical subversion of that will; this remains crucial to his poetic achievement in all phases.

For example, in the period that I know best, that of the "Early" Hayden in the 1930s, the ideology[1] to which he gave credence was an Afro-Americanized Marxism. His orientation is similar in many respects to the 1930s work of Sterling Brown, Richard Wright, Langston Hughes, the young Margaret Walker, Theodore Ward, Ralph Ellison, Frank Marshall Davis, Arna Bontemps, William Attaway, Eugene Gordon, Eugene Clay Holmes, and a number of others who created a Black Marxist discourse that was pro-Communist. In these years Hayden, too, was centrally attracted to the doctrines of Marxism; he believed the Communist movement was the major source of militant struggle to eradicate oppression by class and race.

This chapter was originally presented at the Robert Hayden Memorial Conference in February 1990 in Ann Arbor, Michigan.

But Hayden related to Marxist doctrine through symbolic structures and with qualifications significantly modulated by his sense of himself as an African-American, an identity somewhat influenced by his response to the Negritude themes of the Harlem Renaissance poets. Moreover, both Marxism and African-American identity were refracted through the lens of his own personal traumas and ordeals.

Some information about Hayden's 1930s radicalism appears in interviews such as the following passage from "The Poet and His Art: A Conversation" (Frederick Glaysher, ed., *Robert Hayden: Collected Prose* [Ann Arbor: University of Michigan Press], p. 134):

> I was in college . . . during the thirties, during the depression, and the motivating force behind poetry, behind most writing of the period . . . was social consciousness. Most of the young writers I knew were terribly earnest about changing the world, about politics, about the class struggle. We identified with the labor movement, with the so-called proletariat. We believed that our poems had to have a social message, had to preach, had to offer a solution. These were the passwords into the literary cliques of the time – message, solution, the masses. The Zeitgeist favored poetry that was documentary, realistic, propagandist. As young poets, we were encouraged to take as our masters revolutionary poets like Funaroff, Lola Ridge . . . Sandburg, Langston Hughes. We imitated their styles, their themes.

Hayden told myself and others that he participated in activities of the John Reed Club of Detroit, an organization of writers initiated and led by the Communist Party; that he read at anti-war and pro-union rallies; and that he was at one point dubbed the "People's Poet" of Detroit.

Nevertheless, when we come to the central poetic representation of Hayden's struggle between belief and ideology in his 1930s period, the collection *Heart-Shape in the Dust* (Detroit, Mich.: The Falcon Press, 1940), we are immediately confronted with several complications. One is that Hayden, like several other former pro-Communists, took unusual measures to prevent the reprinting of not only this whole collection but even of individual poems. Indeed, a University of Michigan faculty member or student who is interested in the evolution of Hayden's art will not be able to find a copy of *Heart-Shape* in any of our libraries, although there is a manuscript of it on display under glass in the Rare Book Room.

To the African-American critic Houston Baker, Hayden wrote on November 26, 1969: "I must refuse . . . to allow the poems I have checked on the enclosed form to be reprinted. They are from my very first volume, printed almost thirty years ago, and certainly no longer representative of my outlook, technique, etc." To his permissions editor at October House Publishers, he wrote on November 3, 1970: "Please don't allow anything from *Heart-Shape in the Dust* to be reprinted. Good heavens, the book appeared exactly thirty years ago and contains work that in almost no way represents me now." And to the scholar David Littlejohn he protested on September 2, 1966: "I no longer like any of them [poems of the

1930s and early 1940s] and did not include such 'prentice work in my present volume. I . . . think the term 'communist' applied to my poetry is unfortunate, offensive, and irresponsible, particularly in these conformist times."

There are at least two interconnected issues that one may consider in assessing this response. One is Hayden's judgment of the poor quality of these early writings, an opinion that he continued to maintain in spite of the protests of some younger scholars to the contrary. A second issue is Hayden's famous and completely understandable resistance to having his writing and his artistic self "boxed" under a label imposed by someone else – whether that label be "Negro" or "Black" poet, or "Social" or "Communist" poet.

In regard to the first issue, it is clear that Hayden held his post-1930s styles to be superior artistically to the "message"-, "solution"-, and "mass"-oriented works in the "documentary," "realistic," and "propagandistic" forms that he remembered himself to have written in the 1930s. As for the second issue, it is well known that, in the 1960s, he found himself confronted with a new generation of critics who for various reasons wanted to characterize art by racial or political terminology. In the case of some publishers, the motivation may have been to increase sales. In the case of the Black Arts movement, there was a feeling that writers should identify themselves as Black or Afro-American as a gesture of political commitment and solidarity, as well as a sign of resistance to assimilation.

In response to the second demand, Hayden became embittered about the use of any special characterizations of his poetry as being that of a "Black American," which he saw as a means of narrowing his poetic achievement. He pointed to the case of Yeats, who, though undoubtedly Irish and a political nationalist, is usually presented as a major poet first, with nationality among those qualifications applied secondarily. This is a complex matter and, although one is certainly free to suggest alternative approaches, the literary critic also has a responsibility to try to understand the poet's motives.

However, the devaluation and suppression of poetry is another matter. While it is the responsibility of scholars to respect the taste and opinions of the artists they admire, and to represent them with reasonable objectivity, we also have the duty to try to contextualize and evaluate these opinions. In regard to Hayden's opinions of his early work, I find his judgment misleading in many respects, and even somewhat harmful if not interrogated independently.

First of all, the generic assessment of his first volume as message/solution/mass-oriented writing that is documentary/ realistic/propagandistic in style is, like many memories of 1930s culture, including those of first-hand participants, not entirely accurate. Such one-sided accounts emphasize simple forms and class-reductive content, occluding from vision the trend in 1930s literature that was modernist, feminist, and responsive to cultural difference, as in writers such as Tillie Olsen, Meridel Le Sueur, Thomas McGrath, Carlos Bulosan, Sterling Brown, Henry Roth, and many others.

After all, Hayden's volume is not called "Paeans to Proletarian Revolution"; it is *Heart-Shape in the Dust*. Moreover, Hayden's dialectical theme of human hope, symbolized by the constructed heart-shape, versus transiency, symbolized by the dust of human frailty, is centered throughout this carefully assembled volume in a variety of subtle combinations.

The opening poem, "Autumnal," is a death poem. It moves thematically from plant to animal to abstract human; there is no racial identification. Yet the poem on the opposite page, "We Have Not Forgotten," is a Black pride poem. Turn the page and one is struck by a poem called "He is Foredoomed." This romantic poem is characterized by rhyming quatrains about the lonely fate of the poet, once again in a "raceless" motif. Yet it, too, directly faces a counter-statement: "Sunflowers: Beaubien Street." This Black culture poem reads as follows:

> The Negroes here, dark votaries of the sun,
> Have planted sunflowers round door and wall,
> Hot-smelling, vivid as an august moon.
> Thickets of yellow fire, they hold in thrall
> The cruel, sweet remembrance of down home.
>
> O sun-whirled, tropic tambourines
> That play sad juba songs in dooryard loam,
> recalling chain-gang heat and shimmering pines;
> O sunward cry of dark ones mute within
> The crumbling shocks' bright image of their will
> To reach through prayer, through long belief the sun
> Fixed in the heavens like Ezekiel's Wheel.
>
> Here phonographs of poverty repeat
> An endless blues chorale of torsioning despair –
> And yet these dark ones find mere living sweet
> And set this solid brightness on the bitter air.

Perhaps this is message-oriented and aimed at the "masses"; perhaps it is even "realistic," and in some sense "propagandistic." But there is also a power, vividness, and originality in its language and vision that must be recognized as well.

Hayden's next diptych is comprised of one poem, "The Falcon," describing the killing of a swallow by the war-like, sword-like falcon, placed directly across from "To a Young Negro Poet." "Dedication," a call for the poet to embrace the aspirations of all people, is placed across from "Southern Moonlight," a love song to a Black man by a southern white woman.

The intellectual, political, and personal struggle dramatized in these writings between belief and ideology is the very principle of organization. On the one side of the page is a voluntaristic doctrine of hope; on the other, some sort of complex challenge to that hope. These antagonists square off for the first eight pages of *Heart-Shape in the Dust*, until we encounter the ironical anti-war sequence, "Words This Spring," starting with "Spring Offensive."

Another thirty-eight poems follow. They range from the defiant tribute to "Gabriel" (Gabriel Prosser, hanged for leading a slave rebellion) to an "Obituary" for his father. It is true that many of these are intended as mass chants and recitations, especially "Negro to America, " "Speech," and "These Are My People." But how should we assess them? Most of the dismissals of this kind of writing, including Hayden's own, are based on what might be called "aesthetic dehistoricization." The critic, sometimes even claiming to be impartial and objective, simply does not discuss the writing in light of the goals and models held by the poet at the time.

In the context of the 1930s, when drama was far more central an art form than today, and when galvanizing the exploited into resistance through public readings was regarded as a legitimate artistic objective, much of Hayden's poetry was successful in accomplishing his goals in striking and stirring ways. But such an achievement can only constitute "literary value" if one regards Hayden's poems of the 1930s from the perspective of the literary objectives held by the poet at the time. In particular, one must accept that his literary models were figures such as Sol Funaroff (now-forgotten leader of the *Dynamo* school of poets), Lola Ridge, and the young Langston Hughes. Of course, one's assessment of the early Hayden will be dramatically different if one evaluates his 1930s poems in light of his later literary objectives, in the context of his post-1930s models, such as Yeats.

To invert the situation: Would a critic be able to convince us that a much-admired later poem such as "The Diver" achieved its aims effectively if our model of literary value were, say, the poetic devices of Sol Funaroff's "To the Dead of the International Brigade," or if our literary objective were to motivate striking auto workers to persist in their struggles despite the guns and clubs of the police? Of course, one may hold the categorical view that the kinds of language and strategies promoted by a Funaroff are themselves less worthy than those of a Yeats or Eliot; but here one runs the risk of legislating the "proper" duties for a poet to carry out, a dubious theme in Western culture from Plato to Stalin.

Only if one believes there are aesthetic achievements independent of social context, that there are transcendent models against which everything else must be measured, can one *dehistoricize* artistic objectives and models to conclude that a poem consciously modeled on Funaroff or Hughes is inferior because it fails to measure up to "literary value" based on a model of Yeats. A Funaroff-inspired poem can be evaluated according to Yeatsian norms only if one believes that Yeats provides an all-purpose model of literary value, whether the poet resides in Harlem, a shetl of Eastern Europe, an Ivy League University, a campsite of migrant field workers, or on a Native American Indian reservation.

Of course, it is true that a good deal of traditional literary study has been based on such a transcendent hierarchy of aesthetic value, but a growing number of scholars are recognizing that it almost always turns out that the hierarchy is not "innocent" or "neutral" or "value free," but more or less derived from the British Great Tradition and its version of "Western culture." In other words, there is a correlation between who set the terms of the transcendant aesthetic value system, and those who have held wealth and power in the world.

My argument here, of course, is not to invert the conclusion of Hayden and many others by reversing the schema to valorize the early poetry above the later; this would require transforming the models and criteria of Hayden's early work into the transcendent hierarchy. The point is that assessment of various Hayden texts must be contextualized, which means taking into account a greater variety of influences and models than simply the later or canonical ones. Just as many younger scholars have come to realize that one can hardly even "see" many of the tropes of Chicano, Asian American, and Native American Indian poetry without reconstructing the specific and especially the unique aspects of the cultural soil out of which such syncretic writing grew, so the literature of the particular historical moment of the 1930s African-American Left must be seen in terms of its own social dynamics, its own cultural problematic, and its own models of cultural value toward which writers were aspiring.

But then we have the important question: Was the move to the kind of poetry that Hayden eventually came to write – combined with his active suppression of the earlier work – a natural progression from inferior to superior art? Clearly Hayden believed that to be the case, and clearly he associated the appearance of the Black Arts movement in the 1960s with a regression to inferior techniques, themes, and attitudes he had come to repudiate. But, just as some intellectuals in the Black Arts movement were simplistic in dismissing Hayden in the 1960s as an "Oreo" (Black on the outside, white on the inside), so Hayden was simplistic in his characterization of the Black Arts movement as mere racial chauvinism and anti-art.

In fact, looking back from 1990, I would say that without that stage of vital affirmation and empowerment of the hidden African-American cultural heritage, it is hard to imagine the appearance of and acceptance of the kind of writing we find in Toni Morrison, nor the dramatic resurrection of Zora Neale Hurston (cast into the dustbin by white scholars, and by some African-American ones as well, in the pre-Black Arts period), nor many other extraordinary features of our cultural landscape that were inspired by and revitalized by interaction with that landmark cultural upheaval, whatever the Black Arts movement's excesses or failings. Moreover, what happened in the 1960s was partly prefigured by Hayden and others drawn to Communism in the 1930s.

It is true, of course, that, in the heat of the 1960s, it may have been plausible for Hayden (and also Ralph Ellison) to warn that using "racial" categories to discuss culture embodies certain dangers of polarization and oversimplification. But by 1990 one can say with certainty that the new way of introducing the category of "race" into cultural discourse, like the introduction of the category of "gender," when devoid of biological reference or "essentialism," has complicated and enriched our understanding in innumerable and irreversible ways.

What is interesting is not only that Hayden's post-1930s work survived the hostility of some figures in the Black Arts period, but that his poetry looks better than ever today. I do not believe, however, that such lasting power is because Hayden finally reached the nirvana of the higher transcendent aesthetic realm of the dehistoricized versions of Shakespeare, Milton, and other mystified icons of the ideology of "universal art." I think that the continuing attraction of Hayden's poetry stems from its dialectical tension between belief and ideology that allows him to assume formal positions on the one hand that he challenges in practice with the other.

The enduring presence of this tension is why this poet who said he was not a "Black Poet" continued, among many other things, to write astonishing Black poetry. And why this poet who, after 1940, formally adhered to the Bahai faith, didn't write doctrinaire Bahai poems.

But that creative tension was by no means a late feature; it was there in his artistic origins, and there in his Marxist period as well. So let me end by suggesting that it is time to reject the wholesale dismissal of the early Hayden – time to stop denying ourselves the beauty, anguish and inspiration of so much of *Heart-Shape in the Dust*. It is a fundamental and in many ways formative part of the achievement of Robert Hayden. Moreover, the suppression of *Heart-Shape in the Dust* from Hayden's *oeuvre* is but a microcosm of the exclusion of the complex reality of the 1930s left-wing cultural tradition from our cultural history as a whole.

Notes

1. Here I am using the term "ideology" in its popularized definition as a set of ideas representing a position.
2. For this and all other quotations from Hayden's letters, I am grateful to Dr. Xavier Nicholas, who is preparing a volume of them for publication.

17

John Sanford and

"America Smith"

I

The People from Heaven is a 1943 novel by an unrepentant Jewish-American Marxist about anti-Black and anti-Native American Indian racist culture in the North of the United States. The setting is Warrensburg, New York, then a small rural town in the Adirondack mountains where Sanford vacationed in the summer of 1931 in the company of his personal and literary friend, Nathanael West.[1] Except for a handful of dissenters and outcasts opposed to the local town bully, the subconscious life and daily values of most members of the fictional community are profoundly deformed by the culture and social system evolving from the violent conquest of the continent by Europeans starting in the seventeenth century.

Sanford's bitingly ironic title refers to the reported cry of celebration of the native peoples of the Americas as they hailed the arrival of Columbus and the Europeans who would enslave them – "Come! come to see the people from Heaven!"[2] The pattern of brutality enacted four hundred years earlier underlies the catastrophic events Sanford depicts in 1943: a propertied white man, Eli Bishop, rapes an itinerant Black woman, who is locally referred to as "America Smith," and then seeks to extend his reign of terror against a Native American father and son, an independent-minded prostitute, and, finally, a Jewish refugee from Czarist pogroms.

The advanced thinking underlying the symbolic action of the text is worth noting. Two decades before the writings of Frantz Fanon garnered attention in the United States, Sanford's novel depicts many of the psycho-sexual dynamics of racism, and their disturbing links to the colonization process.[3] Fully five

---

This chapter is based on a talk given at the 1993 national convention of the Modern Languages Association and a version will also appear as the "Introduction" to the University of Illinois reprint of *The People from Heaven* (Urbana: University of Illinois Press, forthcoming).

decades prior to the widespread discussion among scholars about "The Wages of Whiteness," an expression derived from W.E.B. Du Bois for the psychological and public benefits of race prejudice to white workers, Sanford depicts the doubled-edged and ultimately destructive consequences of these "wages" for their presumed beneficiaries.[4] An entire political generation before notions of the right of armed self-defense and autonomous self-organization by people of color became broadly accepted by Euro-American radicals of the 1960s, Sanford's novel promotes a political response in which an African-American woman strikes the first blow for freedom in her own way, violently and with deference to no man.

From a literary perspective, this is a novel that is revolutionary in form as well as content. In its art, *The People from Heaven* brilliantly fuses politics and technique, thus defying the classificatory systems promoted by a half century of literary critics. Yet, the novel's authentic success as literature may have produced the terms for its commercial failure, and, until now, critical neglect; ironically, the "problem" with Sanford's novel is that it didn't fail in the ways that Marxist, modernist, or historical novels are *supposed* to fail in order to conform to these various genres as they were constructed.

That is, even though the author is a Marxist, *The People from Heaven* bears few of the alleged features of the "proletarian novel" or novels about strikes, "bottom dogs," middle-class decay, or conversions to socialism. Hence this work, and all others by Sanford, receives no mention in Walter Rideout's *The Radical Novel in the United States, 1900–1954* (1956), Daniel Aaron's *Writers on the Left* (1961), or any of the substantial scholarship devoted to that proletarian novel tradition usually associated with Mike Gold, Jack Conroy, and the early John Steinbeck. If Sanford's work had ended with the formation of a class-conscious trade union or the heroine picking up a copy of *The Communist Manifesto*, it would have at least received a passing reference in the substantial corpus of books and dissertations about the radical novel.

Moreover, even though the techniques of *The People from Heaven* are aggressively experimental – indeed, in many respects "modernist" – Sanford's anti-racist and anti-colonialist politics are far too central and "in your face" to allow the work to sit comfortably in a genre conventionally represented by James Joyce, Franz Kafka, and William Faulkner, whose politics are often missed or misunderstood by readers. While some experimental novels with technical skill equivalent to Sanford's were produced by open leftists such as Henry Roth in *Call It Sleep* (1934) and Nathanael West in *The Day of the Locust* (1939), none are as direct, unambiguous, and unapologetic in their political message. Again, Sanford "failed" to attenuate his anti-racism into what might be approached as an abstract or allegorical trope for the human condition.

Finally, as indicated by the novel's nine poetic commentaries on episodes of persecution and oppression from the fifteenth through nineteenth centuries, "History" is central to Sanford's understanding of the forces behind contemporary experience; in fact, *The People from Heaven* is partly a "critical realist" text in the way that the term was used by the Hungarian Marxist critic Georg Lukács.[5] Yet this is not a radical "historical novel" in the manner of outstanding Marxist-influenced works such as John Dos Passos's *USA* (1936), Howard Fast's *Freedom Road* (1944), or Margaret Walker's *Jubilee* (1966). *The People from Heaven* proceeds by meditation and a subtle pattern of association, not relentless chronological development and systematic thick descriptions of society. In Sanford, the role of History is perhaps closest to that found in William Carlos Williams's essays *In the American Grain* (1925), albeit Sanford's excursions into the past are poetic and interspersed with a thematically related, taut fictional narrative covering events lasting about a week in the life of the town of Warrensburg. Once again, Sanford "failed" – failed to employ the kind of conventional realism for which historical novelists such as Fast are so often stigmatized as "middlebrow."[6]

Nevertheless, precisely due to the exhaustion of these earlier theorizations of cultural tradition, the moment is ripe in the 1990s for fresh discussions and appreciations of *The People from Heaven*. At one time, these canonical constructs of literary radicalism, modernism, and historical fiction may have been path-breaking explications clarifying specific currents within the larger literary stream, but they now can also serve to obscure vital and noteworthy works such as Sanford's. The past fifteen years have witnessed a dramatic increase of students and scholars grappling to forge a broader and more complex cultural history. They have searched anew throughout many facets of US literary history for alternative "moments" and paradigms, many of which engage precisely the issues central to Sanford's excoriating dramatization of complex interconnections among racism, sexism, and economic privilege and their roots in the history of the United States.

II

The author of *The People from Heaven* is as much an "original" as the work itself. John Sanford, born Julian Shapiro in New York City in 1904, is living testimony to the continuity of the radical literary tradition from the 1930s to the 1990s. At age ninety, Sanford, now residing in Santa Barbara, recently completed his twentieth book, *Maggie: A Love Story* (1993). His nineteen previous books, most of them honed to near-perfection by a singular ability to unite stunning artistry and undisguised social criticism, run the gamut from fiction in the realist and naturalist mode, to historical poetry and prose commentary, to novelized autobiography and other experiments. *The People from Heaven* expresses a distinct stage in the evolution of his craft, yet stands alone as a signal achievement within his *œuvre* as well as in the various sub-genres of US literature to which it has affinities.

The roots of Sanford's art stem from the remarkable cross-currents of the late 1920s and early 1930s, when individuals such as Sanford responded to two trends in US culture, fusing the modernist call to create a fresh language with the radical call to take a stand on behalf of the exploited. The result was a brilliant flowering of literary women and men, writers of color and Euro-Americans. These were people of the Left who consecrated their art of fiction to social emancipation. Nelson Algren (*Somebody in Boots*, 1935), Arna Bontemps (*Black Thunder*, 1936), Edward Dahlberg (*Bottom Dogs*, 1930), James T. Farrell (*Young Lonigan*, 1932), Langston Hughes (*The Ways of White Folks*, 1934), Josephine Johnson (*Now In November*, 1934), Meridel Le Sueur (*The Girl*, 1939), Richard Wright (*Uncle Tom's Children*, 1938) and others established an occasionally prominent but often hidden cultural stream of literary radicalism of uneven quality that would flow through subsequent decades until it was overtaken by new styles of cultural rebellion with the advent of the New Left of the 1960s. Although Sanford was once part of this larger left-wing literary movement of the 1930s and 1940s that more-or-less looked to the Communist Party and Soviet Union for political inspiration, he is among the few who continued to write, and write well, while staying loyal to his fundamental political convictions in the fifty years that followed.

The son of a lawyer, and a lawyer himself by training, Sanford came under the spell of literature through his personal association with Nathanael West, to whom *The People from Heaven* is dedicated. It was West (born Weinstein) who suggested that Sanford change his name, and so he abandoned Shapiro to become John Sanford, the name of the protagonist in Shapiro/Sanford's first novel, *The Water-Wheel* (1933).

Unaffected initially by radical politics in his New York period, Sanford's move to Hollywood, following the minor commercial success of his brutally powerful *The Old Man's Place* (1935), put him in touch with the Communist movement. His connection with the movie industry also brought him immediately in contact with the screenwriter Marguerite Roberts (1905–89), to whom he was married for more than fifty years. Together they shared the ugly "Time of the Toad" of the Hollywood Blacklist era that ended his film career and caused a major disruption of hers.

III

Sanford's political history brings forward important new evidence concerning the controversial matter of US writers and Communism. Due to the Red-baiting that became the official line of the 1950s thought police running the educational institutions and the media (supervised by watchdogs of the FBI and demagogues of the House Committee on Un-American Activities), a social commitment that was once a badge of honor now became highly suspect. Any relationship to the Communist Party, especially an organizational one, became something to be denied, repudiated, or, at least, minimized.

Later on, scholars hoping to redeem the artistic quality of certain writers once on the Left tended to dwell on whatever evidence might be found of a distance from the Communist Party; to be briefly attracted to Communism, like Steinbeck or Dos Passos, might be regarded as compatible with the production of authentic literature, so long as the writer did not actually join or, at least, function loyally for any length of time. This approach reached the point of outright falsification of history when, in 1988, an effort to reclaim Richard Wright's *12 Million Black Voices* (1941) as a quality work of art in a new edition was accompanied by the statement that Wright "never actually joined" the Communist Party.[7] Wright, in fact, was proudly public about his affiliation in the 1930s, and wrote in detail about his Party experiences in later years.[8] Most recently, in a perhaps understandable but nevertheless oversimplified reaction to hostile and reductive treatments of Communism and writers, several scholarly books claim that the cultural movement associated with Communism produced no restrictions of significance in regard to a writer's technical approach or style.[9]

A study of Sanford's experience indicates that, in fact, the Communist movement definitely promoted a strong orientation toward certain literary styles and themes, and had various means of encouragement and discouragement. Imaginative works were frequently judged in reviews and public discussions according to political implications that might be attributed to an interpretation of certain passages and events in the narrative. The institutional mechanisms through which pressure was exerted came through variations of the famous Hollywood "Writers' Clinic" led by Communist playwright and film writer John Howard Lawson, where draft manuscripts were read and reviewed by a committee of Party members. There were also critical notices in the Party press by leading Party spokespersons, who were sometimes full-time paid staff members and who held posts on Cultural Commissions. Less formally, it was not unusual for individuals close to or in the Party to voluntarily share their manuscripts with comrades, especially those who had already published and who were seen as more politically developed, and to welcome feedback of a political or literary nature.

But Sanford's experience demonstrates that it was not always required that one must accede to changes proposed through such institutional constraints, so long as one was otherwise politically and organizationally loyal. In the case of *The People from Heaven*, a draft of the work was judged ultra-Left and even too Black nationalist by members of a Los Angeles committee.[10] This was not surprising in the context of the wartime patriotic orientation that the Communist movement was then promoting. Nevertheless, Sanford refused to alter a word of the manuscript, which was also his policy in dealing with criticisms from publishing houses.

In my view, it would be a mistake to either ignore Sanford's specifically

Communist political commitments, or to try to reduce his novel to a mere function of them, a dramatization of ideology. The overwhelming evidence available from biographical studies of writers, as well as specific evidence from Sanford's own memoirs, indicates that a work of imaginative literature grows primarily out of the unconscious; in Sanford's words, from an "unknown retrieval system."[11]

On the other hand, Sanford's choice of theme, his political categories, and the anti-racist values that shine through on every page cannot be disassociated from his Marxism. This was not a text book Marxism but Marxism of a general character. It was an identification with the underdog against the oppressor, and not, in his literary work, a Marxism dictated by the US Communist Party. His own memory that he "wasn't writing for the Party but out of my own beliefs and sympathy" is confirmed by both the individualistic qualities of the literature itself, and the absence of any evidence that Party cultural leaders ever desired to promote Sanford as a figure to emulate in the way that Howard Fast and several others were lionized.[12]

This is not to suggest, however, that, therefore, Sanford wasn't really a "left-wing writer" or a legitimate part of the Communist cultural tradition in the United States. In a 1947 argument with a Party cultural leader who insisted that *The People from Heaven* was "anti-social" because "it ends with a black woman blowing a white man's brains out," Sanford retorted that he was in his own way true to the much-contested Communist slogan, "Art is a Weapon." He insisted, "If that book isn't a weapon, I never saw one."[13]

However, some parts of *The People from Heaven* originated in stories written from his pre-Marxist phase; in particular, the narrative of the adulterous minister, "Bishop's Story," which was published as "Once in a Sedan and Twice Standing Up."[14] In addition, the novel was partly connected to an earlier novel of the same region, *Seventy Times Seven* (1939), through several characters that he retained. While sketching in the opening vignettes of these and a range of others to populate his fictionalized Warrensburg, Sanford found himself writing the word "Brothers" as the beginning of a sermon by the preacher, Dan Hunter. This was followed by the image of a black woman walking into a white man's store on a rainy cold night to be greeted by, "You want anything, nigger?"[15]

Some of the other autobiographical elements behind the construction of the text have more explicitly radical associations. Sanford had been haunted for some time by an empathy with the Native Americans who thought the Europeans were "The people from Heaven" and he wanted "to write of the hell they brought along."[16] Sanford was also troubled by memories of his attempt to hitch-hike through the Carolinas when he ran away from home at age sixteen; when asked by a man how he felt about the South, Sanford found himself complaining about the lynchings of Blacks, and then the name of Leo Frank, a Jew who was also lynched, came into his mind. Beyond this, the drive to write *The People from Heaven* seems connected with guilt Sanford felt over his failure when he was twenty-four to be aware of the execution of Sacco and Vanzetti.[17]

In any event, the reception of the novel in the public press did not evidence the simplistic equations between the art and Sanford's politics in the way that scholars of later generations would indict and dismiss the literary movement allied with the Communist Party. By and large the response was characterized by a failure to know what to do with the novel. Most reviewers saw many strong qualities in the language and style, although there were complaints that these were not consistently sustained. While most critics also noted the political implications, they did therefore not dismiss the author as a propagandist. What is striking is the inability of the reviewers to come up with many novels for comparison, contemporary or historical; and, when the critics failed to find a context, they seemed unable to recognize that something truly pathbreaking had been produced.[18]

As a result, the richness and complexity of Sanford's vision – the pattern of symbols, the lush allusiveness, the mythological aura – was inadequately recognized and acknowledged. Unfortunately, these very features can preclude a mass audience from spontaneously embracing a work without aggressive intervention by literary critics. Earlier, the left-wing anti-racist satire of Erskine Caldwell in a book such as *Tobacco Road* (1932) was sufficiently direct and straightforward to reach a large public on its own, especially in the political atmosphere of the early Depression. In contrast, *The People from Heaven*, published and reviewed well into World War II, was not by itself able to locate and inspire a popular audience.

However, Sanford's innovative and powerfully focused artistic techniques should have earned from critics and scholars the respect accorded to a Faulkner or some other writer whose "difficulty" (a vague category that varies from reader to reader, depending on prior knowledge and experience as well as one's frame of mind when reading the text) was a mark of high craft. This wonderfully jarring juxtaposition – of the powerful "simplicity" of Sanford's angry anti-racism with the necessity of reading *The People from Heaven* carefully, with attention to detail and an active involvement in constructing meaning – produced an unfamiliar blend that seems to have rendered all the novel's critics of 1943–44 incapable of providing a clear perspective on its meaning and significance.

IV

From the opening scene, as Dan Hunter surveys a congregation comprised of dated tombstones (the dates incomplete for those still living), to the complex closing finale among the ruins of Dan's burned-out church, the reader of *The People from Heaven* is pulled in many directions. We are taken on a tour of sensory and intellectual experiences unlike those produced by any other text in US literature. In the most accessible parts of the narrative, we are presented, following the introduction of much of the Warrensburg community through vignettes, with the appearance of a mysterious stranger.

An unknown and unnamed African-American woman arrives in a tight-knit, repressed, and authoritarian community where the chief shop-keeper, Eli Bishop, is chief lecher and thug. Her appearance divides the town into factions, forcing all to take sides. The miniature civil war that follows is connected with a number of sub-plots that bring to the fore anti-Indian prejudice, sexism, hypocrisy, and anti-Semitism. Undergirding the whole novel is a powerful examination of the historical roots of the ugly racism lying beneath the superficial harmony of a rural community, and the mechanisms by which it is fed by sexual repression and passed on from parents (usually the father) to children (usually the son).

At the same time Sanford employs nine historical inserts to propel us back into into a sequence of events between 1492 and 1863: the journey of Columbus to the New World (1492); the experiences of Pokahontas with the Europeans (1607); the arrival of a Dutch man-o'-war with twenty captive Africans (1619); a recreation of native peoples welcoming whites as the people from Heaven (dated 1620); scenes from the religious conflict between Christians and native peoples (1632); witchcraft trials (1691); an imaginary dialogue called "God in the Hands of an Angry Sinner" (1741); a slave escape (1775); and the story of a former slave who decides to serve the Union army as a spy in the South (1863).

To some readers, who are accustomed to apprehending history as the presentation of "fact," these may well be troubling aspects of the novel. After all, Sanford's poetic commentaries refer to known episodes, yet they are refracted through the individual sensibility of the author. What is "mere" opinionated interpretation, and what is "real," the reader may ask? Indeed, a number of publishing house editors who rejected the book for publication, and critics who commented on the version that was released by Harcourt, Brace and Company, wished the historical commentaries had been removed.

Today, however, Sanford's strategy here appears more like that of a sophisticated modern Marxist who has learned something from critics of the Enlightenment, and even from the post-structuralists: that the boundaries between "objective fact" and "imposed narration" are not always clear but contested by the values of the storyteller, whether in prose or poetry, history or imaginative literature. Like the Marxist playwright Bertolt Brecht, whose aim was to agitate the minds of an audience rather than encourage passive identification and purgation, Sanford encourages readers to think for themselves, to doubt and be vigilant.

A third complicating feature is that the narrative, while propelled along at times with the power of a detective thriller, also crosses over into modernism; it is self-consciously experimental in form and can be difficult and disturbing. At times there are transitions, in setting and character, from "reality" to "fantasy" that are unannounced. Moreover, episodes in the "story" line seem to have sug-

gestive links to many of the historical inserts that precede them, but it is left to
the reader to conjecture the precise relationship or simply intuit a more elusive
connection.

For example, the insert about the "discovery" of the Americas is followed by
the white men of Warrensburg "discovering" and trying to "name" the Black
woman; the insert about the persecution of witches is followed by an episode
where America Smith is persecuted for her race; the insert depicting a slave
escape is followed by a scene where the Native American father, Bigelow
Vroom, seizes a rifle to defend his son, Aben, against Bishop and another racist;
and the insert about the former slave going to spy on the Confederacy is followed by America Smith's decision to enter Eli Bishop's house to confront him.
Virtually the entire text is carefully and complexly interwoven and interrelated
in a series of associations, prefigurings, and other devices.[19] Nevertheless, for the
casual reader there are mysteries, and it is fair to predict that students and scholars of the text will have many opportunities to engage in discussion and debate.

A fourth feature of special concern to readers of the 1990s may be the Jewish-
specific aspects of this novel about anti-Black racism, depicting a rebel African-
American female protagonist. At the excruciatingly high-pitched, violent
climax of *The People from Heaven*, Sanford describes an unforgettably symptomatic showdown. The altercation is between the racist demagogue, Eli Bishop,
and the tiny number of Warrensburg dissidents. First Bishop bashes Dan
Hunter, the iconoclastic town preacher; then he pounds unconscious Bigelow
Vroom, the proud Native American Indian. Standing over his victims, Bishop
turns upon the terrorized onlookers:

"An hour after he can walk," he said, nodding back at Vroom, "we're going to have
a parade in this town, and he's going to head it."

He stooped to pick up a pine cone. "It'll start at the Post Office, and it'll keep
moving till it's out of sight. There'll be four people marching in that parade: this
Indian here, the Indian's boy-bastard Aben, the nigger-woman, and one more." He
cracked a few scales from the cone and let them fall. "The Jew." He looked now at
Novinsky. "The Jew son-of-a-bitch: he goes too. This use to be a white man's town,
Warrensburg, and it won't be long before it's white all over again." A butterfly beat
past, its speckled wings applauding.

America Smith was a grave-length away, her hands, as if in a muff, hidden by the
drape of the spare dress. She brought one of them forth, and the black accusation of
the Colt was leveled at Bishop. "Run," she said.

"Put that gun down, nigger!"

"Now pray and run."

"Did you hear me, nig...!"

A bullet stopped Bishop's last syllable at his teeth, and teeth tumbled from a
second mouth that opened in the back of his head. A dead man did a half-twist, gave
at the joints, and collapsed.

Still holding the Colt, the woman polled the faces of the crowd . . . . [20]

I call this episode symptomatic because it typifies many characteristic features of the Jewish-American literary use of an African-American rebel protagonist in the tradition forged by the mid-century, Communist-led cultural Left. The author is Jewish but the viewpoint is not, at least, not consciously, Judeocentric, Jewish nationalist, or Jewish particularist.[21] The main agent of revenge or retribution, America Smith, is African-American, although the presence of Native American targets of racism and agents of resistance, Bigelow and Aben Vroom, is by no means a casual addition.

The Jewish character, Abe Novinsky, while not among the primary cast of actors in earlier sections, has been referred to in passing. Barely tolerated by the community, Novinsky lives on the borders of racial ostracism. Thus the sudden shift in focus to him by Bishop, which is at first a bit surprising, is not, on second thought, illogical. Indeed, the anti-Semitism of the community has been adequately foreshadowed so that this inclusion of the Jew with the persecuted characters of color germinates new meanings for which seeds were planted in earlier episodes.

Moreover, the introduction of Novinsky as a potential victim just before America Smith downs Bishop, strongly presses toward the following political allegory:

1. Native fascism has its origins in the successful conquest and victimization of indigenous peoples (represented by Vroom), which religious and other Euro-American community leaders (represented by Hunter) failed to halt.
2. The latest group of targets, African-Americans (represented by America Smith), must learn the lessons of the past and not rely on others, but be prepared to defend themselves with arms, if necessary.
3. It is in the interest of all others who are oppressed, first among them Jews (represented by Novinsky), to defend without qualifications the African-American struggle in the United States, because, if the racists are successful against the Blacks, they will next turn on others, starting with the Jews.

Sanford's climax makes this perspective more explicit than many similar texts.[22] But even here the complex relationship must be understood as part of a larger Marxist-internationalist outlook. The Jewish–Black relation is not the fulcrum or single explanatory factor of this fairly substantial tradition of Jewish radical writers culturally "cross-dressing" so as to present their themes through African-American rebel-protagonists. It would be a violation of the known intent and the information we have about the art of John Sanford to center his Jewishness as *the* explanatory factor for the artistic and ideological text. It would also violate the character of the whole sub-tradition of Jewish radical novelists combatting racial capitalism through Black protagonists.

Of course, some Jewish elements are present in the text, as they are in Sanford's self-consciousness as a writer. But *The People from Heaven* is over-determined by his 1930s radicalization, not to mention myriad idiosyncratic matters of personal psychology and literary influence. For such biograph-ical/artistic as well as political reasons, it is probably "no accident," as we Marxists are always pontificating, that *The People from Heaven* contains the Jewish character Abe Novinsky, whose tale of a pogrom is a sensational episode.[23] It is also probably "no accident" that, as the arch bigot Eli Bishop ascends to power at the novel's climax, it is his anti-Semitism that triggers his demise at the hands of America Smith.[24]

This said about the combined possible artistic, biographical, and political motivations, it is important to note that such a climax to the novel was a per-sonal choice of Sanford's – one that was denounced as ultra-Left and ultra-Black nationalist by the Communist Party committee that read over the draft manuscript of his book. As in the case of Guy Endore, whose novel *Babouk* (1934) was likewise sharply criticized as Black nationalist, on that occasion by an African-American Communist critic in the *New Masses*,[25] Sanford was express-ing an anger and empathy that preceded and transcended any formal adher-ence to "Party line."[26]

That John Sanford's uncompromising dissection of racism should be republished after fifty years of obscurity is hardly an innocent or accidental "return of the repressed." The values and behavior dramatized by Sanford are endemic to and long-term features of our country and its culture. Moreover, contemporary trends in literary studies have paved the way for the novel's reception and appreciation by a new generation of students, scholars, and general readers.

Its reappearance confirms the analysis of Marxist critics such as Raymond Williams about the social mechanisms by which some books are remembered and others forgotten.[27] Ideologically and artistically, Sanford's novel raises many of the cutting-edge questions about the selective construction of canons and traditions in a liberal democracy. The book's refusal to die reinforces the assess-ment of scholars such as Cary Nelson who insist that what has been correspond-ingly silenced in this institutionalized process are often works exploring issues beyond the perimeters of acceptable political discourse.[28] As feminist critics have demonstrated in the case of "lost" writings such as Tillie Olsen's *Yonondio* (begun in 1934; published in 1974), Meridel Le Sueur's *The Girl* (1939) and Josephine Herbst's *Rope of Gold* (1939), such issues can be ones that anticipate later concerns, often approached from perspectives far in advance of contemporaries.[29]

Notes

1. Several of Sanford's novels and short stories use an Adirondack setting; six of the stories are collected in *Adirondack Stories* (Santa Barbara, Calif.; Capra Press, 1976).

2. The quote appears on the title page of the 1943 edition, and is attributed to Christopher Columbus in a letter he wrote to Luis de Santangel.

3. See Fanon, *Black Skin, White Masks* (New York: Grove, 1967) and *The Wretched of the Earth* (New York: Grove, 1965).

4. While earlier writers touched on the issue, David Roediger brought the "white problem" to national attention in his compelling study *The Wages of Whiteness: Race and the Making of the American Working Class* (London: Verso, 1991).

5. That is, a twentieth-century "realist" work doesn't simply "mirror" history but offers a perspective compatible with socialist principles of interpretation on the crises of modern society. See Georg Lukács, *The Meaning of Contemporary Realism* (London: Merlin, 1963).

6. "Fast is particularly interesting as the last full-time bard of the [Communist] movement, its most faithful middlebrow servant in the arts." Leslie Fiedler, *To the Gentiles* (New York: Stein and Day, 1971), p. 100.

7. David Bradley, "Preface" to Richard Wright, *12 Million Black Voices* (New York: Thunder's Mouth Press, 1988), p. xiv.

8. The most complete version of Wright's description of his experiences is now contained in *American Hunger* (New York: Harper, 1977); more accurate details can be found in Michel Fabre, *The Unfinished Quest of Richard Wright* (Urbana: University of Illinois Press, 1993).

9. See James F. Murphy, *The Proletarian Moment: The Controversy Over Leftism in Literature* (Urbana: University of Illinois Press, 1991) and Barbara Foley, *Radical Representations* (Durham, NC: Duke University Press, 1993). For a detailed critique of the former, see my study "Literary Leftism Reconsidered," *Science and Society* 57, no. 2 (Summer 1993): 214–22. [See Chapter 10 above, this volume – A.W.]

10. In *A Very Good Land to Fall With*, Vol. 3 of "Scenes from the Life of an American Jew" (Santa Rosa, Calif.: Black Sparrow Press, 1987), Sanford recalls a fall 1941 meeting with a Party literary committee to which he had been "directed" to submit *The People from Heaven*. Sanford claims that he was told to make revisions to eliminate what they believed was the book's call to a premature armed revolt against whites (pp. 202–3).

11. Wald interview with Sanford, July 30, 1989.

12. Ibid.

13. Sanford, *A Walk in the Fire* (Santa Rosa, Calif.: Black Sparrow Press, 1989), p. 79.

14. It appeared in the third and last issue of *Contact*, in December 1932.

15. Sanford, *A Very Good Land to Fall With*, pp. 176–83 passim.

16. Ibid., p. 163.

17. See references in ibid., pp. 162, 174, 175, and *The Color of the Air* (Santa Rosa, Calif.: Black Sparrow Press, 1985), p. 109.

18. Naturally there were passing references to the possible influence of William Carlos Williams's *In the American Grain* for the historical commentaries and Edgar Lee Masters' *Spoon River Anthology* (1915) for the brief but candid biographical sketches. See: Iris Barry, "On Small-Town Morality," *New York Herald Tribune Weekly Book Review*, Jan. 2, 1944, p. 44; "Briefly Noted," *The New Yorker*, Oct. 30, 1943, p. 81; Philip Van Doren Stern, "Sanford's Varorium," *The Saturday Review of Literature* 26 (Nov. 13, 1943): 13; John Hyde Preston, "From the Still Center," *The New Republic* 109 (Dec. 13, 1943): 859; *Saturday Review of Literature*, Dec. 19, 1925, p. 425; Mark Schorer, "Assorted White Trash," *The New York Times*, Oct. 31, 1943, p. 12.

19. Tery Griffin has done an impressive job of correlating the commentaries to dramatic episodes in her unpublished essay "Fiction Wound in Reality."

20. John Sanford, *The People from Heaven* (New York: Harcourt, Brace and Company, 1943), pp. 230–31.

21. Harold Cruse, of course, has argued that virtually all attempts by Jewish-American Communists to write about African-Americans are, in fact, expressions of Jewish chauvinism. See *The Crisis of the Negro Intellectual: From its Origins to the Present* (New York: William Morrow and Co., 1967).

22. A few of the many novels by Jewish-American radicals featuring Black protagonists are Maxwell Bodenheim, *Ninth Avenue* (1925); Laura Caspary, *The White Girl* (1929); Guy Endore, *Babouk* (1934); Len Zinberg, *Walk Hard – Talk Loud* (1940); Benjamin Appel, *The Dark Stain* (1943); Howard Fast, *Freedom Road* (1944); David Alman, *The Hourglass* (1947); and Earl Conrad, *Rock Bottom* (1954) and *Gulf Stream North* (1954).

23. When Novinsky describes how naked Jewish girls were shot from trees, he strongly underscores the novel's theme of the interrelationship of sexual domination and racial hatred – something

about which the reader might think even more after Eli Bishop rapes the Black woman as the culmination of his persecution of her.

24. At the least, one might conjecture that Sanford was dramatizing at the moment of Nazi expansionism how the uprooting of anti-Black racism in the United States now, "by any means necessary," might prevent its logical escalation into other forms of persecution. America Smith's courageous action should be also be supported because it is justified by the failure of others to take steps earlier.

25. See the discussion of this episode in my essay on Endore, "The Subaltern Speaks," *Monthly Review* (April 1992): 17–29. [See Chapter 14 above, this volume – A.W.]

26. That the intensity of personal feelings about racism came before and superseded ideology is documented by an incident in the late fall of 1941, shortly after the Communist Party threw itself into the war effort. At that time an official of the Party committee that read the manuscript calmly explained to Sanford that "[the book's] a plain incitement to revolt, and in the conditions of the day, a revolt would fail." Sanford bluntly replied: "Appomattox was seventy-five years back . . . . If I were black, I wouldn't want to wait another seventy-five for the right to piss in the toilet of my choice." Sanford, *A Very Good Land to Fall With*, p. 203

27. The most compelling explanation of traditions and canons remains Raymond Williams's *Marxism and Literature* (Oxford: Oxford University Press, 1977).

28. See Cary Nelson, *Repression and Recovery* (Madison: University of Wisconsin Press, 1989).

29. See Constance Coiner, "Literature of Resistance: The Intersection of Feminism and the Communist Left in Meridel Le Sueur and Tillie Olsen," in Lennard Davis and M. Bella Mirabella, eds, *Left Politics and the Literary Profession* (New York: Columbia University Press, 1990), pp. 162–85; Elinor Langer, *Josephine Herbst: The Story She Could Never Tell* (Boston: Atlantic, 1984); Paula Rabinowitz, *Labor and Desire: Women's Revolutionary Fiction in Depression America* (Chapel Hill: University of North Carolina Press, 1991); Deborah Rosenfelt, "From the Thirties: Tillie Olsen and the Radical Tradition," *Feminist Studies* 7 (Fall 1981): 370–406.

18

Lloyd Brown and the African-American Literary Left

"Don't think I'm being nationalistic, folks, but it's just that I know my own people so much better."

HENRY FAULCON, *Iron City*

Lloyd L. Brown's 1951 novel *Iron City* is a compelling testament of his love and loyalty to a fellow African-American worker he had known ten years earlier. Twenty-seven at the time, he became friendly with 26-year-old William ("Willie") Jones in the spring of 1941 while Brown was serving a seven-month sentence in Pittsburgh's Allegheny County Jail during an early version of the anti-Communist witch-hunt.[1] Jones had been framed for murder the preceding fall, and would be executed eighteen months later on November 24, 1941, at the state penitentiary in Bellafonte, Pennsylvania. Brown's novel thus has documentary and testimonial qualities. These bind it to a tradition of African-American "resistance culture" dating back to oral tales and stories transmitted by West Africans kidnapped and imported to the North American continent as chattel slaves starting in the fifteenth century. Like nineteenth-century progenitors of this tradition such as Frederick Douglass in his *Narrative of the Life of Frederick Douglass* (1845) and Harriet Jacobs in *Incidents in the Life of a Slave Girl* (1861), and twentieth-century examplars such as Arna Bontemps in *Black Thunder* (1936) and Richard Wright in "Bright and Morning Star" (1938),[2] Brown systematically unmasks the physical and ideological mechanisms of a repressive system. His aim in *Iron City* is to depict strategies of defiance through representative protagonists who are imaginatively rendered even when they are

This chapter is based on a talk given at the Center for the Study of Black Literature and Culture at the University of Pennsylvania in March 1994, and a version will also appear as the "Introduction" to the Northeastern University Press reprint of *Iron City* (Boston: Northeastern University Press, forthcoming).

biographically and autobiographically based. Moreover, from a literary point of view, the behavior of these protagonists is intended to express the authentic patterns of Black life and culture.[3]

The 38-year-old Brown was also a devoted Communist, fully conscious of the main policies and historical practice of his party. His desire to write fiction stemmed from personal, not doctrinal, compulsions; but the analytical categories and political lessons acquired from more than twenty years of activism and study informed the artistic construction of the prison and urban setting. They also shaped his recreation of the unfolding psychological drama of the last months in the life of Willie Jones, who was renamed "Lonnie James" in the novel. Moreover, as a managing editor of the Party-sponsored weekly *New Masses* magazine in the post-war era, and an editor of its monthly successor, *Masses & Mainstream*, in the McCarthy years, Brown relentlessly campaigned against what he saw as the tendency of writers such as Richard Wright (starting with *Native Son*) and Chester Himes to represent African-American characters primarily as victims.[4] *Iron City* was in some respects intended as a corrective.

Beyond this, the moment of publication of *Iron City* was a singularly tense one in US political history. The year 1951 was a crucial juncture in the Cold War witch-hunt. A second set of arrests of the leadership of the US Communist Party under the Smith "Gag" Act, for allegedly advocating the violent overthrow of the US government, had occurred that June.[5] A number of crucial anti-racist defense cases were also under way on behalf of Willie McGee, the Trenton Six, and others.[6] In recreating the events of 1940–41, Brown could not help but be aware of parallels to both the political repression and anti-racist struggles of 1950–51.

Contemporary readers of *Iron City* may also be surprised to discover that a "lost" novel of nearly forty-five years ago focuses on issues that preoccupy radical activists of the 1990s. These include the racist criminalization of the African-American population in the mass media, systematic police brutality against Blacks, and the inherent bias of the judicial system. With a distressingly high percentage of African-American males currently in prison, and the Rodney King beating and outrageous acquittal of the police in the first trial barely out of the headlines, the story of Lonnie James may be dated in details but not in essence.[7] The capture of Lonnie in a racist police dragnet, the forced confession, the incompetent legal representation, and the futile battle against the judiciary suggest that the novel would have served well as required reading over the past decades for anyone wishing to be informed of some of the fundamental truths of racist capitalism in the United States.

Nevertheless, Brown and *Iron City* were consciously erased from US cultural memory by the press and ersatz literary histories. Mostly ignored by the mainstream white media, *Iron City* received favorable notice in a number of left-wing and African-American papers, but was bizarrely denounced as having been based on "improbable circumstances" by the African-American scholar

Margaret Just Butcher in *Phylon*.[8] Robert Bone's influential history of the African-American novel anachronistically describes *Iron City* as "a propaganda tract inspired by the Foley Square trial."[9] Granville Hicks, a former Communist who was at that time an influential book reviewer for *The Saturday Review of Literature*, drafted a review essay in which he conjectured that, if *Iron City* had been written fifteen years earlier, it would have been published by a major press and praised in leading periodicals – but Hicks's article didn't appear.[10]

Perhaps the factor most complicating a contemporary appreciation of *Iron City* is the change of political climate and in the culture of the US Left in the decade following its publication. The 1960s witnessed a dramatic shift in the style and strategy of African-American political and cultural leadership under the impact of the new Black Arts and Black Power movements. Among the results was that the African-American Marxist political tradition represented by Brown, and expressed in *Iron City* through the complex articulation of both class and nationalist themes, became misunderstood and then pilloried as a version of liberal integrationism or even assimilationism.[11] Thus the lines of continuity between Brown's revolutionary political commitments – particularly in the areas of national pride and militant resistance – and the struggles of the African-American radicals who followed were unfortunately obscured.

The Return of a Lost Generation

Indeed, by 1969, the political and cultural terrain of the African-American freedom struggle had shifted so dramatically that *Negro Digest*, a leading intellectual publication with considerable authority, was in the process of changing its name to *Black World*, so that it would not be outdistanced by the very movement it aspired to lead.[12] That June, editor Hoyt Fuller ran a short piece in a column headed "Dissent," by Lloyd Brown, who was identified only by his name. Brown's essay, called "A Middle-Aged Negro Tells It *as* It Is," addresses the new generation of African-American militants, bluntly and ironically, but with humor and sympathy. Although Brown's epistle to the next generation comes late in the decade that is most famous for producing a new brand of revolutionary politics, it has some features of an African-American counterpart to white sociologist C. Wright Mills's "Letter to the New Left" nine years earlier.[13]

Brown begins by taking the young militants to task for their reliance on "obscenities from the speaker's platform." The use of such profanities is "not in the Black cultural pattern," he observes. "It is merely a steal from the revolutionary white kids, especially the upper-middle-class white kids . . . now that you won't let them play with your revolution." Don't "call me a brainwashed Negro," Brown warns, "but if you call me a *mouth*washed Negro – well, you are *so* right."

Brown then quotes the chair of a recent Black Power seminar who interrupted a speaker to admonish that "no Black person who ever respected his
blackness would ever refer to himself as a Negro." In refutation, Brown provides
an impressive compendium of quotations and book titles demonstrating that,
throughout the last two centuries, the terms "Black," "Negro," and "Colored"
had been, at various times, appropriated by freedom fighters and renegades
alike; no term in and of itself guarantees moral and political superiority.

Turning to the issue of "armed struggle," Brown recalls his own initiation in
the tradition of self-defense as an eighth-grader in the 1920s, when he trained
with a real Winchester rifle against imaginary gangs of Ku Klux Klan members.
He was inspired by reading newspaper reports about Ossian Sweet, an African-
American doctor in Detroit, who shot a member of a white racist mob assault-
ing his house. Dr Sweet and a dozen Black friends and family members charged
with murder were acquitted after several trials in which they were defended by
Clarence Darrow and the NAACP. [14]

In the 1960s, Brown ruefully observes, it appears that rifles are not merely an
instrument of self-defense but the magic key to seizing state power. Moreover,
"it now seems [as if I] should have been banging away not at the attacking
Klansmen but at the main enemies of our race – the majority of Negroes (both
in and out of the NAACP) who believe in self-defense but not self-destruction;
and also white liberals like Clarence Darrow who defend them."

In a grand finale, Brown warns that the preachment of any form of racial
superiority or inferiority, even if traditional roles are inverted, is nothing less
than the manifestation of the Western European doctrine. Racism, originally
disseminated to rationalize colonial conquest, is "the most antihuman ideology
ever to inflict mankind"; it reaches "its depth of depravity in Hitlerism," which
Brown describes as "a Ku Klux Klan in power." Racism, Brown implores, "is
not a weapon that we can snatch from the hands of our enemy for use against
him." It must be fought by creating its antithesis, values expressed in W. E. B.
Du Bois's call for a "pride of self so deep as to scorn injustice to other selves,"
and in words from Malcolm X's last formal speech: "The Negro revolution is
not a racial revolt. We are interested in practicing brotherhood with anyone
really interested in living according to it."

The ultimate purpose of Brown's intervention in this debate – where, because
of his age and vocabulary alone, he was likely to be ignored, if not traduced –
was summarized poignantly in a concluding paragraph. To the new militants,
acknowledged as inheritors of his life-long political struggle, he advises more
humility regarding ancestors: "You did not invent the concepts of self-respect
and race pride. You did not start the struggle for liberation and survival. But
those concepts and that struggle are your heritage – a heritage to be cherished
and to be fulfilled." [15]

There is no evidence that Brown's impassioned plea influenced the political
strategy of the African-American Left in the following years, any more than did

the admonitions of white veterans of earlier struggles shape the direction of the newly radicalizing white college students. The preponderance of each rebellious generation strives to make a fresh mark in its own way, often by misreading and then dismissing those who came before. After all, the failures of predecessors seem apparent, since racism, class exploitation, and the waste of human potential persist in spite of the advance of technology and thus the increase in our capacity to relieve suffering.

Still, there come moments eventually in the anti-racist and other struggles when interest in taking a longer view begins to grow; when connections are made, ancestral links are acknowledged, and what was once regarded as ephemeral if not irrelevant suddenly takes on fresh meaning in a new context. Since the 1980s, in fact, a steady effort to reconstruct the US radical traditions, including that of the African-American Left prior to the 1960s, has been in progress, with a special emphasis on ways in which earlier rebels anticipated what were thought to be contemporary problems. Before the late 1970s, studies of the history of African-American Marxism tended to emphasize what was dead, irretrievable, or undesirable, especially in books such as Wilson Record's *The Negro and the Communist Party* (1951) and *Race and Radicalism* (1964), and Harold Cruse's *The Crisis of the Negro Intellectual* (1967). The publication of Richard Wright's bitterly anti-Communist, and, at times, wildly inaccurate, *American Hunger* (1977) was met with national acclaim, while little attention was devoted to Benjamin Davis, Jr.'s *Communist Councilman from Harlem* (1969), William L. Patterson's *The Man Who Cried Genocide* (1971), and Philip Foner's edition of *Paul Robeson Speaks* (1978).

In the late 1970s, however, a new direction was augured by much discussion on the Left of Harry Haywood's *Black Bolshevik* (1978), although it was printed by an obscure radical publishing house, and Hosea Hudson's *The Narrative of Hosea Hudson* (1979), produced in collaboration with the African-American scholar Nell Irvin Painter under the imprimatur of Harvard University Press. These were augmented by impressive works of research such as Abby Johnson and Ronald Johnson's *Propaganda and Aesthetics: The Literary Politics of Afro-American Magazines in the Twentieth Century* (1979), Mark Naison's *Communists in Harlem During the Depression* (1983), Cedric J. Robinson's *Black Marxism: The Making of the Black Radical Tradition* (1983), Gerald Horne's *Communist Front? The Civil Rights Congress, 1946–1956* (1988), and Robin D. G. Kelley's *Hammer and Hoe: Alabama Communists During the Great Depression* (1990).[16]

Yet none of the recent published works touches significantly upon left-wing literary activity of the period of the Cold War and McCarthyism, the years just prior to the Black Power and Black Arts upsurge. Thus the resurrection of the career of Lloyd Brown, including the republication of his unique and well-crafted novel of African-American political prisoners, *Iron City*, has the potential of assisting a new assessment of the history of US literary radicalism in general, and the continuity of the African-American cultural Left in particular.

The integration of Brown's contribution into these two overlapping narratives of culture and politics will hardly settle or exhaust the topics; equally important are the restoration of the achievement of John O. Killens and other writers associated with the Harlem Writers' Guild, the left-wing African-American theater movement of the 1950s, the Cold War cultural activities of W. E. B. Du Bois and Shirley Graham, and many other subjects. But the republication of *Iron City* and a consideration of Brown's views on African-American culture and politics may help stimulate a more favorable climate for such studies by initiating further debate, discussion, and reflection among the communities of scholars devoted to the theory and practice of political and cultural emancipation.

Dialectic of Class and Nation

The world outlook of African-American writers, like that of all other writers, is forged not in isolation but through participation in sub-groups of various kinds. These start with family units or other circumstances of birth and early childhood, but usually evolve more selectively into networks of relatively like-minded thinkers.[17] The mature literary work of many mid-twentieth-century left-wing African-Americans might be theorized as developing in an important (although certainly not exclusive) dialogue with the political and cultural practice of a relatively specific current of political ideology. For the most part, this was the Communist movement and the anti-racist, anti-fascist, and union struggles that it led from the time of the Russian Revolution to the advent of the new left-wing leadership in the 1960s.

Such an approach does not, of course, preclude other major influences.[18] However, many African-American Marxist writers knew each other personally, participated in the same literary clubs, nurtured and mentored each other, read and reviewed each other's works, followed the same publications, and shared many of the same political positions for periods of time.[19] Even where there developed sharp hostilities and rivalries, many of the issues dividing them tended to be associated with that shared Communist tradition. Of course, at the present time, research on the forty or so writers who might constitute this politico-cultural school of African-American literary Marxists is still in its infancy. Indeed, owing to McCarthyism or disillusionment, many left-wing writers have never even gone on record about the details of their ideological and organizational commitments. Lloyd Brown, however, is unabashedly proud of his record as a Communist militant, and his life is testimony to the quality of intellect and political commitment among the cadres of what now must be regarded as the most effective activist organization ever built by radicals in the United States.

Lloyd Louis Brown was born in St Paul, Minnesota, in 1913 to an interracial married couple. His mother, the German-American daughter of a Union Army veteran, died while he was in infancy. His father, a Louisiana-born African-American, worked as a dining-car waiter and Pullman porter. Since there were no Black orphanages, and white orphanages would not admit Black children, Brown was put in the Crispus Attucks Home, an old folks residence for Blacks, with two sisters and a brother. Thus he was raised by elderly African-Americans, some of whom knew first-hand about slavery. The result was a lifelong respect for these elders and their folk and religious culture, which he saw as dignified and highly moral. Brown's short story "God's Chosen People," which was based on that childhood experience, was listed in the O'Brien collection of *Best Short Stories of 1948*.[20]

Self-educated after a year of high school, Brown read voraciously. Everything he laid eyes on seemed to radicalize him, from the *American Mercury* of H. L. Mencken to the *Rubáiyát* of Omar Khayyám. Even before joining the Young Communist League in 1929 in St Paul, he knew about Toussaint L'Ouverture, John Brown, and Spartacus, and considered himself a revolutionary. After a period of YCL activity and a visit to the USSR in 1933–34, he became a YCL organizer in New Haven and Pittsburgh, where he also worked as a CIO organizer. Like other African-American Communists of his generation, Brown was convinced that the Soviet Union under Stalin was advancing toward socialism and then communism, and that it had instituted policies for national minorities that promoted political and cultural autonomy. This conviction about the success of the Soviet Union, seemingly verified by first-hand visits and discussions with others who traveled there, served as a key component in Brown's political outlook regarding international events, even though the sources of his anti-capitalist radicalization were entirely home-grown.

As a writer, Brown received his first serious training by working as the editor of the YCL newspaper, *Young Worker*. In 1937 he married Lily Kashin, to whom *Iron City* is dedicated, a member of the Young Communist League who was born of Polish-Jewish immigrants to Quebec and recently a student at Hunter College. Through World War II, when he served more than three years in a Jim Crow squadron of the Army Air Force, he produced only political journalism, although in the early 1930s he had unsuccessfully submitted a poem to *New Masses*. His view throughout the Depression decade was that most writers were not serious about revolutionary politics. When *Native Son* appeared in 1940, while he was in Pittsburgh, he hated the novel for its portrait of Blacks, believing that left-wing critics were insufficiently critical of it due to Wright's public Party membership.[21]

In the post-war era, he was politically close to Black Party leader Ben Davis, and was influenced in literary and artistic matters by the Marxist critic and poet Charles Humboldt. In addition to *Iron City*, Brown published about a half-dozen short stories in the 1940s-50s, [22] a great deal of political journalism, a dozen critical essays, and, in later years, articles on Paul Robeson, some contributions to *Freedomways*, and many letters to the editor of the *New York Times*. Moreover, he completed a second novel but, due to sharp criticisms of friends such as Humboldt, decided to keep all but one chapter from publication.[23]

Brown remained publicly a Communist Party member until 1952, when he went to work for the great singer, actor, and pro-Communist activist Paul Robeson, writing many of his speeches, columns, and articles, and greatly assisting with Robeson's book *Here I Stand* (1958). He stayed with Robeson until Robeson's passport was restored so that he could leave the country to resume his career, which had been destroyed in the United States by McCarthyism. Although Brown never rejoined the Communist Party, his association with Robeson in the 1950s was consistent with his earlier views, and he has maintained a socialist outlook. In the early 1970s, he visited the USSR a second time and was again enthusiastic about developments among the national minorities.

Much has already been written about the development of the Communist political program to assist in the liberation of the African-American population. As has been well documented, part of the thinking was initiated in the leadership of the Third International with input from US Black Marxists.[24] However, the practical activity of the Party took on a life of is own as it linked up with powerful trends in African-American life in ghettos and rural areas.

What characterizes Brown and most African-American Marxist writers is that they saw themselves as a cultural wing of a social movement that struggled against both racism (white chauvinism, in particular) and class oppression. A narrow, all-class Black nationalism was rejected, but solidarity among African-Americans and recognition of a semi-autonomous African-American cultural tradition were regarded as prerequisites for an interracial class alliance. Wright's 1937 "Blueprint for Negro Writing" – which Margaret Walker believes to have espoused the collective view of the Chicago South Side Writers' Group[25] – is a key text because it expresses a common set of concerns felt broadly among African-American Marxists about race and class. "Blueprint's" perspective is one of going through the national struggle from a proletarian perspective to reach internationalism. While most artistic creation can be neither explained nor controlled by political loyalties, specific issues of form and technique were often discussed and debated within this framework of the dialectic of class and nation.

This development in Marxist theory has the potential of breaking what is often seen as the integrationist/separatist dichotomy; from the 1930s through the late 1950s, interracial class unity was regarded as possible only through Communist and Euro-American support for Black nationalist autonomy based on the hegemony of the proletariat. In literary thinking, following the approach of Wright's "Blueprint," Communist writers often adapted a famous formula from the USSR: the culture to be supported in the African-American struggle was to be nationalist in form (that is, based on African-American life experiences, and using African-American folk expressive culture), but proletarian in content (that is, communicating values leading to interracial working-class unity). Hence, the cultural work of Black writers had to allow space for Black-specific impulses; yet, in the end, to be compatible with political doctrine, their work should motivate interracial alliances on the basis of mutual interests.

The Black and the Red

Lloyd Brown's novel is entirely worthy of the haunting cover of the original *Masses & Mainstream* edition by Hananiah Harari.[26] Tackling a subject virtually ignored by previous novelists – it is possibly the first Black prison novel, and certainly the first depicting the activities of political prisoners in the United States – and artistically driven by a desire to reconcile his strong emotions about the subject with his powerful political convictions, Brown experimented with a multiplicity of forms and styles that he integrated with a craft that is remarkable for a first novelistic effort.

As *Iron City* unfolds, the Monongahela County jail relentlessly discloses more and more features that suggest a microcosm of the state-repressive aspects of capitalist society. Step by step, we are inaugurated into the prison system of enforced segregation, supervision of behavior, spying, and censorship. The jail also has at least one other major characteristic of capitalist society – price gouging for necessary goods is perpetrated by those in power among the prison population, just as merchants increase prices for ghetto residents. [27]

The Monongahela County Court, which works in tandem with the jail and is located on the very next block, may claim to provide "justice for all," but its essential weapons are police terror against Blacks and frame-ups against radicals. The same Judge Hanford Rupp presides over the case of Lonnie James, a Black worker accused of killing a drugstore owner in a robbery, as well as that of the group of imprisoned Black and white Communists charged with violating election laws in their efforts to get Communist candidates on the ballot. In fact, early in the novel a page from an official guidebook to Iron City is produced describing both the courthouse and the jail as gifts of industrial magnate Adam T. McGregor; they are hailed as fine architectural examples of Western culture.[28] The notion that the system is a kind of prison for the workers who, if organized to struggle, might be the gravediggers of capitalism is reinforced by a prisoner's observation that "Half the guys in here . . . have made McGregor steel . . . . we made this here jail for them to put us in."[29]

In a memorable scene, the three Black Communist prisoners survey the cell block across from them; with its gray steel walls and "trellis-work of bars," it resembles "a great ocean steamer, riding high in the water and converging upon them, with all passengers lining the five long decks, facing forward, eager for port."[30] A closer look transforms the block into a fantastic, race-stratified, *Pequod*-like ship of humanity:

220

The top three levels were white men, but directly across, running the length like a waterline, the row of faces was dark; and on the next range down which was the bottom. The men on D could see only this one side of Cell Block two, but they knew that the color line marked this level exactly on each of the five structures.

A thousand men on fifty ranges were standing and waiting – the young and the old, the crippled and the whole, the tried-and-found-guilty and the yet-to-be-tried: the F & B's [fornication and bastardy cases], the A & B's [assault and battery cases], the drunk and disorderlies, rapists, riflers, tinhorns, triflers, swindlers, bindlers, peepers, punks, tipsters, hipsters, snatchers, pimps, unlawful disclosers, indecent exposers, delayed marriage, lascivious carriage, unlicensed selling, fortune telling, sex perversion, unlawful conversion, dips, dopes, dandlers, deceivers, buggers, huggers, writers, receivers, larceny, arsony, forgery, jobbery, felonious assault, trespassing, robbery, shooting, looting, gambling, shilling, drinking, winking, rambling, killing, wifebeating, breaking in, tax-cheating, making gin, Mann Act, woman-act, being-black-and-talking-back, and conspiring to overthrow the government of the Commonwealth by force and violence.[31]

This fine passage, with its energetic and jazzy rhythms, provides a funda-mentally clarifying perspective, but the overall form of *Iron City* may well have presented Brown with something of a conundrum. The essence of the plot is the alliance developed between three African-American Communist prisoners and Lonnie James, aimed at creating a defense committee outside the prison to defend the rights that the police and judicial system had denied Lonnie. In terms of linear chronology, the novel is organized around specific events in Lonnie's life, starting in 1940. On April 10, there is the killing of a drugstore owner. On May 4, Lonnie is picked up by police. On May 20, he is officially arrested and placed in the county jail. On May 21, his confession (achieved through beatings, torture, and sleep-deprivation) is declared. On October 13, there is the announcement of his death sentence. This is followed by an appeal to the State Supreme Court; and when that fails, a second appeal is made based on his lawyer's suicide and the location of a crucial witness, Leroy Flowers, who had disappeared at the time of Lonnie's arrest. Nevertheless, aspects of the work suggest that Brown aspired to realize a highly complex agenda.

Iron City, first of all, is aimed at documenting "real" events. Yet Brown must rely heavily on imaginative techniques to humanize the characters through their thoughts, dreams, and intimate dialogue. While it is a work primarily set in a prison, Brown dramatizes events of the past, and future, and of the imagination, which occur in various regions of the United States and, also, in the Black com-munity just outside the walls of the jail.

Another feature is that there is a large number of characters in the novel (perhaps too many for some readers to remember and absorb) because Brown wants to present a cross-section of the prison population, of the Black Communist cadre, and of the Black community of Iron City. Thus at least a half-dozen life stories are told to one degree or another (some of them with extraor-

dinary beauty, as in the narrative of Zachary's youth in the South), and fragments of the lives of many more are more briefly depicted.

In accordance with the concerns of his literary essays, Brown aspired to
present a counter-model to Black writers who were abandoning Black-specific
topics in the late 1940s and early 1950s (for example, Frank Yerby, Ann Petry,
and Willard Motley), or who were depicting Blacks as brutalized (in the manner
of Wright and Himes).[32] At the same time, *Iron City* must also be understood as
an intervention against larger trends in Euro-American culture in the United
States. Methodologically, the text is designed to take a stand against what Brown
perceived as a retreat from "realism" in literature of the 1950s, typified by
Norman Mailer's shift from *The Naked and the Dead* (1948) to *Barbary Shore*
(1951).[33] While characters in *Iron City* are often vivified by depicting their fantasies and dreams, the plot is structured to continually bring them back to the
material world of hard facts suggested by a frequent use of graphically reproduced newspaper clippings, prison regulations, and reports on world events.

Finally, the novel aspires to dramatize political lessons learned through experiences such as the 1940–41 Pittsburgh struggle. Among the most obvious is that
the rulers of society want through political repression to behead the leadership
of workers' movements; this makes it even more crucial to reunite and organize
under prison conditions, and to fight back through the creation of alliances and
the intelligent use of local opportunities. Another political lesson is that struggles like Lonnie's are ineffective when undertaken individually; the possibility
of success is greatly enhanced when organizational cadres assist. In short, the
prison struggle reflects in miniature the national battle led by leftists against mis-
leaders, police, and stoolpigeons. At the same time, the Communist Party comes
in for some criticism in *Iron City* for a tendency to be too narrow politically – the
Party members had been so concerned with their electoral fight that they were
unaware of Lonnie's life-and-death trial occurring at virtually the same time.[34]

Such a political focus means that *Iron City* is also a novel written against
despair, trying to mobilize hope. And such a fighting, militant theme was an act
of rebellion against conventional literary subjects of the 1950s, especially those
of best-sellers. Moreover, in contrast to works such as *Native Son*, Brown felt he
was depicting "real Communists" – people whose revolutionary politics are part
of the fabric of their whole person, not merely the mouthing of political
slogans.[35]

Above and beyond these specific concerns, however, the novel is structured
to allow the dramatization of the complex Communist perspective on nation
and class. Lonnie doesn't need anyone to tell him to fight; he is already fighting,
but alone. In other words, African-Americans don't have to wait for politicos or
whites to advise them about their need to struggle; they take charge and show
initiative themselves. Still, for ultimate success, a coalition with whites remains
essential.[36]

From the beginning, the perspective of the novel is highly Black-specific.

Although white and Black Communists are imprisoned, we are led to identify only with the Blacks. Henry Faulcon, the oldest Black Communist and a moral center of the story, introduces the theme of Black Pride to the point where he has to defend himself against the charge of being a narrow nationalist: "As long as they got this Jim Crow it's better for a man to be on this side of the line than with the whites . . . . don't come accusing me of nationalism, but I'm telling you the people here are better . . . . you ain't heard nobody Red-baiting us have you? . . . But up on those [white] ranges it ain't like that. All kinds of reactionary bastards up there – Coughlinites, Jew-haters, fascists and everything."[37] Among features of the text specifically reflecting African-American culture are the diction and vocabulary of the Black characters,[38] spirituals, folk songs, humor, and "the dozens." However, Brown's Black population is far from idealized. African-American traitors appear both in prison and in the Party, and one of the Black prisoners, Tuxedo, is described as pimping his own wife.

Iron City also embodies Brown's conviction that nationalism must ultimately be transcended for the sake of interracial unity. Thus, we see Lonnie evolve from believing that what landed the Black Communists in prison was their exploitation by white Communists, to collaborating fully with interracial efforts on his behalf. Still, Black unity and an emphasis on Black culture are never abandoned for the sake of this necessary alliance. Rather, Brown dramatizes both components of the ideological tension. On the one hand, for example, we have Henry, a Communist who leans toward nationalism; on the other, we have Paul, who is drawn toward a class-against-class view of the world.[39] Their separate orientations are reflected in an exchange in which Henry reports to Paul a discussion he heard among Black prisoners to the effect that all humanity is Negro and the Negroes are simply the better part. Half jokingly, Henry announces that he is about ready to demand that, since he is among the better part, he and all the other African-American prisoners ought to be on the upper ranges of the cell block which are warmer and where the food is served first. Paul angrily directs Henry's vision to the top tiers of Cell Block Two: "Maybe you're getting so old you can't see so good any more . . . but those sure look like bars up there to me. Meaning we'd still be in jail just the same, just like the white workers in the mill are still exploited even if they do get a better break than we do." But then Paul realizes that the old man was just "jiving."[40]

Themes of interracial unity are clearly evidenced in many episodes; for example, in the scene where the three Black Communist prisoners learn that white and Black members of the Party are all contributing a day's pay to raise funds for their appeal; in Paul's reminiscences about his Jewish-American friend, Marty Stein, who died in Spain; in discussions of the interracial activities of the International Labor Defense to support the Communists and, later, Lonnie James, after Lonnie's lawyer commits suicide; in the references to an Irish-American union president who supports Lonnie's case; in the return from semi-retirement of the older white Communist leader Archer to work with

Paul's wife, Charlene, on the Defense Committee; and in the appointment of the Jewish liberal lawyer Milton Cohen to defend Lonnie.[41] The linkage between racism and Red-baiting struggles is dramatized when Lonnie's lawyer, Winkel, tries to get Lonnie to break with the ILD by citing Congressman John E. Rankin's denunciation of Archer as a notorious Communist. When Lonnie learns that Rankin is the representative of the racist state of Mississippi, he refuses in a fiesty manner to repudiate the ILD.[42]

"What Can an Old Negro Have to Dream About?"

Subtlety and distinction of characterization are among the artistic strengths of *Iron City*. The portraits of Lonnie James and Paul Harper, who are linked together in multiple relationships of similarities and differences, are fairly detailed.[43] Lonnie is twenty-three years old, and grew up in Ohio in an orphanage. Although strongly alert to possible signs and omens that may affect his fate, he is a person of religious faith, frequently reading a Bible, which seems connected to his will to live and fight back.[44] Previously a laborer in a tin plate mill, Lonnie is now housed in Cell 10. His relations with his main white jailers are contradictory: one guard, Dan, won't mess with Lonnie at all; another, Steve, who himself suffers some discrimination as a "Hunky" but who is politically a reactionary, treats Lonnie with respect; and a third, an older guard named Byrd, has Lonnie terrified.

Paul Harper in some respects recalls the novel's author, Lloyd Brown.[45] He is the leader of the Communists and faces a possible ten-year sentence. Twenty-seven years old, Paul is married to Charlene, a former Cleveland school teacher, and he is reading Victor Hugo's *Les Misérables*. Significantly, Paul is housed in a room directly below Lonnie, in Range D, Cell 10. He is six feet tall and his physical resemblance to Lonnie is frequently noted. Twice it is remarked that he has the same dark complexion as Lonnie, and three times it is said that he "could be kin."[46] Although the most politically single-minded of the Communist prisoners, Paul undergoes a transformative experience in relation to Lonnie because he realizes how easily he could be in Lonnie's place.

Two other Communists, both older than Lonnie, present their life stories in *Iron City*, and their tales are joined by that of another prisoner with whom they become friendly. The Communists, Henry Faulcon and Isaac Zachary, face possible three-to five-year sentences, since they are regarded as less important than Paul. Henry, a former waiter, is sixty-three years old, has gray hair, a round wrinkled face, and is short and heavy-set. He has been imprisoned twice before, and is a veteran of the campaign in defense of the Scottsboro Boys. Isaac Zachary, from the country, is big, tall, broad-shouldered, and solemn-looking. Between forty and fifty years old, he has been married for twenty-two years to

Annie Mae. His dream since his childhood in Mississippi had been to become a locomotive engineer, but the Jim Crow system kept him restricted to the job of fireman.

The third life story is that of Harvey ("Army") Owens, who is in jail because he failed to pay alimony. He is the character with most of the features of a folk hero. In a surprising flash-forward in time, we are told what follows his decorated service in World War II. After falling in love with a woman from Georgia, they travel to her home with another couple and all four are killed by racists who believe Army is acting too "uppity."

The most disturbing relationship in the novel is between Lonnie and "Crazy Carl" Peterson. Described as an "idiot," Carl is one of the three whites confined with Lonnie on Murderers' Row, but is entirely ignorant of racism. Lonnie regards Carl as the "first decent white man I met"[47] and has more close physical contact with him than anyone else, calling him affectionate pet names and even carrying on imaginary conversations with him. Carl, in turn, waits for Lonnie like a puppy dog, offers him simple words of friendship, and is said to be the only person able to reach the "hidden Lonnie within."[48] Moreover, Carl, on his own, surprises Lonnie with the suggestion that the Communists in prison might be of help. Yet Carl has committed infanticide – he bludgeoned his own son to death, and doesn't even seem to realize it!

If the Dostoyevskian Carl adds some "modernist" mystery to what might otherwise be a relatively "realist" plot, there are numerous other elements that enrich and complicate the narrative. For example, references to various kinds of games are interwoven throughout *Iron City*. The pattern begins with a reference to Lonnie's childhood game of Giant Footsteps; but soon he is depicted playing basketball by himself and, then, as part of a baseball team.[49] There are also several episodes involving boxing. One occurs when the prisoners demand to be allowed to hear the Joe Louis fight on the radio; their shouts transform into a cry against white supremacism.[50] Another motif in the novel is ornthological imagery, including comparisons between birds and people – Peterson is compared to an owl; the brutal guard, Byrd, is called a buzzard; and Henry Faulcon's name suggests "falcon."

The climax of *Iron City* also defies what one might expect for the conventional ending of a realist or naturalist novel. On the one hand, the accumulation of evidence begins to clarify the dynamics of Lonnie's frame-up. It appears that a new District Attorney was anxious to find someone on whom to blame the murder, probably in order to make a name for himself and restore confidence among the white citizens. Big John, the bar tender who failed to back up Lonnie's alibi, turns out to be linked to the Police Commissioner. On the other hand, toward the end of the novel, Lonnie has given up all hope, even though the suicide of his lawyer and the appearance of another witness seem to suggest the likelihood of his either gaining a rehearing or having the death sentence commuted.[51]

In a bold move, the final episode of *Iron City* shifts away from Lonnie almost entirely, into the magnificent dream sequence of Henry Faulcon. On night patrol, the brutal guard, Byrd, peers into Henry's cell and sees "the smooth brown face of the sleeping gray-haired" Henry. The guard thinks: "He must be dreaming . . . but what can an old Negro have to dream about?"[52] The dream that follows is a memorable fusion of folk religion and Marxist politics, an Afro-Americanized utopian socialist vision. Politically and artistically, it is a rather striking counterpoint to the horrific fantasy of castration that is the penultimate section of Ralph Ellison's *Invisible Man,* published a year later.[53] Henry's dream recapitulates much of his life and of events in the novel as the imagery shifts from an urban to a pastoral setting, with a euphoric Henry surrounded by celebrating African-American men. Overlooking the crowd from a platform, Henry sees a row of rich whites hogging the front seats and has them ejected by a group that includes the folk heroes Stackalee and John Henry. Next, the men are joined by throngs of African-American women,[54] and finally, the crowd becomes interracial. Lonnie then appears with Peterson on his arm, and Zachary, the frustrated engineer, is shown at last driving the glory train. Henry himself proposes marriage to his longtime sweetheart, Lucy Jackson.

Then, suddenly, in the last three paragraphs we leave the world of dreams and are back with the aging guard, Byrd, who, this time, is peering in on the sleeping Lonnie on death row before continuing his rounds. Thus, although the fight is far from over, the imagery of Faulcon's dream constitutes a powerful affirmation of socialism – not as an externally imposed abstraction, but as the concrete expression of the aspirations of a people. Socialism's universalizing tendencies are depicted as growing out of national culture and experience. Fused with religion, culture, and the history of class and anti-racist struggle, it is figured as the modern expression of the age-old hope that drives humanity toward freedom, despite the prisons and prison-guards of the moment.

Postscript

In a 1988 unpublished reminiscence called "The Inside Story of My Novel, *Iron City*," Lloyd Brown reveals for the first time many of the actual names of the individuals who participated in organizing the Willie Jones Defense Committee in Pittsburgh. He also emphasizes the crucial role played by his wife, Lily, in transmitting Brown's messages from the Committee inside the jail to the "Outside Committee." Finally, he reflects on the considerable trust that the doomed Jones had developed in his new Communist friends, and the feeling of personal responsibility that this engendered in Brown himself. One can hardly imagine a more inspiring symbol of the committed artist than this relationship of Brown to Jones.

"I like to think that in his last moments he [Jones] knew that we had never deserted him," Brown concludes.[55] The republication of *Iron City* at a time when racism is as virulent in the United States as it was in the 1940s and 1950s is a clarion call to a new generation to be as loyal to targets of racist repression in our time as Brown was to Willie Jones in his.

Notes

I am grateful to Lloyd Brown, Robert Chrisman, Lee Freeman, Robin D.G. Kelley, and Richard Yarborough for reading a draft of this essay and offering suggestions, although I alone am responsible for its content.

1. This was at the time of the Hitler–Stalin Pact (August 1939 to June 1941) when US Communists were isolated from their former liberal allies; owing to the Dies Committee Hearings on Un-American Activities, 1938–41, the period is also referred to as the "Little Red Scare." Communist Party leader Earl Browder was indicted on old charges of having traveled under a false passport; the Rapp–Coudert probe of Communist influence in the New York City school system was held; and Communist activists around the country were arrested on various kinds of trumped-up charges. Brown, who was Young Communist League District Organizer for Western Pennsylvania, was arrested along with twenty-seven other Party members for alleged irregularities in attempting to get Party candidates on the ballot. Brown himself anonymously wrote a pamphlet on the case, *The Conspiracy Against Free Elections* (Pittsburgh, 1941). He received and served a sentence of four months, plus another three months for refusing to pay a fine and part of the court costs. Brown and his colleagues were found guilty on October 31, 1940, one week after Jones's conviction on October 24, in the same courthouse.

2. This first appeared as a pamphlet by International Publishers, before its incorporation into *Uncle Tom's Children* in the new and expanded edition of 1940.

3. The most impressive overall theoretical work on "resistance culture" is Barbara Harlowe, *Resistance Literature* (New York: Methuen, 1987). H. Bruce Franklin's *The Victim as Criminal and Artist: Literature from the American Prison* (New York: Oxford University Press, 1987) draws noteworthy links between the slave narrative tradition and contemporary prison literature by writers of color. Barbara Foley's *Telling the Truth: The Theory and Practice of Documentary Fiction* (Ithaca, NY: Cornell, University Press 1986) has a provocative chapter on "The Afro-American Documentary Novel."

4. See, for example, his important review of Chester Himes's *The Lonely Crusade* in *New Masses*, September 9, 1947, p. 18, and a two-part essay, "Which Way For the Negro Writer?" in *Masses & Mainstream* 4, no. 3 (March 1951): 53–63 and 50–59. The latter was a response to the symposium "The Negro in Literature; The Current Scene" in *Phylon* XI, no. 4 (1950): 296–391. Blyden Jackson responded to Brown in "Faith Without Works in Negro Literature," *Phylon* XII, no. 4 (1951): 378–88. Another essay expressing Brown's views about the representation of African-Americans is "Psychoanalysis vs the Negro People," *Masses & Mainstream* 4, no. 4 (April 1951: 16–24.

5. See Michael R. Belknap, *Cold War Political Justice* (Westport, Conn.: Greenwood, 1967), pp. 152–3.

6. Willie McGee, executed in 1951, was a Mississippi truck driver accused of rape in 1946 by a white woman. The Trenton Six were African-Americans originally convicted for murder in 1948, but the Communist-led Civil Rights Congress managed to get the verdict overturned by the State Supreme Court.

7. According to statistics cited by Cedric J. Robinson, "one quarter of Black men in their twenties are under the control of the criminal courts." See "Race, Capitalism and Antidemocracy," in Robert Gooding-Williams, ed., *Reading Rodney King/ Reading Urban Uprising* (New York: Routledge, 1993).

8. See review by Margaret Just Butcher, "Violence and Reform," *Phylon* XII, no. 3 (1951): 294–5. I am grateful to Lloyd Brown for sharing his collection of reviews with me, many of which are not indexed in reference books and would be difficult to locate. In the following list I have provided all the bibliographic information that is available on the materials in possession of Brown. **African-American publications**: "The High Price of Integration: A Review of the Literature of the Negro

for 1951," by Alain Locke, *Phylon* XIII, no. 1 (1952): 7–18; "*Iron City*," by J. Saunders Redding, *Afro-American*, August 4, 1951; "Up and Down Farish Street," by Percy Greene, *Jackson, Mississippi Advocate*, June 1951. **Leftwing publications**: "A Courageous Challenge to Corrupt Literature," by Milton Howard, *The Worker*, March 4, 1951; "A Gripping, Mature Novel of Negro Struggle," by Robert Friedman, *Daily Worker*, June 22, 1951; "The History of Lonnie James," I. Dubashinsky, *Literary Gazette* (Moscow), April 17, 1952; "An Inspiring Novel of Negro Life and Struggle," by Richard Walker (probably a pseudonym for John Pittman), *Political Affairs*, August 1951; "Iron Will in the Iron City," Henry Kraus, *March of Labor*, September 1951; "A New Writer Comes to the Fore," by I. Mikhailova, *Soviet Literature* 5 (1952): 140–43; "A Path-Breaking Negro Novel," by Sidney Finkelstein, *Jewish Life*, September 1951; "Don't Miss *Iron City*," by Sid Gold, *New Challenge*, September 1951; "John Henry's People," by John Howard Lawson, *Masses and Mainstream*, 4, no. 7 (July 1951); "Lloyd Brown's *Iron City* Breaks Cultural Frontiers," by Howard Fast, *Freedom*, August 1951; "Story of a Negro Framed," by Marvel Cooke, *New York Compass*, July 29, 1951; "Without Magnolias – Story of US Negroes," by James Aronson, *National Guardian*, October 24, 1951. **Commercial papers**: "Communists to See Bad Times," by Rev. L. Gillespie, *Cleveland Plain Dealer*, 1951; "Iron City" by G. A. P., *Springfield Republican*, July 15, 1951. The novel, published in both hardcover and paper, went through three printings in the United States, and was also published in Great Britain, the German Democratic Republic (in both English and German), Japan, the Soviet Union, Poland, Hungary, Bulgaria, Denmark, China (separate editions in Peking and Shanghai), Czechoslovakia (in both Czech and Slovak), and Israel (in Hebrew).

9. Robert Bone, *The Negro Novel in America* (New Haven: Yale University Press, 1958), pp. 159–60. The Foley Square Trial was in 1949 and bears no resemblance to the William Jones case. It should be noted that adverse reactions to Brown's and other left-wing novels are sometimes the result of a failure to see what is on the page, due to political prejudice, virulent preconceptions, or simple ignorance. A startling example of this is the 1986 doctoral dissertation by Sam Gon Kim ("Black Americans' Commitment to Communism: A Case Study Based on Fiction and Autobiographies of Black Americans," University of Kansas, American Studies Program), which claims that *Iron City* takes place in the deep South at the same time as the Scottsboro case, on which it is allegedly modeled, and that, as in the Scottsboro case, the defense campaign is victorious in reversing the death penalty. See pp. 173–85.

10. It is undated and can be found in Folder no.104 of the Hicks Collection, Syracuse University Library.

11. Harold Cruse's aggressively anti-Communist Party *The Crisis of the Negro Intellectual: From its Origins to the Present* (New York: William Morrow and Co., 1967) was a major influence, especially noteworthy as an early attempt to bring some theoretical rigor to the prospects of a cultural nationalist position. For an example of Cruse's harsh treatment of pro-Communist African-Americans, see the section called "From *Freedom* to *Freedomways*," pp. 240–52.

12. Abby Johnson and Ronald Johnson, *Propaganda and Aesthetics* (Amherst, Mass.: University of Massachusetts Press, 1979), p. 193.

13. Mills's piece originally appeared in *New Left Review* 5 (September-October 1960) and was reprinted in Mills, *Power, Politics and People* (New York: Ballantine, 1963), pp. 247–59. Mills, of course, was writing on the eve of the 1960s, and his politics was aimed at creating a third way between the "end of ideology" school and those orthodox Marxists who he believed held to a "labor metaphysic."

14. The case is discussed in Wilson Record, *Race and Radicalism* (Ithaca, NY: Cornell University Press, 1964), pp. 47–8.

15. Lloyd L. Brown, "A Middle-Aged Negro Tells It *As* It Is," *Negro Digest* (June 1969): 23–8.

16. This list is only meant to indicate a growing trend; it is by no means an exhaustive inventory of all available scholarship, biography, and autobiography about the African-American Left, nor do I mean to imply that all texts prior to 1980 were hostile and redundant while the more recent ones are uniformly original and sympathetic. A few additional general studies concerning left-wing writers are: Doris E Abramson, *Negro Playwrights in the American Theatre, 1925–1959* (New York: Columbia University Press, 1969); Kenneth Brown, "The Lean Years: The Afro-American Novelist During the Depression (1929–1941)," Ph.D. Dissertation, (University of Iowa, 1986); Donald Gibson, *The Politics of Literary Expression* (Westport: Conn, Greenwood, 1981); Kim, (see n. 9); Edward Margolies, *Native Sons: A Critical Study of Twentieth-Century Negro American Authors* (New York: Lippincott, 1968); Jabarti Simama, "Black Writers Experience Communism: An Interdisciplinary

Study of Imaginative Writers, Their Critics, and the CPUSA," Ph.D. Dissertation, Emory, 1978; James O. Young, *Black Writers of the Thirties* (Baton Rouge, La.: Louisiana State University Press, 1973). Some autobiographies and biographies of African-American activists include Faith Berry, *Langston Hughes: Before and Beyond Harlem*, rev. edn (New York: Citadel, 1992); Martin Bauml, Duberman, *Paul Robeson* (New York: Knopf, 1988); Wayne Cooper, *Claude McKay: Rebel Sojourner in the Harlem Renaissance* (Baton Rouge, La.: Louisiana University Press, 1987); Angela Davis, *An Autobiography* (New York: Bantam, 1974); Michel Fabre, *The Unfinished Quest of Richard Wright* (Urbana: University of Illinois Press, 1993); Lorraine Hansberry, *To Be Young, Gifted and Black: An Informal Autobiography* (New York: Signet, 1970); Angelo Herndon, *Let Me Live* (New York: Arno Reprint, 1969); Chester Himes, *The Quality of Hurt* (New York: Doubleday, 1972) and *My Life of Absurdity* (New York: Doubleday, 1976); Langston Hughes, *I Wonder as I Wander* (New York: Octagon, 1981); Claude McKay *A Long Way from Home* (New York: Lee Furnam, 1937); Willard Motley, *The Diaries of Willard Motley*, ed. by Jerome Klinkowitz (Ames: Iowa State University, Press, 1979); Arnold Rampersad, *The Life of Langston Hughes: Volume 1: 1902–1941. I, Too, Sing America* (New York: Oxford University Press, 1986) and *Volume II: 1941–1967. I Dream a World* (New York: Oxford University Press, 1988); Theodore Rosengarten, *All God's Dangers: The Life of Nate Shaw* (New York: Avon, 1974); Margaret Walker, *How I Wrote Jubilee and Other Essays on Life and Literature* (New York: Feminist Press, 1990).

17. This argument is fundamental to developing a US application of Lucien Goldmann's Marxist theoretical work on the novel. See *Towards a Sociology of the Novel* (London: Tavistock, 1975), where Goldman explores novels as corresponding to the structures of thought of particular social groups.

18. One must consider the specificities of the kind of writing undertaken (fiction, poetry, drama, criticism); the duration and character of the writer's relation to Marxist politics (from ephemeral to lifelong commitment) ; the region of birth and upbringing of the writer (urban, rural); the writer's class background, education, religious training; significant facts of personal biography (sexual orientation, relation to parents and siblings, marital life); and key elements of literary development (early reading, models and mentors, friendships with other writers, networks of friends and collaborators, activity in the other arts, theoretical views).

19. For example, a significant set of personal relations existed among Richard Wright, Chester Himes (who appears to have had Communist associations, if not a brief period of membership, in Cleveland and Los Angeles), Ralph Ellison (certainly a Communist ideologically for a period and possibly in a Party Writers' Unit) and James Baldwin (a Party sympathizer while in high school, a student at the Party-led League of American Writers' School, and a *New Masses* contributor). Wright also knew William Attaway, probably a Party member at some point and certainly a longtime friend of the Party, and collaborated with other Party members and leftists such as Theodore Ward, Dorothy West, Frank Marshall Davis, Marion Minus, and Margaret Walker. Another pro-Communist network involved many participants in the Harlem Writers' Club and Guild, such as John O. Killens and Julian Mayfield, who worked with Audre Lorde (a member of the Communist youth group), Sarah Wright, Maya Angelou, and others. In left-wing theater circles there were a number of associations among Lonne Elder III, Nat Turner Ward, Lorraine Hansberry, Alice Childress, Ruby Dee and Ossie Davis, among others. Langston Hughes and Paul Robeson personally knew many African-American pro-Communist writers, such as Lorraine Hansberry and Lloyd Brown.

20. The story first appeared in *Masses & Mainstream*, 1, no.4 (April 1948).

21. Letter from Lloyd Brown to David Bradley, Dec. 13, 1986.

22. Brown's published stories include: "Jericho, USA.," *New Masses*, October 29, 1946; "Battle in Canaan," *Mainstream*, vol 1, no. 4 (1947), which was listed as one of the distinguished stories for 1947 in the annual O'Brien collection of short stories; "God's Chosen People," *Masses & Mainstream*, 1, no. 4 (April 1948); "The Glory Train" (excerpt from *Iron City*), ibid., 3, no. 11 (December 1950); "Cousin Oscar" (excerpt from unpublished novel, "Year of Jubilee"), ibid., 6, no. 11 (December 1953).

23. Jabarti Simama speculates on p. 238 of his dissertation that Brown's novel-in-progress, "Year of Jubilee," may have been "suppressed by the Party." No serious evidence exists for this view; to the contrary, Brown's correspondence with Humboldt in the Humboldt Collection at Yale University indicates that the problems with the manuscript were purely literary.

24. See Robin Kelley, *Hammer and Hoe: Alabama Communists During the Great Depression* (Chapel Hill: University of North Carolina Press, 1990), p. 238, footnote 1. Communist policy differed from the

WRITING FROM THE LEFT

approaches of all earlier Marxists and socialists in the US. African-Americans were regarded by Communists not simply as an especially-persecuted section of the working class but as a nation within a nation in the US South, a population with a distinct history, territory, culture, and, to some degree, language and cultural expression. Thus the Southern population of African-Americans had the right to its own state, as would a colony. However, the ultimate decision as to whether or not to constitute a state rests with the population itself, as does the form of the state, which could be either capitalist or socialist; otherwise, the notion of self-determination would be a fraud. Moreover, this struggle for national expression of African-Americans, whether or not it took the form of a state, would be most effectively waged if working-class elements came to the fore. However, even though middle- and upper-class elements tended to compromise to save their privileges, these elite African-American groups were relatively insignificant in the South.

Still, in the long run, whatever the dynamics of the national struggle in the South, the Communist view was that the United States as a whole had to be economically reorganized on socialist principles. This couldn't be achieved without unity between the African-American nationality and the white working class, among other allies. In the North, where the Black community was more dispersed among urban ghettos, and more heterogeneous in class composition, the favored Party policy was to form both Black organizations to defend political rights (such as the National Negro Congress) and also interracial unions, political defense committees and other organizations. Of course, the weight given to each component, all-Black and interracial, varied according to circumstances.

The dual elements of this basic formula for the African-American liberation struggle, national and class struggle, shifted in emphasis in different times. The nationalist component was most aggressively expressed before 1935 and during the Cold War. During the Popular Front and World War II, it was somewhat muted, and there was an obvious softening in regard to middle-class Black leaders such as those in the NAACP. Then, due to economic transformations in US capitalism after World War II, the idea of a potential Black state in the South was dropped in 1958. A helpful review of this history and its implications for literary developments can be found in Barbara Foley, *Radical Representations* (Durham, NC: Duke University Press, 1993).

25. Margaret Walker, *Richard Wright: Daemonic Genius* (New York: Warner, 1988), p. 77.

26. The cover depicts the industrial operations of a city (Pittsburgh, renamed "Iron City" in the novel) through the iron bars of a prison (Allegheny County Jail, renamed "Monongahela Jail"). Both jailhouse bars and urban landscape are reciprocal, equally weighted but with different iconic forms that overlap and address each other. From the perspective of the cover, with its bold, red block lettering, the city appears as nothing less than social prison; indeed, it could almost be a group of factories and railroad lines within the confines of a Nazi concentration camp. The overwhelming power of the economic structure is reinforced by the artist's omission of any human workers from the scene. The only activity is the smoke billowing out of factory chimneys, imparting an eerie atmosphere, as if the employees had suddenly died or the machines were being operated by robots.

In contrast, human agency is concentrated entirely in the powerful black hands on the prison bars, which are drawn to suggest a nexus of intersecting cultural meanings. The round poles of the bars directly resemble the round poles of the smokestacks of the mills below, which, in fact, produce the metal used in the bars. In addition, the hands of the prisoner gripping the bars suggest, in the absence of any workers below, that these belong to one who should be working in the factories. When the cover is turned on its side, the bars also resemble stripes of the US flag gripped by the black hands of the person they imprison.

27. *Iron City* (New York: Masses & Mainstream, 1951), p. 36.

28. Ibid., p. 20.

29. Ibid., p. 103.

30. Ibid., p. 31.

31. Ibid., pp. 31–2.

32. In fact, *Iron City* has several features of an answer to *Native Son*. Brown starts with an accused murderer in prison developing a relationship to Communist allies, which takes off from where Wright's novel terminated. Moreover, Paul Harper, the imprisoned Black District Organizer of the Party, is specifically referred to as an example of a "*bad* nigger," a pointed contrast to Bigger Thomas, whose name is a condensation of "bad nigger" and who was said by Wright to have been a composite of various types of the "bad nigger" that he observed in the South. (See Wright's essay, "How Bigger Was Born," which appears in most editions of *Native Son*.) Toward the end of *Iron City*,

a newspaper article is reprinted that describes a lecture by one "Richard Canfield, noted lecturer and sociologist." Canfield refers to the publication of *Native Son* and its protagonist Bigger Thomas to explain pathologies of the Black community by analogizing African-Americans to rats in an experiment. The speaker's remarks as well as name recall Dorothy Canfield Fisher's infamous "Introduction" to the first edition of *Native Son*. That the lecture is to raise funds for "Brotherhood Week" shows Brown's belief that the perspective of Fisher and Wright is an outlook shaped by white paternalism. After reading the article, the Black prisoners laughingly compare themselves to "wild rats" (*Iron City*, p. 209).

33. The literary shift was not unconnected with a political shift on Mailer's part, from sympathy for Communism to the semi-Trotskyist politics promoted by his French translator Jean Malaquais.

34. *Iron City*, pp. 122–3. Brown is also attempting to extend the radical tradition of proletarian literature and Popular Front literature into a new period, building upon the past without repeating its mistakes.

35. Brown may well have been influenced by his friend Charles Humboldt's impressive essay "Communists in Literature," which appeared in two issues of *Masses & Mainstream*, 2, no. 6 (June 1949) and 2, no. 7 (July 1949).

36. Here it may be useful to note that, in the period leading up to the publication of *Iron City*, much debate about racism and the politics of African-American liberation was occurring inside the Communist movement. At the Dec. 3–5, 1946, plenary meeting of the National Committee of the Party, a resolution was passed strongly reaffirming the view of "the Negro question in the United States as a national question" (see William Z. Foster et al., *The Communist Position on the Negro Question*, New York: New Century Publishers, 1947). At the very moment *Iron City* appeared, the Party was engrossed in an internal campaign against suspected white chauvinism in its ranks. Brown wrote an intelligent article on the issue, "Words and White Chauvinism," *Masses & Mainstream*, 3, no. 2 (February 1950): 3–11.

37. *Iron City*, p. 65.

38. In his review of *Iron City* in *Political Affairs*, Richard Walker points out the following about Brown's use of language: "[It shows] sensitivity to the Negro people's idiom and to the *sound* of the language as Negroes speak it. This is a different thing altogether from the customary way of presenting the speech of Negroes as dialect, or as a kind of hodge-podge, distorted, ungrammatical English." In his *Afro-American* review, J. Saunders Redding observed that Brown "has done something quite worthwhile with the race idiom . . . the same sort of thing Ring Lardner did with sport and barbershop idiom – given it elasticity, made it a vehicle not only for speech (dialogue) but of narration and analysis."

39. In this regard the characters somewhat parallel the attitudes of Aunt Sue and Johnnyboy in Wright's "Bright and Morning Star."

40. *Iron City*, p. 104.

41. Cohen is possibly a vague counterpart to Wright's Boris Max in *Native Son*. Another example of interracial unity is the group of students and their teacher who, inspired by the Dreiser investigation of the violence against miners in Harlan County, Kentucky, in the early 1930s, form a committee to investigate James's case. The suggestion came from a white student; after the Committee turns up evidence that strongly supports Lonnie, the white teacher is fired.

42. *Iron City*, pp. 178–9.

43. Some years after Willie Jones's execution, Brown gained access to a number of his letters which he published in *Masses & Mainstream* as "The Legacy of Willie Jones," 5, no. 2 (Febuary 1952): 44–51. The correspondence between the personality of Lonnie James in the novel and that of Jones as revealed in his letters is impressively consistent.

44. On pp. 17–18 of *Iron City*, Lonnie says, "A man has got to believe."

45. Physically, however, Harper resembles James Ashford, a leader of the Young Communist League and a founder of the Southern Negro Youth Congress. Letter from Brown to Wald, March 11, 1994.

46. Ibid., pp. 25–6, 71; pp. 26, 122, 231.

47. Ibid., p. 121.

48. Ibid., p. 235.

49. However, the baseball game, like the prison church services, is subverted as Lonnie and his new friends use the opportunity to transmit information about the defense effort on his behalf.

50. Another reference to boxing is when the guard, Steve, knocks out a prisoner yelling quota-

tions from the Bible.

51. Ibid., p. 237

52. Ibid., pp. 246–7.

53. Brown negatively reviewed Ellison's novel when it appeared in *Masses & Mainstream* 5, no. 6 (June 1952): 62–4.

54. Throughout *Iron City*, issues of gender and sexuality are treated in the conventional and somewhat puritanical manner traditionally associated with male writers on the US Left before the 1960s. For an analysis of the masculinist depictions of the working class and struggle for socialism, see Paula Rabinowitz, *Labor and Desire: Women's Revolutionary Fiction in Depression America* (Chapel Hill: University of North Carolina Press, 1991).

55. These documentary materials are in the possession of Lloyd Brown.

Index

Winwar, Frances 79, 86, 110
Wixson, Douglas 19, 25 n. 3, 186 n. 3; *Worker-Writer* 9, 38
Wolf, Christa 167
Wolfe, Thomas 21, 31
women and the Left, feminism, socialist-feminism 1, 2, 4, 6, 7, 14, 16, 20, 31, 52–6, 69, 71, 73, 77, 78–9, 81, 86, 93, 108, 112, 119, 144, 168, 179
Workers' Party (Brazil) 5
Workers Party of the US 5 n. 13
World War II 49, 98, 110
Wounded Knee 3
Wright, Richard 2, 4, 9, 16, 17, 20, 22, 32, 78, 92, 102, 145, 179; *American Hunger* 216; "Blueprint for Negro Writing" 31, 219; "Bright and Morning Star" 212; *12 Million Black Voices* 203; *Native Son* 30, 31 n. 41, 185, 213, 218, 222, 230 n. 32, 231 n. 41; *Uncle Tom's Children* 174, 202
Wright, Sarah 229 n. 19
Writers' Clinic (Hollywood) 74, 203
writers of color 14; *see also* African-Americans; Asian-Americans; Chicanas and Chicanos; Latinas and Latinas; Native American Indians; people of color; race and racism

Xavier, Nicholas 198, 202

Yeats, W. B. 194, 196
Yerby, Frank 104, 222
Yglesias, Helen 79
Yglesias, José 89, 90, 110, 118; *A Wake in Ybor City* 155
Yiddish-speaking Communists 101
Young, James 229 n. 16

Zahn, Curtiss 90
Zanderer, Leo 106–7, 145
Zinberg, Len (pseud. Ed Lacy) 78, 100–01, 102, 104, 116; *Hold With the Hares* 101; *Room to Swing* 100; *Walk Hard* 81, 101
Zugsmith, Leane 33, 78, 79
Zukofsky, Louis 78